GERMAN MILITARY RIFLES AND MACHINE PISTOLS 1871-1945

HANS-DIETER GÖTZ

GERMAN MILITARY RIFLES AND MACHINE PISTOLS
1871-1945

4880 Lower Valley Road, Atglen, Pennsylvania 19310

All illustrations in this book, unless otherwise noted, come from the
author's archives or were taken by the author.

The author expresses particular thanks to the following institutions
which assisted him on this book:
Bavarian War Archives (State Archives, Section IV), Munich
Federal Archives, Koblenz
Military Area Library VI, Munich
Bavarian Army Museum, Ingolstadt
Military History Museum, Rastatt
In addition, thanks go to all those firms, archive directors and private
individuals who made information available.

Translated from the German by Dr. Edward Force.
Central Connecticut State University

Proofreading and Value Guide by Robert Ball.

ISBN: 978-0-88740-264-7
Printed in China.

This book originally published under the title,
*Die deutschen Militargewehre und
Maschinenpistolen 1871-1945,*
by Motorbuch Verlag, Postfach 10 37 43, 7000 Stuttgart 10,
1985. ISBN: 3-87943-350-X.

We are always looking for people to write books on new and related subjects.
If you have an idea for a book, please contact us at the address below.

Schiffer Books are available at special discounts
for bulk purchases for sales promotions or premiums. Special editions,
including personalized covers, corporate imprints, and excerpts can be
created in large quantities for special needs.
For more information contact the publisher:

Published by Schiffer Publishing Ltd.
4880 Lower Valley Road
Atglen, PA 19310
Phone: (610) 593-1777; Fax: (610) 593-2002
E-mail: Info@schifferbooks.com

For the largest selection of fine reference books on
this and related subjects, please visit our web site at:
www.schifferbooks.com
We are always looking for people to write
books on new and related subjects.

If you have an idea for a book please
contact us at the above address.

This book may be purchased from the publisher. Include $5.00 for
shipping.
Please try your bookstore first.
You may write for a free catalog.

In Europe, Schiffer books are distributed by
Bushwood Books
6 Marksbury Ave.
Kew Gardens
Surrey TW9 4JF England
Phone: 44 (0) 20 8392-8585;
Fax: 44 (0) 20 8392-9876
E-mail: info@bushwoodbooks.co.uk
Website: www.bushwoodbooks.co.uk

Contents

Introduction

The purpose of this book is namely to provide information on German military rifles and machine pistols, and therefore requires limitation to the era of German unity from 1871 to 1945.

The times before, characterized by dozens of small and smaller states going their own ways between Maas and Memel, Etsch and Belt, in which the development of weapons took place in correspondingly many ways, is treated in a separate volume.*

The period after that, in view of the division of Germany into two states, which belong to different military alliances, was not very productive, as so far neither the Federal Republic nor the DDR has emerged with its own individual, significant and really new developments.

Thus the years of the Second and Third Reichs, linked by the short-lived First Republic, remain: the years from the birth to the downfall of a great power.

In this active segment of German history, weapon manufacturers such as Mauser, Luger, Schmeisser and Stange won renown throughout the world and German armaments corporations like Krupp, DWM and Rheinmetall played major roles in the international market. It is not by chance that the beginning and end of this era were marked by wars; the Franco-Prussian, which set everything in motion, and World War II, which the German weapons industry, according to the will of the victors, was not to survive.

It would not make much sense to describe German military rifles and machine pistols from 1871 to 1945 without looking at the political background and economic-technical conditions of the times in which they emerged. For under the influence of constantly changing political and tactical demands in this era, the development of military handguns could not always proceed in peace and according to the rules of logic. This book, therefore, will not tell of great technical achievements alone, but also of missed chances, mistakes and misdeeds. But these are not German specialties; other countries had their armament errors too, and it is no wonder.

Too many new things filled these seven decades, for the development of firearms, characterized by slow, steady progress for centuries, suddenly rushed forward. The metal cartridge, basis of all new developments, got over its teething troubles in barely twenty years, and the repeating rifles were perfected. Smokeless types of powder and jacketed bullets appeared and made the diminution of military calibers from 11 to 6.5 millimeters possible. And that, it must be noted, was before the turn of the century. The first self-loading rifles were in existence shortly thereafter, and in 1918 Germany's infantry combat experience in the World War resulted in the machine pistol.

During the Twenties progress took a break. By the terms of the Treaty of Versailles, the Weimar Republic was forbidden to develop and build military weapons, but neither did other nations create anything earth-shaking at that time. Only in the mid-Thirties, when the impending world conflict could already be sensed, did designers begin to work on a new type of infantry weapon: the rapid-fire rifle, which was to replace the repeater. In Germany this development went on to the universally usable "assault gun", a combination of rapid-fire rifle and light machine gun, made for a "short cartridge" whose conception was already completed by 1945.

Since then the international manufacture of weapons has not experienced any really new impulse. And no one can say at this point whether any further development of military firearms would be possible, thinkable or sensible. For the modern assault guns, those of NATO as well as the Warsaw Pact nations, fulfill every tactically justified wish in terms of precision of shot, range, effectiveness, rate of fire and reliability. It really seems as if the history of the conventional hand firearms has come to a close. Maybe, the development of a useful caseless cartridge and a new assault rifle designed for it opens — whenever — a new chapter.

---

* Götz, H.D., *Militärgewehre und Pistolen der deutschen Staaten 1800-1870.*

How This Book Came About

I have tried to research the history of German military rifles and machine pistols from 1871 to 1945 at the sources, to the extent that this is still possible today. As sources for the period up to 1918, the complete files of the former Bavarian War Ministry on armament and equipment have been available to me. The archives have emerged through World War II almost unscathed and were even saved from the hands of the occupying powers, a better fate than that suffered by most other military document collections in Germany. In one part of the old files I had the feeling of being the first ever to untie them since they were bundled up and put away more than a century ago.

I found in about 10,000 chancellery memos — most of them handwritten — a great many interesting details, names and numbers, which obviously had been forgotten by now. These documents — every page secret in their day — reflect in minute detail the developmental history of the Empire's various rifle models — and not just as seen through Bavarian eyes. The files contain all the important Prussian documents that were sent out routinely for purposes of information, as well as the correspondence with the War Ministry in Berlin, the reports of the Bavarian military representatives in the Empire's capital, production information and calculations of the Bavarian Rifle Factory in Amberg and comparisons with the Royal Prussian armament factories. Not to mention test reports, notes and memoranda.

The information on the period after 1918 comes from correspondence with the manufacturers of those days, to the extent that they are still alive, possess documents and are willing to give out information. I have tried to make contact with still-living technicians and other eyewitnesses from the days before 1945, and I have also examined the military service regulations and any other reliable material, in order to compare and complete data wherever gaps appeared.

The weapons whose pictures you find in this book are for the most part in the collections of the Bavarian Army Museum in Ingolstadt and the Military History Museum in Rastatt, while individual pieces were kindly loaned to me for study and photographing by private collectors.

In the serial development of German military weapons from the Werder rifle to the Assault Gun 45, there are also models that never were introduced for German military use, such as the Belgian M/89 rifle or the Spanish M/93, because they were designed by Mauser. On the other hand, you will also find weapons in this book that were not designed or built in Germany but were used by German troops during the two World Wars. Two such examples are the Mexican-Swiss "Mondragon" self-loading rifle from the First and the Italian "Beretta" M.P. 38/42 from the Second World War. Since the German soldiers used just about any firearms that fell into their hands as the spoils of war during the two World Wars, at least at times, in places and in small quantities, (in World War I alone 28 types were recorded), an account of all of these would stretch to infinity. Therefore I have limited a detailed description to those captured weapons that were used in noteworthy quantities in German service and given German designations.

The German Reich and its Weapons in 1871

When the Prussian King Wilhelm I became the German Emperor on January 18, 1871, the German armies were deep in France. The decisive battles had been fought, the end of the war was just a matter of time. Thus this symbolic act of German unification took place, so to speak, in the field.

In the very proclamation of the Kaiser in the Hall of Mirrors at the Palace of Versailles it was clear that all-powerful Prussia would set the tone of the new Reich, for the Hohenzollern state extended at that time practically from the Baltic Sea to the Main. There also existed the Kingdoms of Bavaria, Württemberg and Saxony with their own national armies, as well as the Grand Duchies of Hessen-Darmstadt and Baden, which followed Prussia closely in military matters.

When the war began, the individual German states had placed their troop contingents under the command of the "Grand General Staff." The fighting began early in August 1870 and just one month later, on September 1, the decisive battle at Sedan had been fought. After that, on every Sedan Day for nearly forty years, German professors wrote poems of praise and German male choruses sang of the "splendid victory of German arms", which could naturally be meant only in a metaphorical sense. For the German weapons, at least those of the infantry, were technically mediocre and far inferior to the French ones in 1870-71.

The fact that the war was won nevertheless was attributable to the overwhelming German superiority in numbers, with 1.2 million soldiers compared to France's 600,000, and also to the strict leadership of the German armies and General Moltke's well-planned advance.

The most important infantry weapon on the German side was the Dreyse needle gun, used in Prussia since 1841 and taken on by almost all the other German states after 1866 without any significant changes. The technology of this once-admired first military breech-loader with cylindrical breech was by then thirty years old and antiquated.

Attempts were just being made to dispose of its chief problems (insufficient gas-tightness at the breech and irregular performance of the paper cartridge with detachable cardboard collar) when the war intervened. As to the modest ballistic performance of the Dreyse design, even the planned "Beck conversion" would scarcely have changed that.

The cartridges used in the Prussian needle gun, caliber 13.6 millimeters, traveled only 296 meters per second and were thus considerably slower than the 11-millimeter cartridges of the French Chassepot rifle, which had an initial velocity of 420 meters per second.

The French rifle was also a needle-gun design. But it had been created in 1866 and thus held an advantage of 25 years' development over the Prussian gun. The Chassepot breech, the gas-tightness, the cartridge with the silk case and cartridge seating were the best that could be achieved before the introduction of the metal cartridge.

The superior performance of the French rifles and other new foreign designs had naturally been known in Prussia long before the war. Parallel to the already noted attempts to improve the M/41

needle gun and its various modifications, extended tests of various new weapons had been made at the Military Gunnery School in Spandau, beginning about 1868, for the purpose of finding a successor type to the needle gun. The urgent "rifle question" was a political controversy of the first rank. It was hoped that the "Rifle Testing Commission" in Spandau, of which more will be said below, would soon come to a decision.

While all the other German states looked to Berlin and waited for the decision, in order to follow the Prussian example, the Kingdom of Bavaria went its own way.

Right after the 1866 war, when the other South German states had decided to introduce the needle gun, the Bavarian War Minister von Pranckh had stepped out of line. He recommended to the young King Ludwig II that the already available rifled percussion muzzle-loader, caliber 13.9 mm Minié, be modified by a system that the Director of the Royal Bavarian Rifle Factory in Amberg, Colonel Philipp Baron von Podewils, had suggested: Cut a piece off the rear end of the barrel, screw on a loading device for paper cartridges and retain the percussion priming. With the Podewils M/67 rifles, which moreover had originated not only by modification but were also being made new, the Bavarian Infantry was almost completely armed in 1870. When the war began, Bavaria possessed 114,000 rifles of this type.

When the M/67 was accepted it was clear that the "percussion breech-loader" could not be the final solution to the rifle problem for Bavaria either, but only an economical stopgap for the time being. Meanwhile, Bavaria made its own search for a new design. It should be, and the gentlemen in Munich and Berlin agreed on this point, a rifle with metal cartridges.

The Bavarians were the first to solve the problem.

Bavarian Werder Rifle M/69

Type: *Bayerisches Infanteriegewehr M/69* (System Werder)
Manufacturer: Royal Bavarian Rifle Factory, Amberg
Function: Single-shot with automatic cartridge ejection
Overall length: 1310 mm
Gross weight: 4.3 kg
Barrel length: 860 mm
Barrel caliber: 11 mm
Number of riflings: 4
Rifling direction: Right
Depth of a rifling: 0.26 mm
Rifling length: 915 mm
Action: Vertical dropping block with hammer concealed
Safety catch: Hammer at half-cock
Sight: Stepped frame sight to 1200 paces

Standard ammunition: Cartridge M/69 long (1875-76 adapted for cartridge 71)
Disassembly: Uncock hammer. Loosen trigger guard screw, unhook trigger guard. Right hand holds upper part of breech casing, right index finger presses cocked breech block down until the forked ejector comes out of its mount in the barrel end. Lift bolt housing out of the frame, remove cover, remove both leaf springs, pull massive parts from the axle bolt.
Safety: (Only possible with system sprung) Release hammer grip with the right thumb, press trigger and slowly move hammer grip forward about two centimeters. Let go of trigger and draw hammer back a bit until it audibly drops into the safety catch. To release it, the hammer is cocked again.

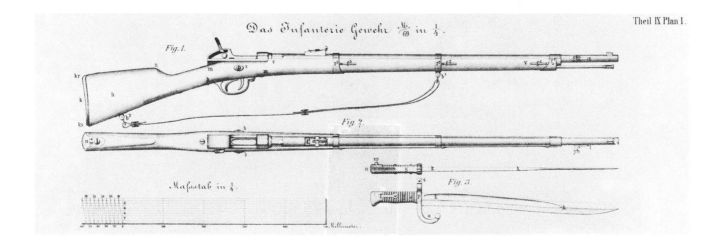

This book begins with a description of a weapon that had already been introduced before the Empire was founded, as the model designation "69" indicates. Nevertheless the Werder rifle clearly belongs in the series of German weapons after 1871. First, because the majority of the rifles were produced during the war and given to the returning troops only in the spring of 1871. Second, because the Werder rifle remained the official infantry weapon of the second-largest German state.

The designer, Johann-Ludwig Werder, Director of the Cramer-Klett Machine Factory in Nürnberg, had made a number of inventions in various areas during the course of his life. He invented tool and

Johann Ludwig Werder (1805-1885)
Photo: Nürnberg City Archives

material testing machines, methods of "instructive" series production, designed steel buildings, orthopedic devices and, along the way, the rifle of which we speak here.

Werder's system is one of the vertical breech types such as were also offered by Peabody and Martini at that time. Their identifying mark is a massive breech block, vertically movable, through the middle axis of which the striker passes, and which closes the open barrel end with its front surface. To load, the front end of the breech block can be lowered so that the cartridge position is accessible. A reliable process, tried and true in hundreds of thousands of guns all over the world, of producing dependable and durable single-shot rifles.

Werder's improvement particularly concerned the process of opening after firing and ejecting the empty cartridge case. He turned this job (which in the other vertical breech systems was done with the rifleman's right hand and a long swinging lower lever) over to a leaf spring, which was cocked simultaneously with the striker spring. A press of a finger on the "brace", which opposes the "sear" (trigger) and is mounted ahead of it under the guard, suffices to open and eject the case. The mechanism is closed and cocked on the grip of the hammer, which projects to the right through a slit in the metal of the breech.

If the "inmost life" of the lock with its strangely shaped and interreacting individual parts is confusing at first, on closer inspection, and especially when using it, all the functions prove to be practical and amazingly simple. In fact the lock, including the two side panels, has only thirteen parts, the same number as the later M/71 rifle, and it can be dismantled by removing just one screw and without tools. This feature was much admired at the time.

Even more remarkable, to be sure, was the "rapid-fire performance" that the Werder rifle achieved through its simple operation and quick ejection of empty cartridges from the bed by a spring. Experienced riflemen could fire 20 to 24 aimed shots per minute with the Werder rifle (with the later M/71, only 12 to 15 were possible). Because of this remarkable performance, the Werder rifle was regarded for a few years as the best infantry rifle in Europe. In the Franco-Prussian War not only the allied Prussians but even the French spoke respectfully of the "Bavarian Blitz rifle" — even though only four Jäger battalions took part in the war with the new weapon.

To sum up its developmental history briefly: In the autumn of 1867, the same year in which Bavaria had decided in favor of the Podewils rifle, Johann Ludwig Werder submitted his design. The Royal Bavarian Hand Firearms Commission, which met on occasion until about 1872 to test new designs that were presented to the War Ministry, took a routine look at the new weapon too.

King Ludwig Decides the Competition

In the literature, old or new, one can always read that the Bavarians let themselves be guided by local patriotism when they chose the Nürnberg inventor's gun. This is not true.

Between the autumn of 1868 and the spring of 1869 the Werder rifle had to prove itself in a rigorous competition against the Austrian Werndl M/67 rifle and, until the very end, against the rifle of the American General Hiram Berdan. Other competitors, including the "Mauser-Norris" system (!), had already dropped out during 1868.

At first 950 Werder rifles were produced in Amberg for mass use and tested along with fifty Werndl models, which the "Austrian Weapon Factory Company" of Steyr had delivered, by the Infantry Guard Regiment and at eight provincial garrisons. When one looks at the old test results, it becomes clear that absolutely nothing was spared the weapons. The rifles stood outside for days and weeks, were often sprayed with water and dirtied with sand, and were then fired uncleaned. Long periods of firing, including the use of cartridges with artificially created faults, alternated with tests in winter cold, in which the loaded weapons were allowed to ice up and were fired in that condition. The only weapon that proved to be equal to the Werder rifle in the end was the Berdan rifle, a single-shot weapon with a cylindrical breech, and it excelled principally thanks to its excellent cartridge. Hiram Berdan, who was traveling through all of Europe with specimens of his rifles, spent a long time in Munich observing the tests. When the head-to-head competition was ultimately won by the Werder rifle, he offered to sell the Bavarians the machines that produced the cartridges that he made. He received a down payment of 25,000 Gulden and disappeared with the money; the cartridge presses never arrived in Munich.

It is hard to imagine that the 23-year-old King Ludwig, who is remembered today only as a Wagner fan and builder of fairytale castles, took an active part in solving the rifle problem. War Minister Pranckh had to report to him constantly on the state of the tests, and finally Ludwig even had both a Werder and a Berdan rifle shown to him — a highly unusual process.

In an "All-Highest Decision" of January 25, 1869, Ludwig decided the "dead heat" in favor of the Werder system, and on April 18 he approved the model weapon.

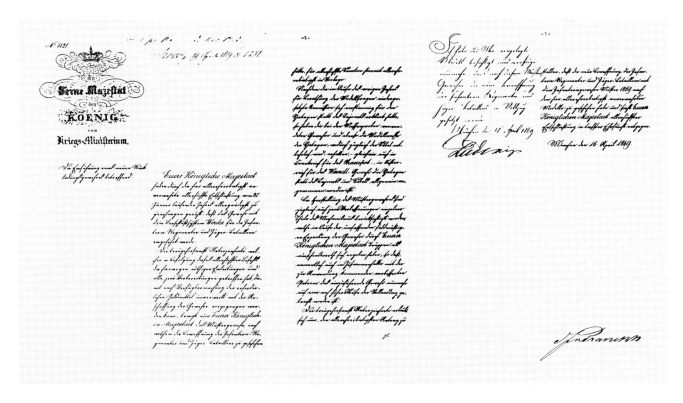

All-Highest order to introduce the Werder rifle in Bavaria. Ludwig II signed it on April 18, 1869.

Meanwhile preparations for mass production of the "Breech-Loading Rifle Model 1869", as it was called officially, were going on at the Royal Rifle Factory in Amberg. Because of the modest technical development of the small rifle factory at that time, the contracts for the complicated individual parts of the Werder mechanism were given to private firms. The main supplier until 1874 was the firm of which the designer of the rifle was the director: Cramer-Klett in Nürnberg. As of 1876 the Augsburg Machine Works took over production of the mechanism.

In addition to the manufacturing contracts, Johann Ludwig Werder also received a Bavarian patent for his system, good for five years, on June 17, 1868, plus a reward of 15,000 Gulden and the Knight's Cross First Class of the Order of St. Michael. In exchange, he turned his patent rights over to the Bavarian government. He was allowed

nevertheless to offer the rifle for sale to other countries.

With an extraordinary credit of 1,100,000 Gulden (granted on April 29, 1869), 100,000 Werder rifles were to be manufactured by mid-May 1872 to arm the Bavarian infantry and Jäger regiments.

At Amberg the barrel and stock production and the final assembly (the mechanisms were delivered) began in the spring of 1870. 1008 guns a week were to be finished and originally stored at the Fortress of Ingolstadt until the Bavarian Army could be rearmed by corps. When the war broke out, only four Jäger battalions, the 2nd (Burghausen), 5th (Zweibrücken, in the Palatinate), 9th (Passau) and 10th (Aschaffenburg) had been issued the new rifles for testing. They went into battle with them. The rearming of the rest of the army was postponed until the war ended, so as not to disturb the uniform ammunition supply of all the troops.

The "Blitz Rifle" in the War

It was not only in Bavaria that men anxiously awaited reports on the experience of the four Werder battalions. The Prussian War Minister von Roon, whose Rifle Testing Commission was then still searching for the best breech-loader with metal cartridges, sent a delegation of officers to Munich to make use of the reports on the Werder rifle's combat use.

On February 4, 1871 the Bavarian Artillery Corps Command already issued a first resumé. Its report to the War Ministry in Munich speaks only of minor technical faults: occasional trouble with the ejector, presumably caused by "swelling of the cartridges."

Weightier problems — so it appears — existed in terms of firing discipline. For the soldiers utilized the superior firepower of the Werder rifle without regard to the limited supply of cartridges in their bullet pouches. In the report it is stated: ". . . the obedient undersigned believes he must draw the attention of the All-Highest to the fact that the corporals as well as the enlisted men must be taught to understand that the excellent performance of this

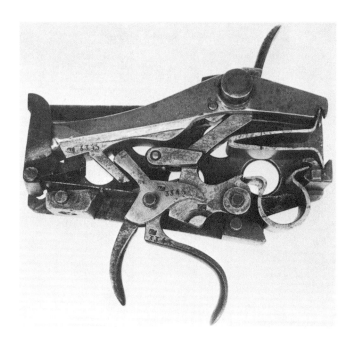

The M 69 rifle with breech housing removed.

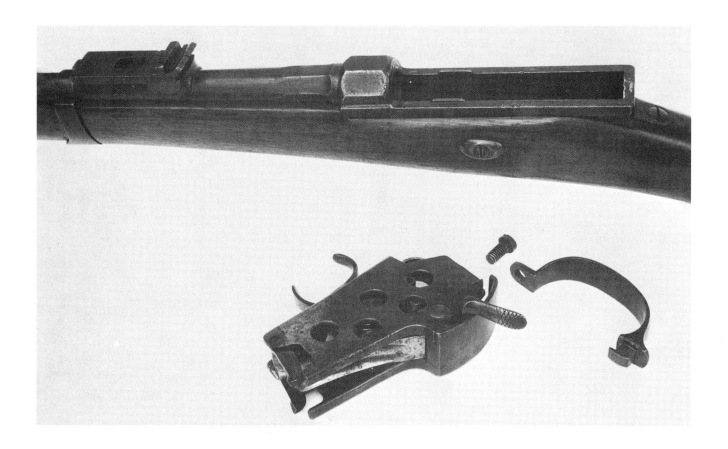

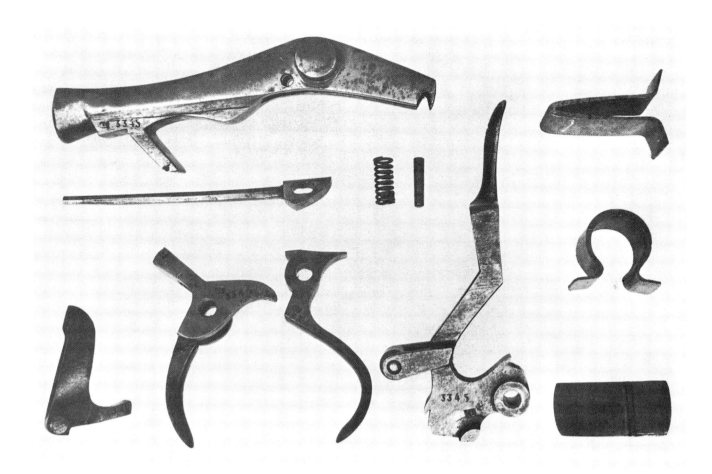

The Werder breech. Parts removed from the axle bolt.

rifle may be brought to full utilization only at the main moments of attack and defense in view of its rapidity of fire . . .''

Now this problem of ''shooting it up'' was certainly not new, but it arose here for the first time in a really threatening form. For under the psychological pressure of a battle, a soldier could use up his supply of cartridges for the Werder rifle within a few minutes.

Another experience resulting from the French campaign, which was particularly rainy in the first few weeks, led to the elimination of the wooden ''rifle plug'' from the soldier's equipment. The plug, intended to protect the muzzle of the barrel, soaked up the moisture and encouraged rust buildup in the muzzle. In addition, there were cases of barrels bursting because the soldiers had forgotten to take the plug out of the muzzle before firing.

The design of the Werder rifle was unaffected by all that. It had proved itself splendidly in its original form that was at hand then. The only actual problem, the result of which would only become apparent years later, was the attachment of a bayonet.

Annoyance at Bent Barrels

During troop testing in 1868 the Bavarian War Ministry had already decided against a removable bayonet and in favor of the then-fashionable "Yatagan", a combined cut-and-thrust weapon, 61.5 cm long, with a 48 cm double bent blade, which was also supposed to replace the saber.

War Minister von Pranckh justified the introduction of this weapon, much too heavy to be used as a bayonet, with the advice that "...in France too, for the Chassepot, in Austria for the Werndl rifle, the yatagan has been generally accepted in place of the bayonet and saber."

The yatagan did not prove itself well in Bavaria. The long and heavy weapon with its correspondingly long patterned handle was pushed through an attachment soldered directly on the barrel, while an arm of the crossguard, in the form of a ring, slipped over the muzzle. Thus this weapon, used as a bayonet, applied a good deal of leverage to the end of the barrel, which often led to bending. What that inevitably meant for the rifle's accuracy is clear.

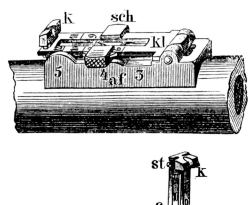

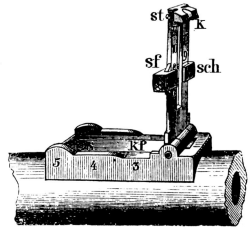

The original sight of the Werder rifle, with step and frame. It goes from 300 paces (210 meters) to 1200 paces (870 meters).

The M/69 yatagan with leather scabbard after the weight was officially decreased. By shortening the crossguard and grinding out the blade, 75 grams of weight were eliminated. (Compare its form with the illustration on page 10.)

To proceed to a solution at once: The "War Ministerial Regulation" of March 17, 1875 began by banning the unnecessary attachment of the yatagan in peacetime, and also ordered that the blade be lightened. At Podewils' suggestion, the crossguard of the yatagan was shortened and the blade ground narrower and thinner in 1876. A reduction of the Yatagan's weight by 75 grams was, in Podewils' opinion, ". . . the extreme limit to which . . . one can go without affecting the necessary durability of it as a thrusting weapon."

This change appeared to be acceptable at all only because the Bavarian infantry had been issued portable entrenching tools shortly before. With that the significance of side arms as economical tools sank, limited perhaps to uses such as splitting wood while encamped.

Back to the year 1872: On May 15 the War Minister reported to the King ". . . that now the rearming of all infantry and Jäger battalions of the Royal Army with the M/69 infantry rifle, the Werder rifle, has been carried out completely." On May 24 the War Ministry ordered another 6000 rifles from Amberg; they were delivered as early as October 1 of the same year and issued to the engineer battalions (according to the All-Highest decision of October 31, 1872).

The "Manufacturing Statistics" of the Rifle Factory in Amberg of October 1, 1872 shows 100,000 finished M/69 rifles. Director Podewils declared: "The order given to the Rifle Factory is thereby filled."

But it was not. Since Bavaria needed a total of 180,000 M/69 rifles in order to have the "double supply" necessary in case of war, another 12,000 or so Werder rifles a year were to be produced in Amberg. The factory could not accomplish more, as in the summer of 1872 a Prussian order for M/71 rifles had been received and was to run until the end of 1875.

In retrospect it is at first incomprehensible why the Bavarian government, despite its own unfulfilled needs, put its production capacities at the disposition of a "foreign" state. We will see later, though, how this particular Prussian order helped the Bavarians out of a serious crisis.

How to Make a Good Weapon Bad

The problems with the Werder rifle, which had drawn nothing but fervent praise from all over the world until then, began when Prussia and the other states of the German Empire introduced the Mauser infantry rifle with the M/71 cartridge. This cartridge was developed from the Werder type, being lengthened, with a stronger charge of powder, and thus faster. This fact, as well as a probable desire for unity in infantry ammunition in the whole German Empire, led to the attempt to make the M/69 usable with the M/71 cartridge.

A series of tests at the Bavarian Military Gunnery School in Augsburg in the autumn of 1874 gave encouraging results at first, which were summed up in an evaluation of November 7, 1874:

Using the "Le Bouléngé" electric chronograph, the following muzzle velocities were measured:

M/69 rifle with 69 cartridge: 385 meters per second

M/69 rifle with 71 cartridge: 432 meters per second

M/71 rifle with 71 cartridge: 430 meters per second

In addition, the English Martini-Henry rifle, model 1871, with its own ammunition, was compared: 384 feet per second. Not only the initial velocity (which at that time was not yet stated as V_{25}, but as V_{25} increased when the 71 cartridge was used, but naturally, so did the range. At an elevation of 32 to 37 degrees, the shot of the Werder cartridge covered 2200 meters, the M/71 shot, on the other hand, 2800 to 3000 meters. Besides, the Director of the Military Gunnery School, Oberst von Reitzenstein, took the liberty of "humbly suggesting" that when the 71 cartridge was used in the Werder rifle, the dirtying of the barrel by remaining bits of powder, and the filling of the riflings with lead were noticeably less. He attributed this to better Prussian powder and paper wrapping of the 71 cartridge's projectile, which was 0.51mm smaller in caliber than the Bavarian type.

All of this could not fail to have an effect in the Munich War Ministry.

On December 11, 1874 a large-scale test with Bavarian guns and Prussian cartridges was ordered. For this purpose the rifle factory was given a contract to adapt 200 Werder rifles to take the M/71 cartridge, which meant lengthening the bed and attaching M/71 sights.

These rifles were at first supposed to be fired with 500 M/71 cartridges each, and 40 of them with another 2500 cartridges each, in order to test the durability of the Werder design when using the stronger ammunition. The tests were made separately in the spring of 1875 by four companies in their Munich, Augsburg, Ambergand Nürnberg garrisons, and the results, summed up in a report of May 5, 1875, were in no way as encouraging as those of the Gunnery School tests the previous autumn. There were numerous jamming cartridges, breeches and hammers.

Despite this cause for alarm, the causes of which were attributed to faulty ammunition, an order was given remarkably quickly, barely a month later, on June 5, 1875 to adapt all 127,000 Werder rifles. For this purpose the weapons were to be sent to Amberg gradually, one battalion at a time.

The money allotted for the adaptation amounted, in Reichsmarks, to 8 Marks 68 Pfennig per rifle. The new M/71 sights came from the firms of Loewe & Co. of Berlin, M. H. Kernaul in Berlin, and Mauser Brothers & Co. in Oberndorf.

The biggest problem was the lengthening of the bed. This was done at Amberg as handwork, using reamers. Many of the adapted beds turned out to have step-like irregularities or were not exactly centric. But that was just one of the reasons that led to a great crisis in Bavaria in the summer of 1876, while the adaptation was still going on.

An adapted M/69 Werder rifle. In 1875-76 all these rifles were reworked with cartridge beds and sights for the 71 cartridge. This weapon, bearing number 90274, was made in 1870.

The Great Crisis

In the troops' very first firing tests with the adapted Werder rifles, faults appeared in such numbers that the readiness of the entire Bavarian army to defend itself was called in question at one stroke.

Many units reported load problems with 60 to 70% of all their rifles, essentially caused by the same faults that had already been seen in the troop testing: fired cartridges jammed in the bed such that the ejector was bent and eventually did not work at all. Breech parts were damaged by the powerful recoil of the M/71 cartridge, with the arched frontal surface of the breech pushed into the base of the cartridge so that the breech could no longer be opened.

Such damage, relatively easy to repair in a vertical breech, completely crippled a design like the Werder rifle. With a rigid case and a stuck breech block, a gunsmith at the factory had his hands full for hours. A soldier to whom such a misfortune occurs in battle has absolutely no chance of getting his rifle back into order.

Because of alarming reports on the failure of the adapted M/69 rifle, the main responsible officers were ordered to the War Ministry on July 24, 1876. Oberst von Reitzenstein (Military Gunnery School), Lieutenant General von Podewils (Rifle Factory), and Captain Dekinder (Main Laboratory in Ingolstadt) were to take a position on the question: "Is the adapted M/69 rifle to be regarded as a weapon fully usable in war?" The form of this question underscores the seriousness of the situation.

Is Bavaria Unarmed?

Behind closed doors and with the strictest secrecy, the gentlemen conferred for two days. The faults and their causes were analyzed. But the decision that the adaptation was hasty does not appear in the reports. The fault, it was stated instead, lay partly with the unskilled battalion gunsmiths who had neglected to replace insufficiently hardened breech parts with new ones at the right time. On the other hand, the malfunctions were caused by faulty cartridge cases and percussion caps: The private suppliers and the Main Laboratory in Ingolstadt, where ammunition production had just been switched to M/71 cartridges, were to blame.

On July 29 and 30 the Bavarian Ordnance Master, His Royal Highness Prince Luitpold, finally called the expanded group together again. This time the possibilities of solving the problem were discussed, for there was no longer any doubt: the adapted M/69 rifles were no longer fully usable in war. Since the faults had not been found in the Werder rifle "Type 69 New Model", which had already been introduced in July of 1875 (see the next chapter), Prince Luitpold at first asked for the replacement of the adapted rifles by "M/69 new models." But that was no longer possible. Since the Prussian contract, the Rifle Factory at Amberg was completely set up to produce M/71 rifles. To resume large-scale Werder production, much too much would have to be changed, which would cost much money and even more time. When most of the other participants in the conference also repeatedly stressed the advantages of the cylindrical breech, Luitpold finally gave in. In Bavaria, it was decided, the M/71 rifle should be introduced.

How much the prince regretted dispensing with the home-grown Werder rifle can be seen clearly in his last comment recorded in the report. He mourned: "The somewhat flattering and pecuniarily advantageous contract to manufacture the M/71 for Prussia leads us to a bitter result . . ."

Werder Rifle, New Model (M/69 n.M.)

Type: *Bayerisches Infanteriegewehr M/69 n.M.* (System Werder)
Number: 121
Year made: 1876
Manufacturer: Royal Bavarian Rifle Factory, Amberg
Function: Single-shot with automatic cartridge ejection
Overall length: 1310 mm
Gross weight: 4.6 kilograms
Barrel length: 860 mm
Barrel caliber: 11 mm
Number of riflings: 4

Rifling direction: Right
Rifling length: 550 mm
Rifling depth: 0.3 mm
Rifling width: 4.5 mm
Breech: Vertical dropping block with inside hammer
Safety catch: Hammer half-cocked
Sight: Upright, no flap, and sighted to 1600 meters
Standard ammunition: Cartridge 71
Disassembly: Like M/69 rifle
Safety: Like M/69 rifle.

While the attempts to make the Werder rifle suitable for the M/71 cartridge, a commission of the Bavarian Military Gunnery School in Augsburg had considered desirable innovations for subsequent production. For in 1874-75 Bavaria still had a need for 78,000 rifles; the requirement for "twice the number" had not yet been met.

The new production of M/69 rifles, intended for the M/71 cartridge, was to include the installation of a stronger ejector and barrel walls as thick as those of the M/71 rifle.

The Munich War Ministry, influenced by Rifle Factory Director Podewils, went even further in its recommendation of March 17, 1875: The bayonet was no longer to be attached to the barrel, but to the upper band, as on the M/71 rifle, in order to avoid bending the barrel. The ministry also recommended that the interior construction of the M/71 rifle barrel be used for the Werder rifle, so as to take the new cartridge. That means the rifling length of 915 mm for one revolution of the riflings should be reduced to 550 mm.

The Gunnery School at Augsburg raised a protest against these two suggestions. In a report of May 1, 1875 the Commandant, Baron von Reitzenstein, declared that the upper band attachment of the M/71 was criticized in Prussia, since it prevented the free vibration of the barrel when firing and thus unfavorably influenced accuracy. He showed in firing tests with M/71 rifles, of which some had had the upper bands and some the entire shafts removed, that the weapons now suddenly shot lower than before. This fault had also been recognized in Prussia.

How strongly the barrel vibration had been hindered was shown by the fact that in many M/71 rifles the upper band screw, which firmly connected the band, shaft and barrel, bent and its threads were damaged. Reitzenstein also suspected that the much stronger rifling of the M/71 rifle unnecessarily intensified the vibration. Thus he advocated retaining the old Werder shaft fastening.

But the Rifle Factory brought forth a — financially — weighty argument against this:

"In the Rifle Factory here as well as in all German factories in which M/71 rifles or their parts are manufactured, the machine facilities for the production of the M/71 rifle are at hand in such a manner as they were never in use for any previous rifle model, and this fact suggests that the rifle to be produced will probably be suitable for the M/71."

After the Werder rifles with M/71 barrels had proved their superiority over Werder rifles with their old barrels at a new comparison test at the Military Gunnery School in Augsburg in September of 1875, all doubts were finally laid to rest and the new model could be defined.

The Werder Rifle M/69 n.M. had the same barrel and overall dimensions as the old M/69, as well as the same mechanism, though with a strengthened ejector. The shape of the barrel, chamber and rifling as well as that of the forearm including the band attachment and the sight, though, corresponded to those of the M/71 rifle. The wooden stock on either side of the mechanism was strengthened. This resulted, along with the somewhat heavier barrel, in a weight increase of some 300 grams, which was nevertheless not undesirable in view of the heavier recoil.

Its introduction had been ordered by a War Ministry directive of July 21, 1875, thus before the aforementioned Gunnery School tests. The cost projection from Amberg (9/19/1875) for the new model cites 57.50 Marks, including the cost of the mechanism delivered from Augsburg.

At this time, though, the Bavarian Rifle Factory was still occupied with filling the Prussian M/71 contract and could not even think of making the required number of the M/69 n. M. for some time.

Therefore the War Ministry in Munich inquired of the rifle manufacturers in Suhl and at once received a militant protest from the Prussian War Ministry. All Suhl manufacturers — it was stated — were engaged in manufacturing M/71 rifles to the extent that an additional Bavarian contract was not wanted, since it would endanger the quality of the work and the keeping of the schedule.

Thus the contract eventually went to Austria. Josef Werndl's "Austrian Weapon Factory Company" in Steyr contracted to deliver 20,000 M/69 n.M. rifles at a price of 35 Gulden apiece. At the same time, Amberg completed another 5000 of them and charged 31 Gulden apiece. A total of 25,000 mechanisms were produced in Augsburg.

Contrary to the original viewpoint, no M/69 n.M. rifles above and beyond these 25,000 were made. In the meantime, Bavaria had decided in favor of the M/71 rifle.

The old yatagan was no longer considered as a bayonet for the new Werder rifle model. Therefore Bavaria ordered 25,000 M/71 bayonets from the Weyersberg & Stamm firm in Solingen. They cost 4 Marks 38 Pfennig apiece.

The M/69 n.M. rifles were in service until the end of 1882. In the end they were found only in the depots of the replacement battalions. In 1883 they were mustered out and sold.

The Werder Carbine

Type: *Bayerisches Karabiner M/69* (System Werder)
Number: 93
Year made: 1871
Manufacturer: A. Francotte Weapons Factory in Liège
Function: Single-shot with automatic cartridge ejection
Overall length: 800 mm
Barrel length: 365 mm
Barrel caliber: 11 cm

Number of riflings: 4
Rifling direction: right
Breech: Vertical with inside hammer
Safety catch: Hammer half-cocked
Sight: Standing, no flap, to 500 paces (365 meters)
Standard ammunition: M/69 short cartridge
Disassembly: As M/69 rifle
Safety: As M/69 rifle

In their initial enthusiasm over the quick-firing Werder rifle, the Bavarians also wanted to have a carbine and a pistol with the same mechanism right away. The two short weapons were intended for the cavalry, which was still equipped with old-fashioned smooth-bore muzzle-loading pistols in 1869.

The Prussian example may have played a role in these thoughts of developing a whole family of weapons out of the Werder system. The Prussians had likewise built carbines with shortened Dreyse needle-gun systems after 1841 and experimented with pistols and revolvers. Naturally new, less powerful cartridges had to be introduced for them, which naturally made the supplying of ammunition in case of war more difficult.

This problem now faced the Bavarians as well. Of course it would have been possible to build a Werder carbine for the rifle cartridge with its load of 4.3 grams of powder. Something similar was actually done later for the M/71 carbine with the considerably stronger M/71 cartridge. For the planned Werder pistol, though, the rifle cartridge could not be considered. Since both the carbine and

the pistol were intended for the cavalry, it was decided to build both weapons for a weaker 11 mm caliber cartridge that would be produced. This solved the problem of uniform ammunition for the cavalry on the one hand, but on the other, it limited the Werder carbine to unsatisfactory performance from the start.

On February 19, 1869 the Rifle Factory in Amberg received the order to provide a model carbine and twelve experimental examples for troop testing. The new weapon was to be only 80 centimeters long, have a 36.5 cm barrel and an 11 cm mechanism. This mechanism, shorter than the rifle's by four centimeters, was scaled down precisely. In order to exclude unintentional cocking and re-leasing of the hammer during use on horseback, the cocking lever had an additional spring lever to hold it in the safety position. Later the projecting cocking lever was given a slight inward bend.

To attach the carbine hook in front of the rider's chest, two interlocking rings were attached under the small of the butt. A massive iron cap at the front end carried and protected the foresight at both sides and attached the barrel to the shaft.

Insufficient Performance From the Start

The model cartridge for the carbine and pistol had already been approved on April 26, 1869. It had a brass case 35 mm long (the rifle cartridge measured 50 mm) and held a 22-gram soft lead bullet with a diameter of 11.51 mm, the same as the rifle bullet. The load of powder weighed 2.5 grams (the rifle's weighed 4.3 grams), and its total weight was 33 grams (the rifle's weighed 36 grams).

The performance of this cartridge, as used in the carbine, was never satisfactory. The relatively heavy bullet did penetrate four one-inch spruce boards at 300 paces (216 meters), but the trajectory over this distance had already curved so much that its zenith was 29'' rh (75 cm) over the sight line.

In later years there were several attempts to upgrade the performance of the carbine cartridge. The Rifle Factory and the Military Gunnery School in Augsburg experimented between 1873 and 1875 with cartridges that contained 3, 3.8 and even 4 grams of powder, almost as much as in the rifle cartridge. To improve the carbine's performance, it would even have been acceptable at that time to introduce three different types of cartridge for the rifle, carbine and pistol. But it soon became clear that even this sacrifice would have been pointless. The strengthened and lengthened test cartridges gave the trajectory sufficient power to reach 600 paces (432 meters), but the accuracy of the carbine declined, to say nothing of other unpleasant factors that now appeared: Muzzle puff, recoil and problems in inserting the long cartridges into the short carbine mechanism. So the weak cartridge was retained, along with its shot performance.

There were also difficulties in producing the 4000 carbines with which the privates and corporals of the six Bavarian light cavalry regiments were to be equipped, as long as they were not regarded as ". . . blacksmiths, saddlers, trumpeters, stretcher bearers, engineers, blacksmith trainees and officers' servants in regimental marches." The latter, along with the Uhlans and cuirassiers, were issued Werder pistols.

According to a cost projection at the Rifle Factory, a carbine would cost 22.30 Gulden. But since Amberg was fully occupied with converting the factory to Werder rifle production in 1869, the contract had to be given to a private firm. It went to the renowned weapons factory of August Francotte in Liège. The Belgians were required to use Werder mechanisms from the Cramer-Klett Machine Factory in Nürnberg.

On July 1, 1869 King Ludwig finally approved the introduction of the new cavalry weapons, but several changes to the model still ensued. The carbine's stock became slimmer, and the original fixed sight with a hole for short-range and a V-notch above it for long-range aiming were replaced by a fixed sight with a deep V-notch, with which either the fine or the thick foresight could be used.

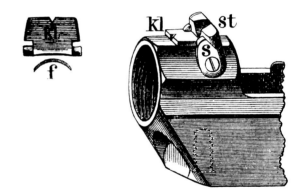

The sight of the Werder carbine in its final form: fixed sight and flap.

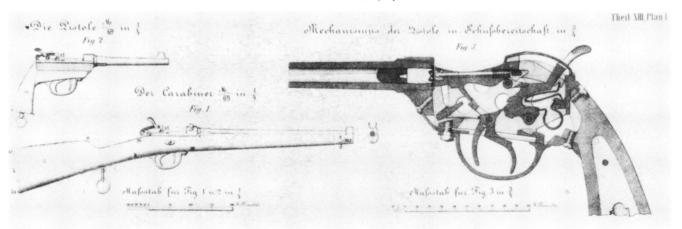

On August 31, 1870, when the 4000 carbines should already have been delivered according to the original production schedule, the War Ministry in Munich demanded a new sight for the third time. This time it was a fixed sight for up to 300 paces and a high flap for up to 500 paces. Beyond that, the chamber was changed in small ways.

Why the Bavarian Cavalry were Given Prussian Carbines

As long as the carbine model had not been finalized and approved, the Francotte rifle factory naturally could not produce. The result was that as July changed to August 1870 and the war with France began, the Bavarian light cavalrymen were left without carbines. So as not to have to send their cavalrymen into battle with muzzle-loaders against the French cavalry, who were armed with Chassepot carbines, the Bavarian War Ministry sent a call for help to Berlin as mobilization was ordered. The Prussians helped their South German allies as well and as quickly as they could. On July 27 and 28 the arsenal administration in Magdeburg sent 500 needle-gun carbines and 150,000 M/57 cartridges, on loan for the duration of the war. Every light cavalry regiment received 80 to 90 carbines. But that was naturally just a drop in the bucket.

The Rifle Factory Director Podewils suggested that within two or three weeks 600 old experimental Werder rifles be shortened and turned into make-shift carbines. In one test model, Director Podewils reported, ". . . no disturbing recoil whatsoever has appeared . . ." The shortened rifles were, of course, a pound heavier than the planned carbine model, but for this reason they could use the stronger rifle cartridges.

This suggestion was rejected and Bavaria thus missed a chance to obtain a carbine with ammunition that performed well. Munich was still hoping for deliveries from Belgium.

On August 18, 1870, as the fighting in France neared its high point, the first 624 carbines finally arrived in Amberg. At the same time there came a message from the manufacturer August Francotte that the Belgian government, in order to stress their neutrality in the German-French conflict, had forbidden the export of weapons. Therefore no more carbines could be delivered until the war was over.

And that was that. The light cavalry got by for the duration of the war with the few needle carbines, and only in July of 1871 were five of the six regiments, still on duty in France, issued the Werder carbines that had been produced by then. The Fourth Light Cavalry Occupation Regiment in Brie was the last to receive the new weapons, only in August of 1872, as French railway officials (surely not by accident) had sent the cases with the 80 Werder carbines astray. The shipment turned up in a Paris railroad station a year later.

In a Bavarian War Ministry decree of May 24, 1872 it was stated: ". . . M/69 carbines and pistols . . . with which the primary needs of the ten cavalry regiments have been met, (are) not to be produced further for 1872-73."

In 1875 the sights of the 4000 Werder carbines were changed for the fourth and last time. Along with the adaptation of the M/69 rifles for the M/71 cartridge, Bavaria had changed its military range-finding system from paces (0.72 meter) to meters. As a result, the carbines now had to have sights with metric calibration. They took the form, though, of the old pace sights, with fixed sights and flaps. August Francotte delivered the new parts.

This last change took place at a time when the mustering-out of the Werder carbines was as good as agreed on. In May of 1875 Prussia had accepted the M/71 carbine for the 71 cartridge. Since Bavaria had meanwhile also modified the rifle for this ammunition, the Werder carbine, with its inferior ammunition, no longer fit into the scheme of military armaments.

And in 1877 the M/69 carbine was replaced by the M/71 carbine.

The Long and Short M/69 Cartridges

Cartridge: M/69 (long)
Overall length: 65 mm
Gross weight: 36 grams
Case length: 50 mm
Case weight: 9.3 grams
Bullet length: 24.3 mm
Bullet weight: 22 grams
Bullet material: Soft lead
Bullet form: Round head with three grease grooves and small hollow in base
Bullet caliber: 11.51 mm
Charge weight: 4.3 grams
Type of powder: New Bavarian gunpowder (black powder)
Lining: perforated sheet cardboard

Cartridge: M/69 (short)
Overall length: 50 mm
Gross weight: 33 grams
Case length: 35 mm
Case weight: 8.2 grams
Bullet length: 24.3 mm
Bullet weight: 22 grams
Bullet material: Soft lead
Bullet form: Round head with three grease grooves and small hollow in base
Bullet caliber: 11.51 mm
Charge weight: 2.5 grams
Type of powder: New Bavarian gunpowder (black powder)
Lining: Perforated sheet cardboard

The production of metal cartridges with their industrial manufacturing process, which was brand new and untested at that time, was much more difficult in the late Sixties of the 19th Century than the series production of the weapons in which they were used.

In particular, the pressing and drawing of long cases for rifle cartridges could not always be done with the necessary degree of perfection. Impurities or different alloys of raw materials also made large-series production difficult. At first there were a great many torn, jammed and otherwise faulty cases, not only for the Werder cartridges, but also for the M/71 and, even later, the 88 cartridges. Such faults could be dangerous for the riflemen when they, under high pressure, drove powder gas at a

temperature of about 1000 degrees backward from the bed. Severe facial burns and many blindings were the results.

At that time, though, there was a second reason why attempts were made to improve case quality as soon as possible: the cases were so expensive that they were supposed to be reused as many times as possible.

In peacetime the soldiers had to pick up the empty cases, remove the percussion caps, wash the cases carefully in a series of operations, clean the ignition channels and dry the inside of the case with a stick wrapped in cloth. There were specific instructions as to what was to be done and how before the cases could be returned to the ammunition factory for reloading.

There they were generally given full loads four or five times, and when the first tears and bulges appeared in the material, the cases were still good enough to be used for blank or dummy cartridges. Only with the 88 rifle were "one-time cases" introduced in Germany, to be melted down after being used.

At first it was thought that production could be made simpler and cheaper if the cases were not pressed and drawn out of one piece, but were made with separate base and jacket and riveted together in the end. The first cartridges for the Werder experimental rifle mechanism were also made with two-piece cases. The base, including the cap chamber, was made of iron, the jacket of the case of copper. The detonator of the percussion cap was

Long and short M/69 cartridges The case construction with insertion ring and Berdan ignition (r) is the same, likewise the lead bullet (right). The 71 cartridge was developed from the long cartridge.

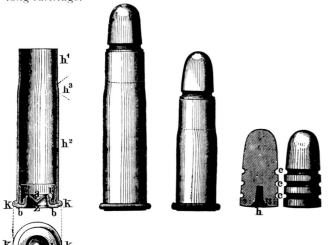

stamped out of sheet metal, in the Englishman Edward Boxer's system, and lay loose in the cap chamber.

Berdan's Patent Affair

During the comparison testing of the Werder and Berdan mechanisms in the winter of 1868-69, the cartridge of the Berdan rifle proved to be more durable and function more safely. It had a one-piece drawn copper case with a shoulder, weighing 9.6 grams, was loaded with 4.5 grams of black powder and carried a 26-gram cylindrical-ogival soft lead bullet without channels or hollow space. The .42 caliber (10 mm) bullet's cylindrical section was wrapped in paper; between the powder charge and the bullet was a grease pad which was supposed to keep the remains of the powder soft while passing through the barrel.

General Hiram Berdan had carefully patented the manufacturing process for his cartridges when he came to the firing tests in Munich. His Bavarian patent of September 12, 1869 describes the "...fixed detonator at the base of the percussion cap chamber and the production of the percussion cap orifice of the same piece of metal of which the head is made."

Berdan's cartridge with its projecting rim was pressed of thin sheet metal and had the same thickness everywhere. Cleverly arranged grooves and channels served to stiffen the sheet metal of the case. To provide additional firmness for the particularly burdened base section, a ring of sheet metal was inserted into the lower part of the case.

Bavaria wanted to use this case construction (which you see in the cutaway drawing of the M/69 cartridge) for the Werder cartridge, changing only the measurements. Berdan promised to deliver the necessary case presses to the main laboratory in Ingolstadt, took a down payment of 25,000 Gulden, and disappeared without fulfilling the contract.

Yet he had the effrontery to demand damages from the War Ministry for the use of his case patent. Strangely enough, nobody in Munich seemed to remember the Berdan affair any more. Thus it happened that the government seriously considered paying the American 6000 to 10,000 Gulden in compensation "honoris causa." But then the old act of 1868 suddenly popped up again and it was recalled that Berdan's contract default had delayed

M/69 (Werder) cartridges: Left: the rifle cartridge; right: the carbine cartridge.

ammunition production in Bavaria for months at that time. Berdan got nothing.

The dimensions of the cartridges for the M/69 Werder rifle and carbine, both adapted from the Berdan cartridge, are listed in the tables at the beginning of this chapter. The stamped soft lead bullet with the diameter of 11.15 mm, when fired, was pressed into the grooves of the 11-mm rifling. The three grease grooves were filled with grease (a mixture of five parts tallow, six parts yellow wax and one part spermaceti). The grease was pressed out in the deformation of the bullet during its passage through the barrel and lubricated the barrel walls. In this way, leading and crusting of the barrel were to be prevented.

The significance of the hollow area in the base of the bullet is explained in the service instructions for the Werder rifle: It "brings the bullet's center of gravity somewhat further forward and makes pressing easier during production."

The "igniting capsule" (percussion cap), an arched pan of sheet brass, held the primer, which was covered in turn by a piece of sheet metal. The primer consisted of four parts of explosive quicksilver, 2.5 parts of potassium chlorite, 1.5 parts of antimony and two parts of pulverized glass.

Lastly, the powder: The "Bavarian new gunpowder" consisted of 76 parts saltpeter, ten parts sulfur and 14 parts coal. It was made in the Ebenhausen powder mill and was not regarded as one of the best types of powder.

In 1874 the Military Gunnery School in Augsburg, in a report to the War Ministry, decried the poor quality of the Ebenhausen powder: ". . . residues of sulfur-potassium and coal dust in the barrel, then the unburned grains of powder being flung out and great differences in performance from shot to shot . . ."

In the cartridge, the load of powder and the bullet were separated by the "covering sheet", a cardboard sheet with a small hole in the middle, of which it was then believed that it could ". . . contribute to the prevention of the powder gas penetrating between the bullet and the case when fired."

Blank and Dummy Cartridges

Along with the full-strength cartridges for the M/69 rifle and carbine, there were also "blind" or blank cartridges which contained three plugs of gray blotting paper, one on top of another. Blank cartridges were marked by a collar around the case near the base and a red spot on the base. Dummy cartridges had the interior of the case filled with a piece of beechwood which projected and simulated the shape of the bullet.

For reasons of economy, the War Ministry wanted to have production done from the beginning at the Main Laboratory in Ingolstadt. But as production awaited the delivery of the case presses, the private ammunition factory of M. Utendörffer in Nürnberg received the contract to produce the first ammunition. Only at the beginning of 1871 was the Main Laboratory in Ingolstadt supplied with two sets of machinery. As of that March the Laboratory delivered half a million cartridge cases a month.

Costs and Problems of the First German Metal Cartridges

At that time, 5000 rifle cartridges cost the Bavarian government 216 Gulden and 34 Kreuzer. This was a lot of money in comparison to the old muzzle-loader ammunition. And then too, the expensive new cartridges were as yet nowhere near perfect. The poor quality of Bavarian gunpowder was already being talked about. And there were faults in the preparation of the cartridges.

In an investigation report of the Bavarian "Hand Firearms Testing Commission" of November 21, 1871, on the causes of barrel rupturing in new M/69 rifles, it was said: "It has been shown that cartridges occur at times which receive absolutely no or only a very meager charge of powder. As experience shows . . . a powder charge of 0.1 gram is sufficient to drive a bullet far enough into the barrel so that another cartridge can be loaded, and since only a charge of 0.25 grams is sufficient to drive the bullet out of the barrel with certainly, thus it can occur in cases of insufficient attention that, after a presumed failure, two bullets can be in the barrel at the same time and therefore . . . the barrel is torn apart in firing."

Production of the long Werder cartridges was halted after the rifles were adapted for the M/71 cartridge in 1875. The carbine and pistol cartridges, though, were still made in small quantities until 1907. In that year the Bavarian police, who had previously used a "police rifle" similar to the M/69 carbine, were given a new weapon.

The Mauser Brothers

The story of Paul and Wilhelm Mauser, two factory workers who rose to international fame, began under wretched conditions in the rural regions of Swabia. Wilhelm, born in 1834, and Paul (1838), the eleventh and thirteenth children of a 'parts filer' in the Royal Württemberg Rifle Factory in Oberndorf on the Neckar, were already working at lathes at the age of twelve in order to improve the big family's income. The Mausers were so poor that the Oberndorf city government did not even grant them the rights of citizenship.

The childhood experience of poverty was doubtless the most important motivation for Paul and Wilhelm Mauser's strivings for success. Along with that, two characteristics that are particularly attributed to the Swabians played a role too: diligence and tough perseverance.

Today it is difficult to determine which of the two brothers achieved more of their success. When both of them were dead, their heirs quarreled and tried to decide the question in court. They did not succeed.

Certainly Paul Mauser was the more talented designer. But without Wilhelm's capable negotiations with potential customers, some of whose contracts extended over many years, there probably would never have been a weapon factory named Mauser.

The foundation of this world-renowned firm has a rather complicated prehistory.

Since the early 1860s the brothers had worked intensively on their own breech-loader designs outside their working hours in the factory. In 1867 one model had developed to the point that they could venture to make it known. It was a cylindrical breech mechanism with a chamber case, similar to the Dreyse needle gun. The lock was a completely new design and improved with a striker for the central ignition of metal cartridges.

It is indicative of the limited opportunities of the two Oberndorf inventors that they could not personally exhibit their model weapon to the appropriate foreign governments, but had to limit themselves to presenting it to the embassies in nearby

Wilhelm Mauser (1834-1883)

Paul Mauser (1838-1914)

Stuttgart. There, of course, the brothers had to deal with diplomats, most of whom were scarcely qualified or interested enough to recognize the good points of the Mauser rifle.

"Of Faulty Construction"

The Prussian ambassador brushed off the inventors at once, advising them that no change from the proven Dreyse rifle was contemplated, which was probably untrue. The representative of the Kingdom of Bavaria, though, sent the model gun to Munich, where it was judged and rejected by the Hand Firearms Commission in a memorandum of January 16, 1868: "Errors in design principle," it was said, "that cannot be disposed of. Danger of cartridge self-ignition if a foreign body gets into the lock..." and finally: "Three of four springs (in the lock) are of faulty construction..."

The Mauser rifle was well received only in Vienna. The Imperial and Royal War Minister was so impressed by it that he showed the weapon to the agent of the American arms firm of Remington with the comment that he would choose this rifle if his government's decision had not already been given in favor of the Wänzel conversion mechanism.

In fact, the Mauser breech was particularly suited for use in the conversion of muzzle-loaders, and such mechanisms were wanted by practically all the European states at that time. The Remington agent, Samuel Norris, hoped to make a business deal of his own when he visited the brothers in

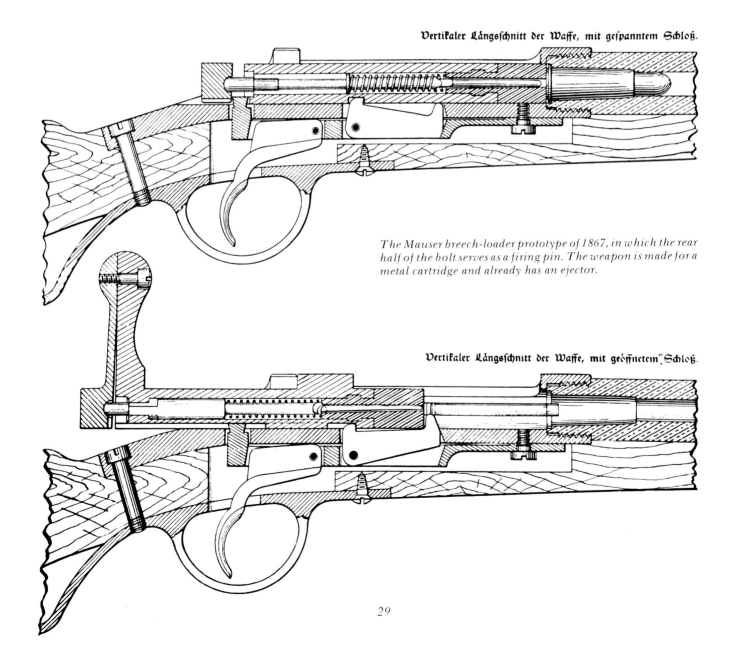

Vertikaler Längsschnitt der Waffe, mit gespanntem Schloß.

Vertikaler Längsschnitt der Waffe, mit geöffnetem Schloß.

The Mauser breech-loader prototype of 1867, in which the rear half of the bolt serves as a firing pin. The weapon is made for a metal cartridge and already has an ejector.

Oberndorf on September 13, 1867 and persuaded them to come to Liège and work for him there.

The Mausers in Liège

For a payment of 60,000 Francs, payable in ten yearly installments, the Mauser brothers declared that they were ready to decline all rights to their inventions in favor of Norris. Financially, the Norris contract did not bring the Mausers the advantages they had hoped for, since their partner did not keep his promises. Their stay in Liège, at that time the center of the weapons industry, was nevertheless to be important to the two designers' further work. They got acquainted with machines and production methods of which no one in the little Oberndorf rifle factory had the slightest idea. And what may have been even more important: they got the chance to experiment with the very latest things in the world of weapons: metal cartridges.

The most important work done by the Mausers in Liège was a conversion mechanism with which the French Chassepot needle gun could be prepared for metal cartridges. The patents for this came in 1868. How well the Mauser brothers had already accomplished their task became obvious some five years later, when great numbers of Chassepot rifles were converted in a very similar manner, in Germany as well as in France. The simple and well-designed bolt covers of the Chassepot rifle were used by Paul and Wilhelm Mauser later, in scarcely changed form, for the prototype of the Model 71. Used, to be sure, in connection with their own, meanwhile much improved breech piece of 1867.

Probably the last favor that the businessman Norris did for his partners was to put them in contact with the Prussian Military Gunnery School at Spandau in 1869. For attempts to develop a new infantry rifle were already going on then, and will be described in detail in the chapter on the Model 71.

From that time on, the Mausers were in constant contact with Spandau. They pinned all their hopes to a big Prussian contract that could make possible the founding of their own factory. But they could not bank on the Prussians. Of course the Mauser rifle was eventually introduced, but the inventors received no contract; they did not even receive license rights. They were brushed off with a mere pittance.

In spite of that, Paul and Wilhelm ventured to build their own small factory in Oberndorf in 1872. The manufacture of sights kept the business just barely afloat. Only at the end of 1873 did a big contract come their way. The government of Württemberg ordered 100,000 M/71 infantry rifles and at the same time offered to sell the brothers the unprofitable state rifle factory. The needed capital came from the Württemberg Union Bank. On February 5, 1874 the corporation of Mauser Brothers & Co. was founded.

This day marked the turning point. The Mauser firm made progress from then on, though the founders were no longer the masters of their own house, but only minor partners. After Wilhelm's death in 1884, the firm was turned into a stock company, whose shares were obtained three years later by the wealthy competitor firm of Ludwig Loewe in Berlin. From then on, Paul Mauser was a mere employee in his factory. The great profits from the worldwide business that was done with his name and his inventions were taken by others.

Under these conditions the countless honors that were accorded Paul Mauser in the last years of his life must have been only a poor consolation. In 1887 he had already been named a Royal Kommerzienrat, in 1898 his countrymen elected him to the Reichstag, in 1902 he became an honorary citizen of Oberndorf, in 1912 he, who was never an engineer, was awarded the Grashof Memorial Medal of the Society of German Engineers, and in the same year he received the Cross of Honor of the Crown of Württemberg. Along with this, he was raised to the nobility. When Paul von Mauser died in 1914, at the age of 76, he was portrayed as a national hero and a brilliant inventor. But was he really?

The "National Hero" Paul Mauser

From the perspective of the summer of 1914, at the end of which millions of men carried Mauser rifles into the World War, Paul von Mauser may well have been a national hero. His portrayal as a genius, though, is inaccurate. His career and the chronological order of his many patents show that a great awareness never struck him. Instead he worked steadily, industriously from one small success to the next for decades. For an absolutely

The first factory of the Mauser brothers, built in Oberndorf on the Neckar in 1872-73.

straight line leads from the first Mauser breech-loader of 1867 to the last repeater of 1898. How could it have been otherwise?

Paul Mauser, who only attended elementary school and had no knowledge of the laws of mathematics and physics, had to derive this basic knowledge from the experience of his daily practice.

His designs were not born on the drawing board, but in the interrelationship between the workshop and the firing range. This is probably also the reason why the Mauser repeating system reached the highest degree of perfection and has been copied about a hundred million times in the last eight decades without the slightest change.

Infantry Rifle M/71

Type: *Infanteriegewehr M/71*
Number: 55744
Year made: 1878
Manufacturer: Royal Bavarian Rifle Factory, Amberg
Function: Single shot
Overall length: 1350 mm
Gross weight: 4.5 kg
Barrel length: 830 mm
Barrel caliber: 11 mm
Number of riflings: 4
Rifling direction: right
Rifling length: 550 mm
Rifling depth: 0.3 mm
Breech: Cylindrical, opening lever

Safety: Leaf, works only when cocked
Sight: Standing sight, small flap and frame, to 1600 meters
Standard ammunition: Cartridge 71
Disassembly: Turn bolt handle up, loosen bolt stop screw, lift washer, press trigger through, draw bolt out of receiver to rear. Right hand holds bolt, left hand turns cocking piece 90 degrees. Bolt head removed including extractor.
Place bolt vertically on point of firing pin and push down until firing pin nut can be unscrewed. Release firing pin, take firing pin and main spring out of bolt. Assemble in opposite order.
Caution: Screw firing pin nut all the way in!

Since Wilhelm Mauser's first visit to the Prussian Military Gunnery School at Spandau in 1869, the "Mauser-Norris" design participated in the tests of the Rifle Testing Commission for the purpose of finding a new Prussian infantry rifle. At first this was of no significance, for at that time the Prussians tested everything new that existed in the area of handguns in Europe.

At first the competitors of the Mauser design were: Henry-Martini (England), Comblain (Belgium) and Beaumont (Netherlands). Added later were: Berdan II (USA), Vetterli (Switzerland) and Chassepot (France). The most serious competitor, though, was the Bavarian Werder rifle. Of course the Prussians had reservations about the vertical breech, for they were accustomed to the Dreyse cylindrical breech after thirty years. But the Werder cartridge, which was later adopted in modified form for the new rifle, drew their interest.

After the Mauser brothers had broken with Samuel Norris at the end of 1869 and moved back to Oberndorf from Belgium early in 1870, Wilhelm immediately resumed his contact with Prussia. He traveled to Spandau to find out for himself what was happening in the rifle tests.

On May 10, 1870 he wrote to his brother in Oberndorf:
"That a new rifle is sought in Prussia is definite, and ours is surely at the head of the list. In terms of simplicity it stands alone among all the rifles they have there. In any case, they are making very few tests . . ."
According to the wishes of the commission members, the Mauser rifle underwent several significant modifications thereafter, for the Prussians kept offering new constructive criticism. Wilhelm Mauser sent them on to his brother in Oberndorf, and Paul went to work on them in the small workshop that he had set up in his father-in-law's house. The Franco-Prussian War interrupted the tests for some time, but in the summer of 1871 Wilhelm again took his usual place in Spandau. The Mauser rifle became better and better; the Werder rifle lost ground.

On September 18, 1871 the Bavarian military envoy, *Oberst* Theodor Kries, reported from Berlin that the commission had judged the Werder mechanism unsatisfactory and also decried the heavy dirtying of the barrel and the difficulty of cleaning the Bavarian rifle.

On November 7 the commission had already agreed on several principles of the new rifle to be accepted: Barrel and stock lengths had been determined, the caliber was to be eleven millimeters, but no decision had yet been made as to the mechanism.

Of course the Mauser cylindrical breech had meanwhile become the uncontested favorite, but according to the opinions expressed by the dominant members of the Rifle Testing Commission, the problem of the safety catch had not yet been solved satisfactorily. The Mauser brothers agreed to make new attempts to solve the problem within two months, and so the first decision, on December 2, 1871, was made in favor of their rifle. It was immediately given the M/71 designation, although it did not yet exist in its final form. 2500 test rifles like the current model were produced at the rifle factory in Spandau. Paul Mauser solved the safety problem within the time limit. On February 14, 1872 Wilhelm was able to consent two alternative breeches at Spandau, one of which suited the conceptions of the commission.

In a note from the Prussian War Ministry it was finally stated: "His Majesty the Kaiser and King, through the All-Highest Cabinet Order of March 22, 1872, has condescended to approve the test of the Infantry Rifle M/71 and to command most graciously that rifles of this type be produced for the rearmament of the infantry . . ."

It was clear that the other states of the Reich would introduce the new rifle along with Prussia. With the exception of Bavaria. In a ministerial memorandum from the War Ministry in Munich, the following observation is found:

"If, as it appears, the Mauser rifle were to be accepted for the other German states in the future, the main reason would be . . . not the greater advantages of this weapon as compared with the Werder . . . but quite definitely that the relationship of the Mauser to the needle gun in terms of design, manufacturing process and use offers advantages in terms of allowing quick production and rearmament, quick familiarity with the new weapon for the troops equipped and familiar until now with the needle gun . . ."

This was surely a correct interpretation. It was true that the Mauser breech closely resembled that of the needle gun, not in its outward appearance but in its loading process, but was considerably less complicated.

The Mauser Mechanism

The bolt of the M/71, with the bolt handle turned up 90 degrees, can be pushed back and forth in the receiver. Its rearward motion is limited by the washer-shaped bolt stop screwed to the bolt guide, contacting a rounded shoulder on the receiver bridge. With the bolt fully retracted, a cartridge can be placed in the loading ramp through the opening in the side of the receiver. Pushing the bolt forward will seat the cartridge in the chamber. When the bolt handle is pushed down, the rounded corner on the back of the bolt handle engages the locking cam on the front of the receiver bridge, forcing the bolt slightly forward and helps to seat the round in the chamber.

In the Mauser M/71 receiver, as in almost all subsequent Mauser systems, cocking occurs almost completely as the bolt is unlocked through engagement of the cam nose on the cocking piece with the cocking cam on the rear of the bolt . When the bolt is pulled to the rear, the bolt guide follows the lengthwise slot in top of the receiver bridge. When the bolt is open (and cocked) the cocking piece is held, aginst the pressure of the main spring, against the rear surface of the bolt.

To prevent the cocking piece from turning when the bolt is drawn back, the firing pin which holds the entire bolt together is flattened at the left rear. This flat in the end of the firing aligns with the flat in the cocking piece, fixing the position of the two pieces. At the same time, a flat-topped section behind the head of the firing pin extends into a slot in the bolt head, which also cannot be turned because the extractor runs in its slot in the receiver. Thus only the central portion of the bolt can turn, while the cocking piece and bolt head cannot change their position in regard to one another.

At the rear end of the cocking piece is the firing pin nut, which engages the threads of the firing pin; holding it in place. The safety catch extends longitudinally, with a bolt flattened on one side, into the opening at the rear of the cocking piece. With the bolt cocked and locked, the safety can be moved from the left, or 'off' position, to the right, or 'locked' position. In the process, the rounded half

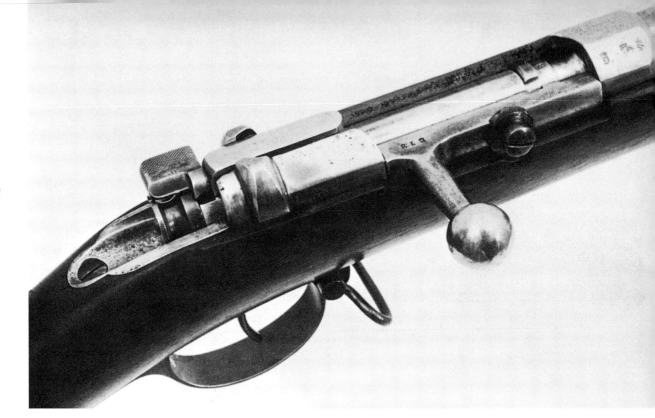

The M/71 receiver, closed and uncocked.

of the safety-catch bolt fits into a companion notch in the cocking piece, and thus prevents the opening of the bolt, as well as premature release of the firing pin.

In its cocked condition, the cocking piece is held with its front end against the rear which projects in front of the cocking piece from below. A pre-liminary pull on the trigger (the slack) levers the sear downward, almost out of engagement with the cocking piece. A slight additional pull will lever the sear downward enough to release the cocking piece; the coil with attached cocking piece and firing pin nut forward igniting the cartridge.

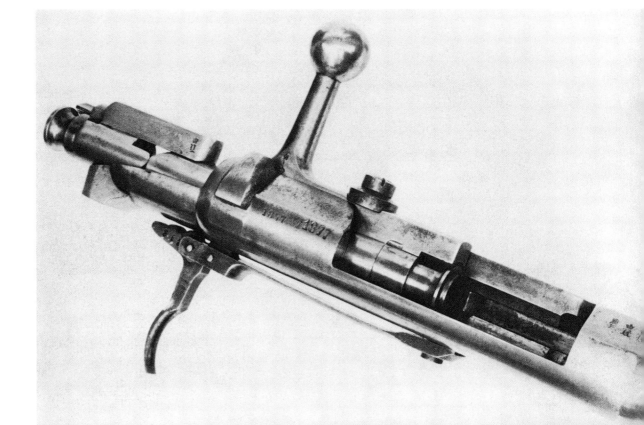

The M/71 receiver complete with trigger; the barrel is detached, the bolt half-open.

The M 71 bolt, removed from the receiver.

A Perfect Safety System

Several details of this breech deserve special attention and make the handiwork of Paul Mauser evident. The perfected safety mechanism, which was used again and again with scarcely any changes in his later models, was already being talked about, as was the bolt tension that was compelled to take place on opening. Also involved is the curve on the rear of the case head which, when the breech is opened, causes the fired cartridge first to be loosened in its bed before the actual process of extraction takes place.

In the M/71, exactly as in all later designs, Mauser gave particular concern to the safety of the rifleman. He may well have been thinking of his

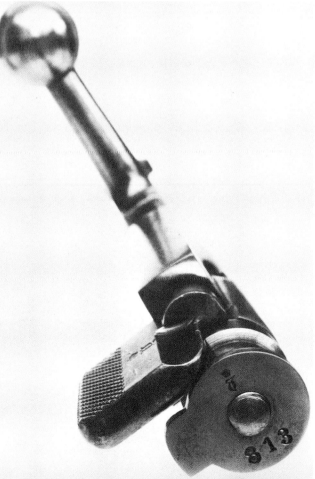

The M.71 bolt; a view of the bolt head with "plug" and extractor (left), and of the firing pin nut and safety catch (right).

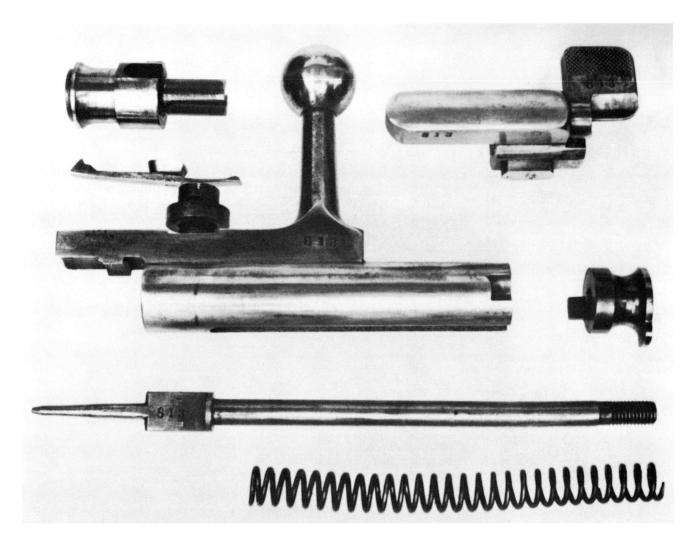

The M/71 breech bolt disassembled. The parts from top to bottom: bolt head with extractor, cocking piece with safety, bolt with bolt stop and screw, firing pin nut, firing pin and main spring.

own safety too, for to the end of his days he tested all his weapons himself and thus knew the dangers. Despite this, accidents with the prototypes were not completely prevented. In 1901, at the age of 63, Paul Mauser lost his left eye in a firing test with one of his first self-loading rifles.

At the time when the Model 71 was created, the greatest danger was caused by faulty cartridge cases which did not contain the gas pressure and tore. Thus high-pressure hot gases could shoot backward out of the cartridge bed. The breech needed to be fitted with a system that prevented the gas from shooting into the rifleman's face.

For this purpose the bolt head was fitted with a "plug" and a ring-shaped flange which worked together to close the chamber as tightly as possible at the rear. If a cartridge ripped and gas still managed to find its way out of this labyrinth, then

it was collected in a ring groove at the front end of the loading opening and safely directed up and out.

Two additional "gas catchers" are located in the ejector groove of the receiver. This groove, which extends from the chamber to the end of the case, is blocked once by the cocking piece lug and again by an addition at the left side of the firing pin nut.

Parts Not Made by Mauser

Aside from the breech mechanism, not much more of the M/71 rifle was made by the Mausers. The 11-millimeter barrel with its four riflings measuring 550 mm is a copy of the French Chassepot barrel, the trigger mechanism comes from the Dreyse needle gun, the measurements of the gun, its stock form and parts were set by the Rifle Testing

Commission — the cartridge was developed in Spandau.

This did not happen because the Mauser brothers had made no suggestions of their own, but rather because the Spandau commission, under the leadership of Colonel Kalinowski, wanted to realize their

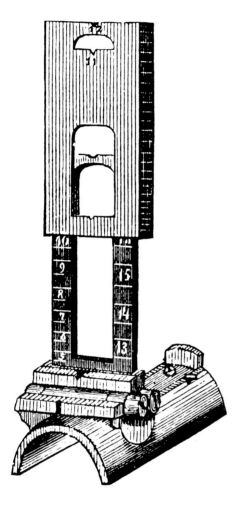

The sight of the infantry rifle, flap up and frame drawn out.

own conceptions at that time. Despite that, the cooperation between the designers and the commission was still excellent then, though the situation was to change later. The one incomprehensible point is why the cartridge ejector, which was already present in the Mauser model rifle of 1867-68, was not retained for the M/71. This simple mechanism, which would have increased the rate of fire of the cylinder breech considerably, was forbidden the Mausers. To remove the fired cartridges, the soldiers were supposed to tip the rifle to the right on its long axis so that the case fell out of the

loading opening. The elimination of the ejector may also have been connected with the fact that in 1871 no value was placed on a fast rate of fire. The fear that soldiers could shoot up their supply of ammunition too fast was great, and was not entirely unjustified, as the Bavarian reports on experiences with the Werder rifles in the 1870-71 war had shown. For the same reason, the Swiss Vetterli rifle, a repeater with a tubular magazine for eleven cartridges, was not even included in the short list during the tests at Spandau, although the weapon was ten years ahead of its time.

Faults of Model 71

The M/71 infantry rifle has a reputation "like rolling thunder" among connoisseurs in all the world. Obviously, the past hundred years have erased the memories of this model's weak points. For the Model 71 had its faults, like any other. First of all, there was the problem of "weak igniting ability", with which the Rifle Testing Commission had concerned itself until 1876. There were misfires because the firing pin often did not push far enough into the percussion cap. At first attempts were made to improve the ignition by changing the cocking piece. In order to strengthen the impact of the firing pin point, three possibilities were tried. The strength of the coil spring could be increased (stronger push), the cocking piece could be lightened so the firing pin had less weight to carry forward. But one could also — and that would have been the finest solution — attach the firing pin firmly to the cocking piece and thus increase striking power. (In the M/71 the cocking piece sits loosely on the striker.)

In 1875 the Prussian First Lieutenant Wind had been the first to suggest the coupling of the cocking piece and bolt, a small modification that would have cost three to four Marks per gun. And in October of 1876 the Prussian War Ministry approved the adaptation of 500 rifles to the Wind system for troop testing.

In the meantime, though, the problem of weak ignition capability had solved itself: by a change in the ammunition. As of 1876 the M/71 cartridges made in Prussia no longer had an arched (Bavarian) percussion cap, but a flat one that offered less resistance to the striker.

Two other problems of the rifle could not be solved, as they were based on the design and affected the accuracy of aim: the upper band attachment on the barrel and the one-sided attachment of the cocking piece through the bolt guide. The importance of the one-sided attachment was not recognized at all at first, since the deviation of aim that resulted was covered by the first and even greater weakness.

But at the beginning of 1873 a report from the Military Gunnery School at Spandau on "the varying relations of the striking point to the aiming point of the M/71 rifle" circulated through the war ministries of the states, as did the transcript of a report that a Major Peterson had given at Spandau, which had attracted much attention. His subject: "Deviations of the striking point of the M/71 rifle with the same aiming point."

The chief cause of these phenomena was the screw connection between the upper band and the barrel. The decision had originally been made in favor of this attachment in order to give a secure grip to the bayonet, whose attachment was on the right side of the upper band. The iron ring encircled the barrel (which had a plate on its underside at this point), the cleaning rod and the front end of the forearm. A roundhead screw was screwed through the upper band and the barrel plate from the left. This firm connection prevented the barrel from vibrating while firing and led to a change in the impact point. How great the eliminated vibrating power had been was shown in terms of damage to the upper band threads, which occurred in many rifles.

The M/71 Bayonet

The bayonet for the infantry rifle had a single blade 470 mm long with a ridged back and two hollows. Only the point was two-bladed. The crossguard was curved in an S shape and encircled the muzzle of the barrel with a ring. The massive brass ring with an attachment slot in the end of the handle,

Upper band attachment of the M/71 (seen here dismantled and displayed on the Jägerbüchse). The screw attachment with the barrel plate had an unfavorable effect on the aim.

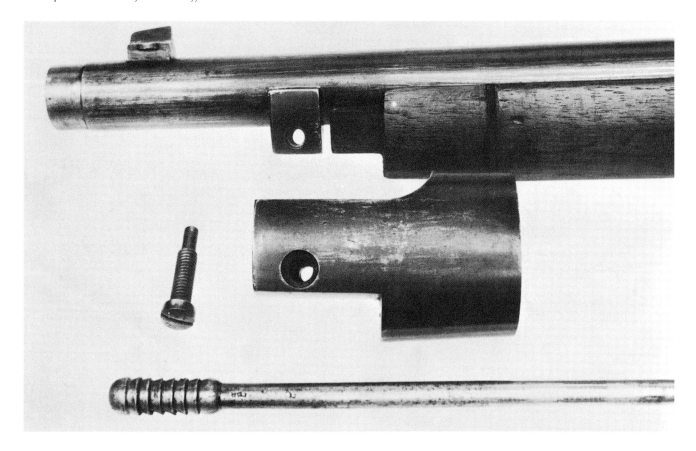

made to be pushed onto the bayonet lug, is made with diagonal ribs on the right side, while the left side is smooth. The pressure spring, visibly set on the right side, ended in a button that projected on the left. The mouth and locating panels of the sheath are made of sheet metal, and the leather is blackened. Six percent of the bayonets had sawtooth backs and could be used as tools in the field. (Not to be confused with the engineers' bayonets that had the same handle and crossguard but a considerably wider blade.)

The M/71 bayonets were made by the firms of Weyersberg, Kirschbaum & Co. of Solingen, V. Jung & Son of Suhl, and others, and cost about four Marks. To make them all uniform, the following specifications were agreed on:

Every bayonet blade had to be turned twice to either side on the turning board for 46 millimeters. This showed whether the blade returned to its straight position afterward. In the following striking test (twice each with blade and back against a piece of hardwood), the blade was not to bend, nor was the cutting edge to flatten.

Changes to Model 71 as of 1882

After being used by the troops for ten years, the following changes were ordered for further M/71 production: The small flap of the sight (for the foresight to 360 meters) was equipped with a small coil spring on the right side of its frame which made folding simpler. This change was later made to some of the rifles made before 1882.

In order to make repairs to the receiver bolt guide easier, since its rear surface was damaged by rubbing on the receiver, a hardened "receiver attachment piece" was inserted in the end of the guide and held in place by a transverse pin. From then on the bolt stop and its holding screw could no longer be removed. The screw was held by a transverse pin in the bolt guide and could be unscrewed only as far as was necessary to dismantle the bolt.

The M/71 bayonet (fixed) with leather scabbard (above). The M/71 engineers' bayonet (below) with saw teeth.

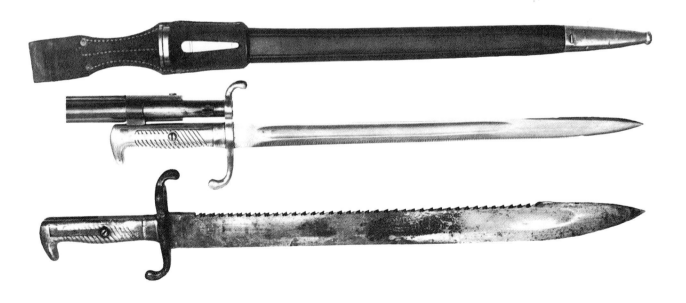

M/71 Production and its Costs

When the Model 71 was introduced, Prussia maintained three state — "royal" — rifle factories in Spandau, Erfurt and Danzig, in which most of the required new weapons were to be produced. The rifle factory in Spandau, having the advantage of being close to the Gunnery School and Rifle Testing Commission, was able to commence production of the new type in 1872. Danzig and Erfurt began in 1873. These delays took place because of the necessary reequipping of the factories and the wait for the many new production machines, almost all of them made by the firm of Pratt and Whitney in Hartford, Connecticut. The drop forges and milling machines arrived gradually between the autumn of 1872 and the beginning of 1874.

In the "dimension tables" for M/71 production, tolerances had been reduced for the first time to hundredths of a millimeter, and thus complex standards of precision had to be prepared before production began. For the M/71 barrels, for example, the following conditions were established: "The caliber measures 11 cm and the barrel cylinder (one of the measuring standards) of 10.95 mm must go into every barrel, while one of 11.1 cm must no longer fit . . ." The dimensions and the "centricity" of the cartridge bed were determined with the help of a sulfur casting and the strength by a charge of ten grams of powder (twice the normal load) and one lead shot 47.5 mm long and 10.2 mm in diameter.

The strictness of the Prussian Inspection Commission was well known; only first-class parts received their stamp of approval.

As always, when a new rifle model was introduced, production was under great time pressure. With the M/71 too it was clear that the Prussian state factories would not be able to meet the army's needs within the stipulated time of five years. Thus the Prussian War Ministry gave a whole series of contracts to firms outside Prussia. In May of 1872 an order for 10,000 rifles was given to the Royal Bavarian Rifle Factory in Amberg. The "Production Society of Spangenberg & Sauer, Schilling, Haenel" in Suhl made a total of 180,000 rifles for

Prussian orders by February of 1876, and contracts were even given outside the Reich. The Austrian Weapons Factory Co. in Steyr made a total of 293,876 rifles from the beginning of 1874 to the beginning of 1878, and the English "National Arms & Ammunition Co." in Birmingham accepted a contract to make 75,000 rifles.

It is all the more remarkable that Paul and Wilhelm Mauser came out empty-handed. They had staked all their hopes on an M/71 contract but were only allowed to make a few thousand sights. The brothers were robbed by the Prussian state, in a scarcely credible manner, of the fruits of their years of labor.

It was typical of the Prussian attitude that the state did not let anyone set up conditions for it. Thus the Mauser brothers did their developmental work without knowing what they would receive for the acceptance of their rifle. They had suggested 60,000 Taler (at that time 180,000 Marks), a sum that the President of the Rifle Testing Commission, Colonel Kalinowski, had recognized as fair in a private conversation with Wilhelm Mauser. But the War Ministry in Berlin had a different view of the matter.

In February of 1872 the "Royal General War Department" informed the two designers of its decision to ". . . offer you in recognition of all the aforementioned conditions as well as in particular consideration of the situation that you have devoted yourselves in the past years almost exclusively to the improvement of your rifle which took part in the tests here, and have worked diligently and incurred costs, a compensation of 7000 to 8000 Taler . . ."

The Mausers finally received 8000 Taler (then 24,000 Marks) and could not even hope for M/71 contracts from foreign countries, as the design of the weapon had been declared a "government secret." A further result: The Mausers could obtain no patents within the country and were not allowed to obtain any outside. The secrecy was lifted in 1874, but the patent ban remained in effect. In this way the Prussian state wanted to prevent the possibility of the Mausers charging licensing fees. As compensation for the loss, King Wilhelm granted an "unconditional authorized cash gift" of 12,000

Marks on March 18, 1876. Along with the first compensation, then, Paul and Wilhelm Mauser received a total of 36,000 Marks. What saved the Mausers was that the War Ministry of Württemberg finally took pity on the Mausers and gave them an order for approximately 100,000 M/71 rifles in December of 1873, to run until July of 1879. An order from the Chinese Empire for 26,000 M/71 rifles also arrived, plus one from Serbia in 1878 for 100,000 of the Mauser-Koka Model 78/80 rifles, a slightly changed version of the German M/71.

The Württemberg contract settled the following prices: For the first 11,000 rifles, 22 Taler (66 Marks) each, for the rest 18 Taler 55 silver Groschen (about 55 Marks).

By way of comparison: National Arms & Ammunition of Birmingham sold M/71 rifles for 55 shillings (about 55 Marks), Steyr had also agreed on 55 Marks, and Amberg reckoned on 28.5 Gulden (about 57 Marks) for Bavaria's own use, thus without profit.

The M/71 Jäger Rifle

Type: *Jägerbüchse M/71*
Number: 5419
Year made: 1883
Manufacturer: Royal Prussian Rifle Factory, Danzig
Function: Single shot
Overall length: 1245 mm
Gross weight: 4.33 kg
Barrel length: 720 mm
Barrel caliber: 11 mm

Number of riflings: 4
Direction of riflings: Right
(other rifling data same as M/71)
Action: Bolt action, cocking on opening
Safety: Leaf, working only when cocked
Sight: Standing sight, small flap and frame, to 1600 meters
Standard ammunition: 71 cartridge
Disassembly: Same as M/71 infantry rifle

It was part of a century-old Prussian tradition that the Jäger troops carried different rifles than the infantry. This custom went back to the times when the "Jäger" troops were usually foresters and were equipped with rifles exactly like the hunting rifles then in use. They were rifled guns known as "Büchsen." The infantry, on the other hand, used smooth-bore guns, "Flinten."

When the Prussian infantry also learned to shoot rifled guns after 1841, the Jäger rifles became superfluous in principle. Yet in 1865 the Jäger troops were again given a special weapon.

Aside from the Dreyse uniform needle breech, the classic characteristics of the old Jäger rifles had been carried over to the new model: octagonal barrel, stock all the way to the muzzle, barrel attachment by side bolts and levers, trigger guard with a curved handrest, hunting-style strap and hair-trigger.

The next model, the M/71 Jäger rifle, was the last authentic special model of this kind among German military armaments and retained only two of the classic characteristics: It was about ten centimeters shorter than the infantry rifle, and had a trigger guard with a curved handrest extending to the rear. The other differences from the infantry rifle resulted from the shorter construction.

M/71 infantry rifle (above) and Jäger rifle (below), showing comparative lengths.

The shortened barrel had the same thickness and form as that of the infantry rifle, and therefore had to have a 10-mm extension on the muzzle so that the ring of the bayonet would fit. The sight had the same construction as the infantry rifle with adjustment to a maximum range of 1250 meters (1200 meters for the infantry rifle). Aside from the bottom cap of the shaft, the trigger panel, the cleaning rod and the breech mechanism, all the metal parts were blued (those of the infantry rifle were browned).

The bayonet used on the Jäger rifle was traditionally called the "stag catcher." It had a blade ten centimeters longer, in order to equal the length of the infantry rifle with the bayonet fixed. The iron handle bore riveted black leather grips with fish-skin patterns. The decorations on the scabbard were also made of iron.

The M/71 Jäger rifle was used in all the states of the Reich except Bavaria. The Rifle Testing Commission had received the assignment of designing this special weapon after the rifle model was finished, in the summer of 1872. The exact date on which the Jäger rifle was introduced can no longer be determined exactly; it was presumably 1873. In any case, delivery to the troops took place only after 1876. The Danzig rifle factory was set up to produce it, and there the series ended in 1884.

The Mauser factory in Oberndorf produced some 3000 of them for use in Württemberg, plus 100,000 Jäger rifles that the Prussian War Ministry had ordered from the "Austrian Weapons Factory Co." in Steyr. The weapons were delivered between January 1874 and December 1875. The price: 57 Marks.

Troop marking on the shaft plate of an M/71 Jäger Rifle.

The M/71 Carbine

Type: *Karabiner M/71*
Number: 9485
Year made: Not known
Manufacturer: "AGH", Suhl (Arbeitsgemeinschaft Haenel)
Function: Single shot
Overall length: 1000 mm
Gross weight: 3.47 kg
Barrel length: 485 mm
Barrel caliber: 11 mm

Number of riflings: 4
Rifling direction: Right
(Other rifling data same as M/71 rifle)
Action: Bolt action, cocking on opening
Safety: Leaf, works when cocked
Sight: Step frame sight up to 1100 meters
Standard ammunition: 71 cartridge
Disassembly: Same as M/71 infantry rifle

In the 1870-71 war the proud German cavalrymen had learned the meaning of fear. High on their horses, with glittering cuirasses or glowing uniforms, they offered every rifleman a target scarcely to be missed. And the precise-firing, long-range Chassepot rifles of their enemies had to be faced by the Uhlans, heavy and light cavalrymen with nothing more than old-fashioned smooth-bore pistols and needle-gun carbines, with which one could, after all, still hit a target with certainty at a hundred meters.

The feared "Franctireurs", French marksmen who fired from under cover, soon found out that mounted messengers, post riders and small mounted patrols were completely in their hands. In the end the cavalry only dared to march with an infantry escort. For then the "Franctireurs" left them in peace.

These experiences, recorded in many reports, showed how urgently the creation of high-performance weapons for the cavalry had suddenly become. It seemed as if the time when a cavalryman could safely rely on his saber or lance was over once and for all.

Thus King Wilhelm of Prussia announced on March 6, 1873:
"1. A carbine corresponding to the M/71 infantry rifle is to be produced.
2. With this carbine are to be armed: all light cavalry regiments in place of the needle-gun carbine.
3. Of every squadron of Uhlans and heavy cavalry regiments, 32 privates, in place of the same number of cavalry pistols.
4. The mounted men of the supply-train battalions and administrations . . .
5. Until the new carbines are produced, Chassepot carbines or shortened Chassepot rifles are to be used. Each rider receives 48 cartridges . . ."

The German Kaiser and Prussian King Wilhelm had his own personal opinion of the carbine. He feared for the men's morale in battle and therefore added a noteworthy warning:
"I express the definite hope that the cavalry, after receiving the finished weapons, will be able, true to their glorious traditions, to maintain the ever-proven old Prussian cavalry spirit. The cavalrymen

The M/71 customs carbine with bayonet attachment, made by Mauser at Oberndorf in 1876. A police weapon.

The sight of the M/71 carbine. The fixed notch is at the foot of the (here folded) frame. The small flap is up.

shall continue to seek their first and truest occupation in throwing themselves at the enemy with cold steel as soon as the enemy is within reach in the open field. The firearms shall, in addition, never be put to use in a closed troop. They are, rather, intended solely for use by individual cavalrymen, vedettes, patrols and flankers, as well as for those rare cases in which fighting on foot becomes unavoidable . . .''

It was clear from the start that only a carbine in which the long, strong rifle cartridge could be used would be considered. Since on the other hand the weapon was supposed to be as short and light as possible for use on horseback, the designers on the Rifle Testing Commission took quite a long time until they had found the best compromise between these opposing demands.

Just two years later, in January of 1875, the guidelines for the new carbine were set for the time being. The most important of them in brief were: Overall length one meter, barrel with octagonal form and rifle-type cone, possible simplification of the case similarly to the Chassepot. The carbine was to have a cleaning rod, a sight similar to the Jäger rifle, and bent bolt handle.

The model weapon, which was finally accepted in May of 1875, had the same mechanism as the longer M/71 with the exceptions of the bent bolt handle and a small change in the crosspiece. The frame sight with fixed sight (270 meters) and a small flap could be adjusted to 1200 meters, and a test report notes in particular "that the actual effective range ends only at 1400 meters."

The cleaning rod was done away with. The stock reached to the muzzle and was connected to it there by a massive upper band with front sight protectors. The form of the butt was like that of the rifle, but the end plate was made somewhat wider in order to conduct the strong recoil of the carbine to the

shooter's shoulder somewhat more favorably. For the sake of durability, the carbine's trigger guard and trigger plate were made as a single piece; likewise the base of the sight was not soldered to the barrel but worked as an integral part of it. The carbine was one meter long.

It is really surprising what kind of performance the M/71 cartridge produced in connection with the barrel, which was only 48.5 cm long. Initial velocities were measured at Spandau in 1875 at 395 meters per second. (That of the rifle: 430 meters per second.)

Creation of the M/71 Carbine

In the summer of 1875 the War Ministry in Berlin was already negotiating with the "Austrian Weapons Factory Society" in Steyr for the delivery of 60,000 carbines. Since at that time all state weapons factories were still fully occupied with the production of infantry rifles, only private firms were considered for the contract. The Steyr director, Josef Werndl, was ready to deliver them for 47 Marks. Production was to start at the beginning of 1876. In the final contracts between Berlin and Steyr for a total of 65,000 carbines, delivery dates between June and December 1876 were set. In 1877 Saxony ordered another 10,000 M/71 carbines from Steyr.

Meanwhile the Kingdom of Bavaria had reorganized and equipped its cavalry in the Prussian manner and thus suddenly needed 10,000 carbines (the old Bavarian equipment plans had called for only 4000 Werder carbines). The state's needs, they thought, might also be met in Steyr. The negotiations were almost completed when another, much more favorable offer arrived in Munich.

The "Manufacturing Society of Spangenberg & Sauer, Schilling, Haenel" of Suhl offered M/71 carbines for 36 Marks and was also ready to take 14,000 Chassepot rifles captured by Bavaria in the war in return at the rate of 15 Marks apiece. The Bavarians agreed.

In Oberndorf, Mauser received an order for some 3000 M/71 carbines for the Royal Württemberg Cavalry.

The M/71 carbines disappeared from German armaments after 1892, for from that time on all mounted soldiers were gradually issued the new 8-mm caliber 88 carbine. The mustered-out black-powder carbines were sold to soldiers for two Marks apiece. A thousand leftover carbines were sent to China in 1906.

The 71 Cartridge

Cartridge: M/71 (11 x 60 R) until 1884
Overall length: 78 mm
Gross weight: 43.4 grams
Case length: 60 mm
Case weight: 12 grams
Bullet length: 27.7 mm
Bullet weight: 25 grams
Bullet material: Soft lead
Bullet shape: Round head, smooth, cylindrical part wrapped in paper
Bullet caliber: 11 mm
Charge weight: 5 grams
Type of powder: Gunpowder 71 (black powder)
Cross-section pressure: 26.3 grams/cc
Lining: Wax plug between two sheets of cardboard

Cartridge: M/71 (11 x 60 R) as of 1884
Overall length: 76.5 mm
Gross weight: 43.4 grams
Case length: 60 mm
Case weight: 12 grams
Bullet length: 26.2 mm
Bullet weight: 25 grams
Bullet material: Soft lead
Bullet shape: Round head with flattened head, paper wrapping
Bullet caliber: 11 mm
Type of powder: New gunpowder 71 (black powder)
Cross-section pressure: 26.3 grams/cc
Notes: As of 1884 the M/71 cartridges were made with modified bullets and percussion caps. These new cartridge components were designated: Bullet 71/84 and Percussion Cap 71/84. Every soldier had 100 cartridges in his pack.

71 cartridges in cross-section. From left to right: Base of case with 71/84 percussion cap, live cartridge with 71/84 bullet, blank cartridge 71 with paper plug, blank 71/84 with paper plug and hollow wooden bullet, dummy cartridge.

When Wilhelm Mauser introduced the breech-loader prototype at Spandau in 1869, from which the M/71 rifle was to develop later, he also offered a metal cartridge of which, unfortunately, only a very vague description has been preserved: short, bottle-shaped cases, formed from one piece, cap chamber with Berdan detonator. The case held 4.5 grams of the older Prussian gunpowder and carried a 25-gram lead bullet with an oval head. The bullet had three ring grooves on its cylindrical part which

were filled with grease. A cardboard disc separated the charge of powder and the bullet.

There are indications in the Mauser history that Samuel Norris could have obtained Austrian Werndl cartridges for his partners' experiments in 1867-68. The description of the Mauser test cartridge given above actually fits the original type of the Austrian M/67 rifle cartridge in several ways. It might be possible that the Mausers had worked with a slightly modified Werndl cartridge at that time. The choice of ammunition in Europe at that time was not very great.

As for the test cartridge, there were still many features of it to be determined: On account of the compression of the soft lead bullet when fired, all the grease was forced out of the grooves. Thus the lubrication was only enough for the rear part of the barrel, and lead was deposited in the forward section.

The "older Prussian gunpowder" also showed its failings: too many deposits and weak performance.

The results improved when English "Curtis & Harvey" powder was used in the tests and the charge was increased from 4.5 to 4.67 grams. In addition, the bullet was given a doubled paper wrapping on its cylindrical section. The cardboard disc between the charge and the bullet was replaced by a plug of grease that took over the lubricating function.

That was the situation in the summer of 1870, when the Franco-Prussian War interrupted the tests.

In the summer of 1871 the tests were resumed at Spandau. Since the Bavarian cartridge of the Werder rifle had worked so well in the war, it was now used in place of the Mauser test ammunition. On July 27, 1871 the General War Department in Berlin requested 5000 Werder cartridges and two bullet molds from Munich for the tests at Spandau.

The one-piece brass case of the Werder cartridge, made completely of thin sheet metal, had an inset ring of brass in the base, a strengthening that was supposed to prevent cartridges from tearing.

To increase the capacity of the cartridge and therefore its performance, the Prussians lengthened the cylindrical front section of the Bavarian case from 50 to 60 millimeters. Thus the paper-wrapped lead bullet could be set deeper in it (10.7 mm), and there was still room for the wax plug and five grams of "Metz powder."

This new propellant, made in the Metz powder factory in annexed Lorraine, had been created during testing with the help of a better process to imitate the English "Curtis & Harvey" powder. The Metz powder, to be sure, did not quite equal the quality standard of the English powder, but it was considerably better than the "older Prussian gunpowder." Production of Metz powder began in the autumn of 1871. It was later designated "Rifle Powder 71."

The plug, originally of pure beeswax and set between two cardboard discs, had a slight hollow in the side turned toward the bullet, which was supposed to assure that the grease could not stick to the base of the bullet.

The "ogival" soft lead bullet also had a slight pit in its base, to make room for the ends of the paper wrapping. The wrapping of hemp paper surrounded the shaft of the bullet to a height of 15 millimeters, measured from the base. The bullet itself had a diameter of 11 millimeters and weighed 25 grams. It was set so deep in the case that, what with the space the grease plug behind it took up, there was no more air space between the powder and the bullet.

The Bavarian percussion cap of the Werder cartridge had been retained. With its arched surface, it was set 0.1 millimeter below the "friction surface" of the cartridge base.

The overall length of the cartridge was 78 mm, its weight 34.3 grams. The cartridge that was designated M/71 at the end of the tests and used in the infantry rifle, Jäger rifle and carbine appeared as described here. It was retained, with slight modifications, until 1888 as the standard cartridge of the German Reich.

One- and Two-Part Cartridge Cases

At first the modifications concerned the cases. There were still cases of the thin-walled, lengthened Werder cartridges tearing. The reinforcing ring did only an unsatisfactory job and did not seem to stay in place firmly enough, for in a Rifle Testing Commission report the "pushing forward of the reinforcing ring" in firing is mentioned. All suggestions for improvement were directed at strengthening the particularly stressed base of the cartridge, meaning making it out of heavier material. The difficulties in making such cases were still considerable, and attempts were made to circumvent them by making the case of two parts and then riveting them together. This was done as follows:

The case jacket was produced as a tube closed at the rear, its wall thickness gradually decreasing toward the opened end. A hole was bored in the base, in which a hollow cylindrical extension of the separately made base would fit. The overlapping rim of the hollow cylinder was riveted into the inside of the case jacket.

Cases of this type were later designated "2A./C." This meant: two-part case, older construction. The originally one-piece case with the inset ring was called — in retrospect — "1A./C." to differentiate it.

The two-piece cases with heavy bases, made by Utendörffer of Nürnberg and the National Arms & Ammunition Company of Birmingham, among others, also had its shortcomings. There were "bulges" at the riveted joint, and sometimes the bases were riveted on crookedly or not centered.

Only the third — and final — case type for the M/71 cartridge was successful: the one-piece drawn "Nietzke system" cartridge, which was given the military designation "N.C." (new construction).[*] Production began about 1874. Some of the manufacturers were:

Utendörffer of Nürnberg, Georg Roth of Vienna,

---

[*] In the Eighties this was written "N.K." instead of "N.C."

the ammunition factories in Spandau, Danzig and Erfurt, Ludwig Ammunition Factory of Karlsruhe and Karlsruhe Artillery Depot. The Bavarian Main Laboratory in Ingolstadt began production only in 1876. The Artillery Workshop in Munich joined in later.

The new one-piece case was somewhat longer because of its reinforced base, and the length of the finished cartridge thus grew to 78 millimeters. The igniting channels were also changed. Instead of the formerly customary four square, stamped channels, now two round ones were bored, one over the other. The interior of the case was covered with a thin layer of colorless paint, so as to avoid chemical reactions between the powder and the brass in cases of long storage. The best case material proved to be a mixture of 66% copper and 34% zinc. From then on, all cases were made of that material.

Because of the original difficulties with ignition, which have already been noted in connection with the M/71 rifle, the cartridge was fitted as of about 1876 with, instead of the arched Bavarian "capsule", a flat percussion cap whose base could be struck more easily by the striker. The primer was covered by a sheet of tinfoil. To keep moisture out, the ring of the percussion cap was also sealed from outside with paint.

Strong M/71 cartridges in blue cardboard boxes with white labels were used throughout the Reich. A box held ten or twenty of them. Boxes and cases were reused. Tests had shown that faultless cases could be reloaded 25 to 30 times. In every reloading process the cartridge cases were marked with a dot or star on the "friction surface" on the base.

Changes to the 71 Cartridge in 1884

When the M 71/84 rifle, a repeater with a tubular magazine in the front part of its stock, was introduced in the German Empire, the M/71 cartridge was given a new bullet and percussion cap. Both were designated 71/84.

The changes to the ammunition were necessary for safety reasons, as self-ignition was a danger on account of the ammunition's position in the magazine tube of the new rifle (bullet tip against cartridge base). For that reason the 71/84 cartridge had a bullet head flattened to a diameter of six millimeters. The loss of weight incurred by

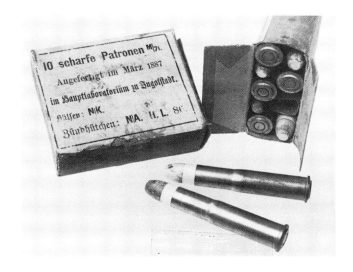

71 cartridges with 71/84 bullets and original blue boxes.

flattening the rounded tip was compensated for by lengthening the cylindrical shaft of the bullet.

The 71/84 percussion cap is somewhat higher than the old cap, which was 2.3 mm high. It sits with its rim on the bottom of the cap chamber, which was not the case with the old capsule. In addition, the material of the bottom of the percussion cap was now thickened again. By now misfirings were no longer to be feared, as the weight of the firing pin in the M 71/84 rifle had been increased by attaching it firmly to the bolt.

Bullet Lubrication

In the tests at Spandau it had been seen that the grease plug placed in the case between two cardboard discs behind the bullet, was not always sufficient to lubricate the barrel and bullet in every situation.

Of course the black powder residue in the barrel could, when the gun was fired slowly, absorb enough of the moisture in the air to make the deposits soft enough that the majority of the residue would be pushed out the barrel by the next shot. But during rapid fire the short pauses did not suffice. The powder deposits remained hard, formed crusts in the riflings, and collected lead on them.

For this reason the bullets had to be given an additional coating of wax. It is noteworthy that this layer of lubricant was not applied in the factory when the cartridges were being made, but — at least in peacetime — by the soldiers on the eve before rifle training. The reason: It was feared that the bullet coating could melt off or be rubbed off during longtime storage at varying temperatures. In addition, tests had shown that the lubricating material encouraged the formation of oxides on the bullet. For that reason the application of the lubricant was turned over to the troops.

A particular requirement governed the work process: The grease, which was delivered by the artillery depot, was a mixture of tallow and paraffin. 180 grams of wax per 1000 bullets had to be heated in a water bath, and then every cartridge was dipped in from the tip of the bullet to the case.

The "New 71 Gunpowder" (n.Gew.P.71)

The propellant from the Metz powder factory, known as "Gunpowder 71", had been regarded from the start as only a makeshift solution. Since efforts at the time had not been successful in attaining the quality of the English powder made by Curtis & Harvey, attempts to improve the powder continued after the M/71 cartridge was introduced. Finally, in 1881, they ended in success. The "new 71 gunpowder", "n.Gew.P. 71" for short, had a greater cubic and specific weight (943 and 1.74 grams) than the old powder. The attempts to achieve a more even grain size had also succeeded (0.76 to 1.5 mm). This was all beneficial to firing accuracy in particular, as the differences in performance from one cartridge to another were decreased.

71 Blank and Dummy Cartridges

Blank cartridges — as opposed to the live ones —were delivered in red packages. The base of the cartridge was painted red. They were made only from cartridges that were no longer suitable for firing with full charges. The powder too consisted of leftovers that were regarded as inferior because of long storage or faulty production. The charge was smaller than that of the regular cartridges.

Until 1884 three paper plugs, inserted in the cartridge case one on top of another and reaching about to the mouth of the case, served to plug it. As of 1884 the blank cartridges were made with red wooden bullets that splintered when fired.

This modification of the blank cartridges had become necessary because the old type could not be used in the new M 71/84 repeater rifle.

The dummy cartridges had a wooden bullet until 1884 and, instead of the percussion cap, a lead filling in the cap chamber. After 1884 dummy cartridges were made with a soldered-in sheet-metal dummy in the shape of the 71/84 bullet. Instead of the "striker lead" in the cap chamber, which had worn down with long use, an iron buffer with rubber springing was used.

To show the difference between them and live bullets clearly, the cases of the dummy bullets had been equipped with a circular ring about a centi-

The 71 cartridges, from left to right: a loaded cartridge with original bullet, a loaded cartridge with bullet 71 84, and a dummy cartridge.

meter from the base. Dummy bullets too could be made only out of mustered-out cartridges.

The manufacture of M/71 cartridges was halted early in the Nineties (probably 1893). The many millions of cartridges that were still stored as mobilization supplies were sold off in part, while the rest were used up gradually by the troops in practice outside their usual activities.

The Adapted Chassepot M/71 Carbine

Type: *Aptierter Chassepot-Karabiner M/71*
Number: D96022
Year made: 1866
Manufacturer: Manufacture Imperiale Mutzig
Function: Single shot
Overall length: 1000 mm
Gross weight: 3.5 kg
Barrel caliber: 11 mm
Number of riflings: 4
Rifling direction: Right
Rifling length: 550 mm
Rifling depth: 0.3 mm
Rifling width: 4.5 mm
Action: Bolt action with manual cocking
Sight: Step frame sight from 220 to 1300 meters
Standard ammunition: Patrone 71 (Vo: ca. 400 meters/second)

Note: The bolt of the Chassepot carbine can only be opened when the cocking piece has already been drawn back.
Disassembly: Loosen receiver screw (right on receiver bridge), press trigger, withdraw cocking piece from receiver by turning, take extractor out of the channel. Take bolt in left hand, right hand turns cocking piece to left. Unscrew the bolt screw with special wrench; the bolt can now be lifted out. When the coil spring is compressed, the firing pin mechanism complete with firing pin can be pushed to the side.
Safety: Cocked cocking piece the bolt is turned to the left about 1/8 of its diameter, pressing the trigger. The weapon is now locked.
Release: Pull the cocking piece back by the thumbgrip until it is behind the sear, push the cocking piece lever down.

In the Franco-Prussian War the German troops captured great numbers of French Chassepot needle guns and carbines. How many were taken in all cannot be estimated today. There may well have been some 600,000 of them; the Kingdom of Bavaria alone had 44,000.

Needle guns of this type, made for an 11-cm cartridge with a silk case, were already issued to German troops in small numbers during the war. Right after the war attempts were made to adapt the Chassepots for metal cartridges, in order to include them in the regular German military weaponry. No problems were expected, since the Mauser brothers had already presented a usable Chassepot adaptation mechanism in 1868.

The War Ministry of Württemberg wanted to buy Chassepot carbines captured by the Bavarians in 1870-71 and arm their own cavalry with them.

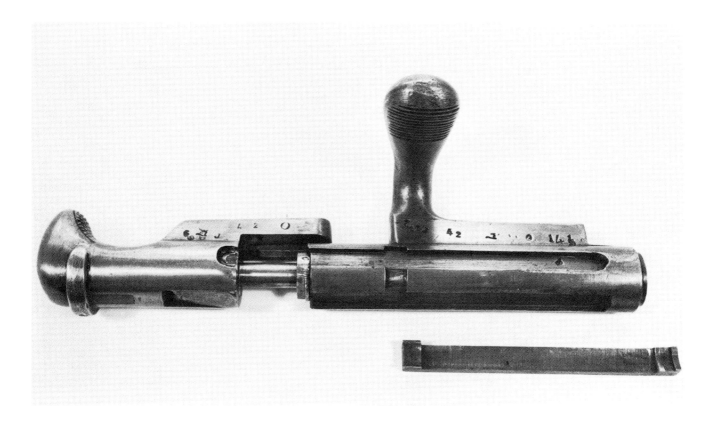

The complete bolt of the adapted carbine. The extractor is placed in the visible groove. It is new, as is the crescent-shaped guide on the bottom of the cocking piece.

Since the Mausers later included the barrel and breech case of the Chassepot mechanism in the line of development that finally led to the German M/71 infantry rifle, there was now a close relationship between the two models. The riflings with four grooves and a length of 550 millimeters were identical, and thus it was encouraging to "adapt" the captured Chassepot weapons for the German M/71 cartridge. The necessary modifications concerned the cocking piece, the bolt, the barrel and the sight. The originally hollow front part of the bolt was boxed out, the typical Chassepot rubber plug with the steel front panel was removed. Since the firing pin was made in two pieces anyway, only the long, thin front part had to be replaced by a short, heavy firing pin.

In the original Chassepots the bolt moves on a guide roller in the guide rail. In the course of German modification, this roller was removed and replaced by a heavy brass guide. The extractor for the metal cartridge cases was made new (the original Chassepot cartridges had silk cases that burned completely when fired).

The following description of the modified mechanism is taken from the service manual for the "Adapted Chassepot Carbine M/71" (Berlin 1881): The bolt consists of:

1. Receiver with trigger mechanism
2. Bolt with curved handle and guide rail, ejector, cocking piece screw, firing pin, striker point, coil spring and bolt holding screw.

The bolt contains three bored holes: the front one, shorter and narrower, formed by a bored-out cylinder soldered in the bottom of the bolt, holds the cylindrical part of the striker point, the middle one, conical, holds the heavier part of the firing pin bar, the rear one, longer and farther, holds the striker with the firing pin bar hook and coil spring and bears on its lower end the threading for the cocking piece. The front, narrower hole of the bolt lies exactly in the longitudinal axis of the last and generally corresponds to the form of the firing pin point moving in it.

At the front of the bolt is the bolt head which, when the action is closed, moves into the cut out in

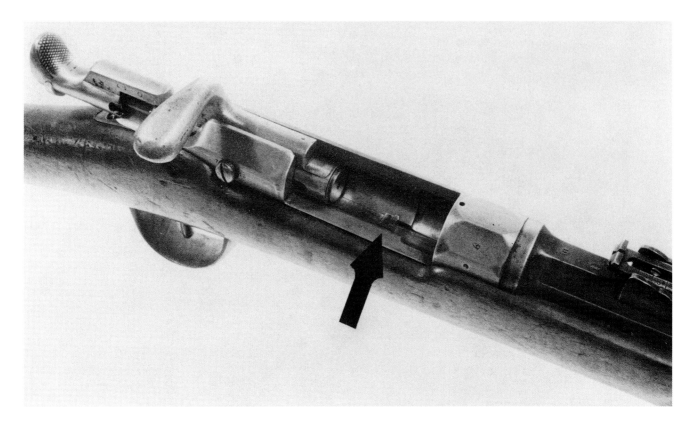

The bolt is opened and half drawn back. The extractor (arrow) can be seen in the bolt.

the barrel for the rim of the cartridge case.

On the right side, taking up almost all of the right side, is the groove for the shaft of the chamber holding screw, and below it is the groove for the sear. Both are linked by a transverse groove to the passage of the foot of the ejector. The sear groove is shaped on its walls in swallowtail fashion, holds the similarly formed foot of the ejector and regulates its movements. On the rear end of the bolt are three grooves for the attachments of the bolt, of which the larger one makes possible the triggering of the cocked bolt, the next largest allows the resting position and the smallest serves to cock the bolt or hold the bolt fast when it having been removed from the carbine, is replaced in it.

The Extractor, of hardened spring steel, consists of the hook, the long part and the foot, made in so-called swallowtail form, which is shaped to fit the extractor groove. This moves in the extractor groove of the receiver, the inserted cartridge brings it forward by means of the bolt, the bolt takes it back and thereby also removes the empty cartridge case. The extractor is to extend 68.2 mm over the head of the bolt when it lies with its foot at the front end of its groove in the bolt.

The cocking piece serves to guide the movement of the firing pin and to fire, cock and put the carbine on safety.

Suggestions for Adaptation

The modifications to the barrel of the Chassepot weapons which were made at that time may be described today, a century later, as bungling: To create a new chamber, the barrel end had to be bored out and an insert screwed in. This makeshift method was unsuitable because the dimensions of the chamber for the Chassepot silk cartridge were larger than those of the new M/71 cartridge. As a "safety valve" in case of torn cases there is a bored hole about two millimeters wide, which leads vertically from above to the rear end of the cartridge case. So much for the individual details of the modifications to the Chassepot mechanism, which were made to rifles as well as carbines. The states of the German Reich scarcely needed modified Chassepot rifles anyway, since they began to rearm with the new M/71 rifle shortly after the 1870-71 war. The Chassepots were of importance mainly in

The Chassepot action un-cocked. To open it, the bolt has to be half-cocked by the thumb grip.

shortened form as a transitional weapon for the cavalry in the period before the new M/71 carbine was available.

The Director of the Bavarian Rifle Factory in Amberg, Philipp Baron von Podewils, had already reported to the War Ministry in Munich on March 20, 1871 on the successful modification of a captured Chassepot rifle to take Werder cartridges. But this one model was all that existed at first, as the Rifle Factory was not free to modify the captured weapons. The project really got started only when the Prussian King Wilhelm I ordered on March 6, 1873: ". . . until the completion of the new carbine (M/71), Chassepot carbines or shortened Chassepot rifles should be used (by the cavalry). Every cavalryman is to receive 48 cartridges . . ."

The Prussian solution was also a guidepost for the other states of the Reich. The search began for a method of conversion by which Chassepot rifles could be made into usable carbines as quickly and cheaply as possible. As far as modifications to the mechanism was concerned, they have already been described above. Here are the alternative ways to shorten the barrel and shaft:

In July of 1873 the Kingdom of Saxony presented a carbine model that the Saxon Captain Bremer had developed in cooperation with the Dresden armory gunsmith Einhorn. The test model is interesting in that Bremer and Einhorn had tried to circumvent the boxing out of the cartridge bed. They cut off the original Chassepot barrel just ahead of the head of the case and shortened the barrel from the rear by the length of the Chassepot cartridge bed. An M/71 cartridge bed was machined in the new barrel end, and on the outside a thread was cut to screw into the head of the case. Since the new end of the conical barrel had a smaller diameter than the original one, the sawed-off threaded stump of the original barrel was inserted into the head of the case and the new threading for the shortened barrel was cut in the old stump. In order to reduce the Chassepot rifle barrel to the size of a carbine, a piece naturally had to be taken off the front end as well.

The bed would no longer fit into the moved-back, shortened, conical barrel now. It had become too wide. Bremer and Einhorn solved the problem in a radical way: they simply cut off the front shaft. The Saxon test carbine thus had a free-standing barrel. The total length of the weapon was under one

A detail of the butt of the adapted carbine. The old French burned-in markings have been bored out and plugged (left). Beside it are the new "Deutsches Reich" stamp and monogram with crown.

The muzzle ring of the adapted Chassepot carbine with cleaning rod and foresight protectors.

meter, and an additional safety device was attached to the left side of the breech case.

At the beginning of 1874 a Prussian "shortened Chassepot carbine" appeared in competition with the Saxon model. It was one meter long and the shaft reached to the muzzle. There sat a heavy iron cap which linked the barrel and shaft and bore two foresight panels on top. This upper ring had a point at the bottom that covered the head of the sprung unloading rod. To draw the unloading rod, the head first had to be pushed toward the barrel and turned.

The sight of the "adapted Chassepot carbine M/71", a so-called step-ladder sight, could be adjusted from 220 to 1300 meters. In this Prussian version the cartridge bed, as described above, was boxed out.

In the autumn of 1874 the testing of the adapted rifle began at the Military Gunnery School and the Rifle Testing Commission in Spandau. As of 1875 the modification went on in grand style. It was a task that private firms above all applied to share, as the required machines were not too expensive.

Prussia had work done by, among others, the rifle factory at Herzberg in the Harz as well as several manufacturers in Suhl. But 53,000 carbines for Prussia and 1800 for Saxony were adapted at the "Weapons Factory Society" in Steyr in 1875-76 too. The War Ministry in Munich also negotiated with Steyr for adaptation work. But in the end it seemed more reasonable to introduce new 71 carbines. So Bavaria sold the greatest part of the captured Chassepot rifles in their original condition, charging 15 Marks apiece. The cost of modifying them by the Prussian system would have been 18 to 24 Marks each. In the other German states, the adapted Chassepots still saw service with the cuirassiers and home guards in the Eighties.

Above: a Saxon Chassepot carbine "Mod 73", adapted by the Bremer-Einhorn system, no. 3407. Overall length: 95.5 cm, barrel: 45 cm.

Right: A look at the bolt, half removed from the receiver. It is already set for self-cocking; the cocking piece need not be cocked separately by hand. Einhorn achieved this by adding a projection under the guide rail, to fit into a machined curve on the bolt (arrow). The hole in the cocking piece (B) forms a bed for the safety bar, which can be moved in and out with the lever (front). The cartridge ejector is designed more practically than that of the Prussian adaptation. Here it is set in the hollowed-out guide rail (not visible in the picture) and is held by the screw (A).

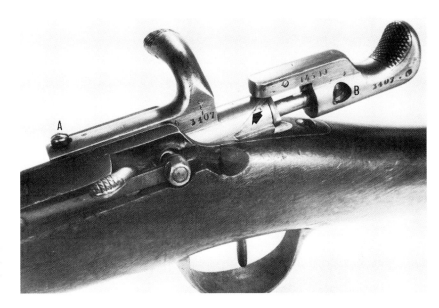

The Serbian M 78/80 Infantry Rifle (Mauser-Koka)

Type: *Serbisches Infanteriegewehr M 78/80* (Mauser-Koka)
Year made: 1882-1884
Manufacturer: Mauser Brothers & Co., Oberndorf on the Neckar
Function: Single shot
Overall length: 1290 mm
Gross weight: 4.5 kg
Barrel caliber: 10.15 mm
Number of riflings: 4
Rifling direction: Right
Depth of a rifling: 0.15 mm
The width of the wedge-shaped riflings decreased from 4.7 mm to 3.9 mm at the muzzle.
Rifling length: 550 mm
Breech: Cylinder breech similar to M/71 but with ejector

Safety: Wing, working only with cocked breech
Sight: Standing sight with large frame (300 to 2025 meters)
Standard ammunition: Patrone 10.15 x 63 R (Serbian), Vo: 510 meters/second
Disassembly: Essentially as M/71
Cartridge: 10.15 x 63 R (Serbian)
Overall length: 79 mm
Weight: 40 grams
Case length: 62.8 mm
Case weight: 13 grams
Bullet length: 29.2 mm
Bullet weight: 22.1 grams
Bullet material: Hard lead (100 parts lead, 7 parts tin)
Charge: 4.8 grams of black powder (Serbian gunpowder)
Lateral pressure: 27.8 grams

The "Congress of Berlin" had recognized the independence of the former Turkish province of Serbia in 1878. The Serbians wanted a king again. But before the monarchy could be established, armed forces had to be built up; Serbia needed weapons.

As early as 1879 the government in Zagreb had announced an international competition to choose the best infantry weapons. The ammunition was supplied to the participating firms; it was a black-powder cartridge with a hard lead bullet in 10.15 mm caliber and a brass case 62.8 mm long. The case was substantially like the German type; the bullet had a paper wrapping.

The Mauser brothers, who competed vigorously with the great international armaments firms for the first time in Serbia, offered an improved version of their successful M/71 model, with coupled striker and cocking piece as well as a cartridge extractor that simultaneously worked as an ejector. The coupling effect, which increased the weight of the firing pin and made ignition more sure, was accomplished by Paul Mauser with a simple conical "step" at the rear end of the firing pin. The design of the combined extractor-ejector was also very simple. When the opened bolt was drawn back, the sprung shaft of this element pushed against the screw that rose up from the left rear into the extractor groove. This made the extractor turn a little, and the front end of the withdrawn empty cartridge case at first struck against the left inside of the receiver, bounced off and fell to the right and out of the cartridge entrance.

In the bolt, the changed form of the firing pin head (heavy, with grooves for gripping) is eye-catching. So is the design of the safety lever, which is set in the bolt with a small coil spring for the first time and can be removed when the bolt is disassembled (in the M/71 the safety lever was held in the bolt by a transverse rod).

The long receiver tang, unlike that of the M/71, is lengthened somewhat to the rear, to the neck of the butt. It is meant to give the cocking piece, a projection of which extends into a groove in the case for the first time, a steady position and prevent its turning, even when the bolt is drawn back. Thus the "scoop" on the front of the firing pin, which had reached into a slit on the head of the M/71 bolt and guided the position, becomes unnecessary. The changes to the bolt described here were essentially used again on the later Mauser repeater M 71/84.

The barrel of the Serbian model had four (tapered) grooves, which became narrower from the breech to the muzzle. The rifling length is the same as that of the German M/71 infantry rifle, but the Serbian rifle, with its only slightly changed cartridge, has considerably better performance. The muzzle velocities form a ratio of 440 to 510.

The fittings differ only slightly; the German rifle has closed lower and central bands, the Serbian rifle has them open at the bottom. They are held together by set-screws.

Wilhelm Mauser's Last Success

Wilhelm Mauser traveled alone to Belgrade in June of 1879 to present the competition weapon. It was almost a wonder that this simple man from Oberndorf could win out against the clever agents of the international armaments industry and survive in the jungle of corruption in the Balkans. But the battle cost him almost a year's time and his last bit of strength. At the end of 1880 the Mauser model was accepted by the Serbian War Ministry. In mid-February 1881 Wilhelm Mauser returned home to Oberndorf with a contract for 100,000 M 78/80 infantry rifles. It was the salvation of the factory, which had not received a large order for years. The citizens of Oberndorf honored Wilhelm Mauser with a torchlight parade. They new that the small city on the Neckar only prospered when the chimneys of the Mauser factory smoked.

Two months after his last triumph, Wilhelm Mauser sickened, dying on January 13, 1883. The production of the Mauser-Koka rifle began in the summer of 1882. By the beginning of 1884 the contract had been fulfilled. The gunpowder factory in nearby Rottweil could also gain from the Serbian contract. It delivered three million 10.15 mm caliber cartridges.

Infantry Rifle M 71/84

Type: *Infanteriegewehr M 71/84*
Number: 6554
Year built: 1888
Manufacturer: Royal Prussian Rifle Factory, Spandau
Function: Repeater
Overall length: 1294 mm
Gross weight: 4.6 kg
Barrel caliber: 11 mm
Number of riflings: 4
Rifling direction: Right
(Other rifling data same as the M/71)
Breech: Cylinder breech, same as M/71

Safety: Wing, working only with cocked breech
Magazine: Tubular, for eight cartridges, in front part of shaft
Sight: Fixed sight, small flap and frame (200 to 1600 meters)
Standard ammunition: 71 cartridge with 71/84 bullet and percussion cap
Disassembly: Before the bolt is disassembled, the cut off on the left of the receiver must be moved to its central position! Bolt disassembly is essentially like that of the M/71.
Note: The cut off can only be used when the bolt is drawn all the way back and the cartridge carrier is in its upward position!

The first magazine rifle among German military weapons had no chance from the start of making a name for itself. Technically it was only a halfhearted further development of the model 71, and it came a decade too late as well. For in 1884, the year of its introduction, engineers and ballistic experts all over the world were already discussing a small-caliber new generation of weapons, compared to which the German repeater rifle for 11-millimeter black-powder cartridges looked downright old-fashioned.

The fact that the decision was made as it was undoubtedly was influenced by the political situation in France at the time. There the War Minister, General Georges Boulanger, had ceaselessly stirred up his countrymen's feelings of revenge since they had lost the war. In the mid-Eighties it really seemed as if a new campaign was coming in the near future, and it was uncertain how the Russian Empire would react in this conflict.

In hopes of gaining a tactical advantage, the German leaders decided in favor of a repeater rifle that could be introduced quickly without tedious testing and, above all, without having to produce new ammunition. Thus the least risky course was chosen, though it included the danger that after just a few years a new rifle would have to be developed and manufactured.

In the early Eighties there were already a whole line of proven repeater systems in Europe, with cylinder breech and tubular magazine in the front shaft. Examples are the Swiss Vetterli rifle of 1869, the Austrian designs by Fruwirth and Kropatschek, and the French M/1878 naval rifle using the Gras-Kropatschek design.

Director Josef Werndl of the "Austrian Weapons Factory Society" in Steyr, which produced M/71 rifles for Germany, had already offered the Rifle Testing Commission in Spandau an M/71 rifle with a Kropatschek tubular magazine in 1875. But the test rifle gained nothing more than polite interest. The need for it, so it seemed, was not yet at hand at that time.

The situation changed lightning-fast two years

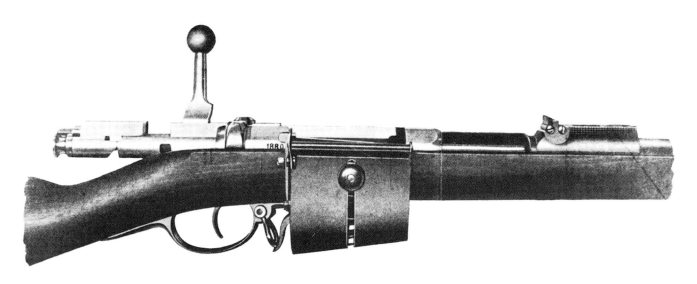

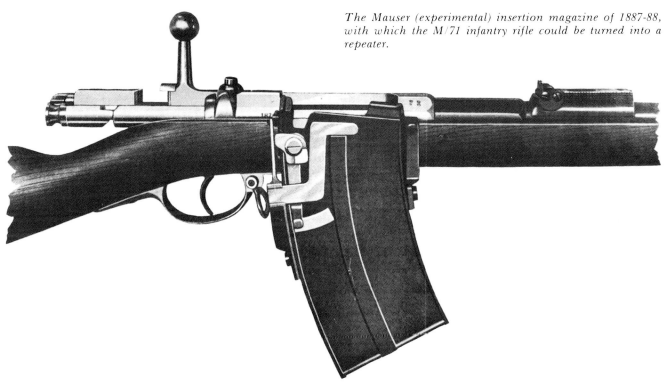

The Mauser (experimental) insertion magazine of 1887-88, with which the M/71 infantry rifle could be turned into a repeater.

later, when the news of the battle of Plevna ran through all of Europe. For in this 1877 battle in the Russo-Turkish War, Turkish troops in a hopeless position had been able to hold their own against vastly superior Russian troops with their Winchester repeater rifles. In Oberndorf, Paul Mauser immediately recognized the signs of the times. He designed a whole series of insertion magazines, some in boxes, some U-shaped, that could be attached to the M/71 rifle. This economical solution would have allowed the single-shot rifle to be turned into a repeater. But in Spandau they said no.

Two years after that, when the Serbian government announced its new international competition for new army rifles, Mauser designed his first repeating rifle for it, including a tubular magazine and based on the M/71 design. Though the repeating rifle did not come into use in Serbia, Kaiser Wilhelm I soon took a personal interest in the design.

On September 27, 1881 the Kaiser visited the State Trade Fair in Stuttgart, spent a long time at the display of the Mauser brothers, and had all the details of the repeating rifle explained to him. The effect was not lost.

In the very next year, 1882, troop testing of 2000 Mauser repeaters took place. Four battalions in Darmstadt, Königsberg and Spandau tested the rifles that had been made by Mauser in Oberndorf: 500 with and 1500 without a cleaning rod.

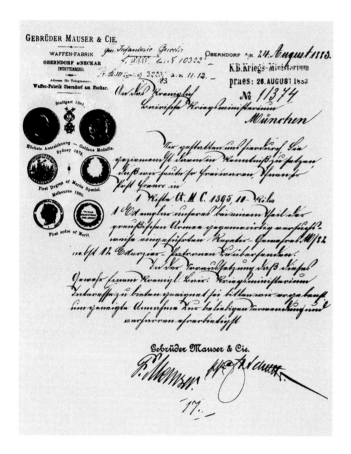

Paul Mauser offers the Bavarian War Ministry an example of the M/82 experimental repeating rifle.

In the provisional instructions distributed for the troop tests, "The Infantry Repeater Rifle of 1882", it is stated that the new weapon corresponded completely to the Model 71 and had been modified solely in the repeater mechanism under the receiver and the magazine tube under the barrel. But it was not that simple. Paul Mauser had designed the repeater mechanism as a completely new unit, and the only part that he retained from the M/71 unchanged was the steel stock forend.

The experience gained in the troop testing during the winter of 1882-83 led to the following changes in the rifle:

The capacity of the tubular magazine was reduced from the original nine cartridges to eight. Thus the barrel, stock and magazine tube could each be shortened by five centimeters. Aside from the saving in weight, this improved the weapon's center of gravity. For the center, which lay too far forward when the magazine was filled, had to change with every cartridge that was taken out of the magazine. The shortening of the rifle succeeded in minimizing to some degree this natural weakness of all tubular magazine rifles.

Because there had been a few magazine explosions during troop testing, The M/71 cartridges had to be equipped with new 71/84 flat-topped bullets and more firmly seated 71/84 percussion caps (see "The M/71 Cartridge").

In addition, the barrels were equipped with a lower rifling. The depth was reduced from 0.30 to 0.15 mm (in Prussia by order of 11/14/1883, in Bavaria when production began at the end of 1886).

Description and Operation

The octagon at the rear end of the barrel is grooved on its underside to make room for the snugly fitting steel magazine tube. It is fully bedded in the wood of the forearm and closed at the front end with a corrugated steel screw cap. From the screw cap a small pin with a round head projects, used to hook several rifles together for stacking arms.

The rear end of the magazine tube empties directly into the "area" at the underside of the receiver, in which the "carrier" can move up and down. In the magazine tube lies a long, soft wire coil spring that pushes a cylindrical piston toward the open end of the tube, which also pushes the cartridges when the magazine is filled.

The "carrier" takes up one cartridge at a time, lifting it into the feedway when the bolt is drawn back. It lowers again when the bolt is moved forward as soon as the front end of the advanced cartridge is pushed into the chamber by the bolt head.

The movements of the carrier are guided by a groove in the ejector. The ejector, a long rail that reaches into the bolt head with a half-ring, runs in a

Das abgedrückte Schloss zum Magazinfeuer gestellt.

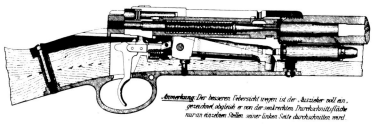

Anmerkung: Der besseren Uebersicht wegen ist der Auszieher voll an. gezeichnet, obgleich er von der senkrechten Durchschnittsfläche nur an einzelnen Stellen seiner linken Seite durchschnitten wird.

Das gespannte Schloss zum Magazinfeuer gestellt.

Anmerkung: Um die Wirkung des Auswerfers auf das Anschlag. stück sichtbar zu machen, ist die Stellfeder vorn. abgebrochen gezeichnet.

Das Schloss bei geöffneter Kammer
zum Magazinfeuer gestellt.

Anmerkung: Um die Wirkung des Auswerfers auf das Anschlag. stück sichtbar zu machen, ist die Stellfeder vorn. abgebrochen gezeichnet.

groove in the left wall of the receiver. The extractor of the M 71/84 is attached to the breech head with a tail piece at the upper right. The bolt corresponds essentially to that of the Model 71. The firm attachment of the cocking piece to the firing pin and its thread was new and made it possible to increase the firing pin's weight considerably. For this purpose the firing pin was given an offset area on which the front surface of the cocking piece bore leaned firmly when the firing pin thread was screwed on. The firing pin had also lost its "leaf" in the front. It became superfluous because now a

The M 71/84 bolt seen from the left side, showing the long ejector rail.

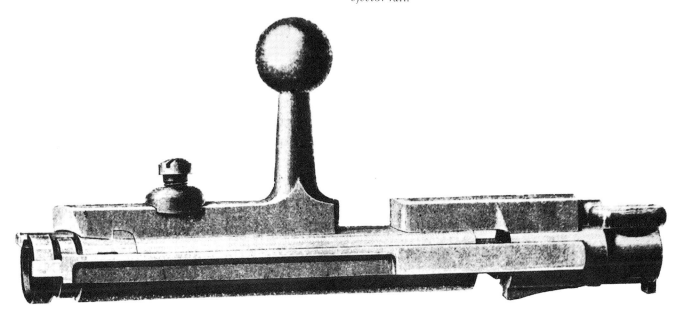

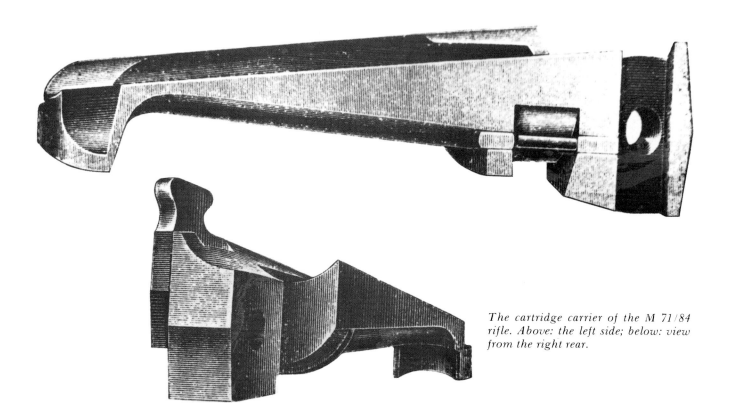

The cartridge carrier of the M 71/84 rifle. Above: the left side; below: view from the right rear.

projecting point on the underside of the cocking piece runs into a groove on the bolt body and guarantees the correct position. The safety was set with a small coil spring. It could be removed.

The rear end of the M 71/84 barrel has no "bored-out flange" any more to enclose the rim of the cartridge. Instead of that, the bolt head has a corresponding cutout area that surrounds the rim of the cartridge.

The rifle can be set optionally for magazine firing by using the magazine cutoff lever on the left side of the receiver (lever backward) or for use as a single-shot rifle (lever forward). In the latter case, the repeating mechanism is disengaged.

The Bayonet for Model 71/84

With the exception of the Prussian Guards, who continued to use the M/71 bayonet, the German infantry was issued a new bayonet for the M 71/84 rifle. It had a blade only 25 cm long and a black

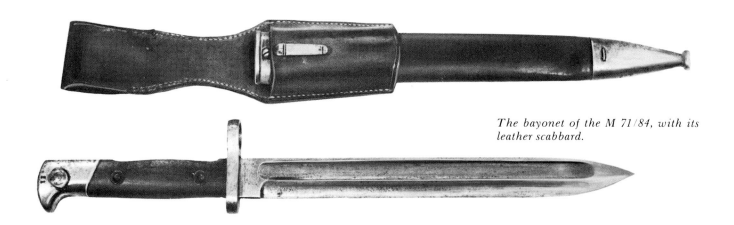

The bayonet of the M 71/84, with its leather scabbard.

leather hilt with steel trim. Manufacturing was done in Solingen. The price was 5.47 Marks.

Special Wishes of the Jäger

According to the original plans of the War Ministry in Berlin there was to be just one version of the new rifle. In spite of that the Prussian Jäger corps, who had had special weapons for a century, were able to obtain a small modification. As of 1886 each M 71/84 that was intended for a Jäger battalion was fitted with a separate sling loop, its base attached to the wood 19 centimeters from the stock cap. The hole in front of the trigger guard, in which the lower sling loop was mounted on all other M 71/84

rifles, was bored out to a diameter of six millimeters on the Jäger repeaters and used "to hold the sling." There were also special wishes in terms of the sight.

Within the parameters of a troop test that began in March of 1886 in Prussian Jäger Battalions 1, 3, 9, 10 and five infantry battalions, the decision was to be made in favor of the most useful graduations of the sight.

The competitors were:
The "Infantry Sight" and the "Jäger Sight"

	Infantry Sight	Jäger Sight
Fixed sight	270 meters	200 meters
Small flap	350 meters	300 meters
Large flap	400 to 1600 m	400 to 1600 m

The sight of the M 71/84, with sliding flap. The highest notch, for 1600 meters, is cut into the very top of the frame.

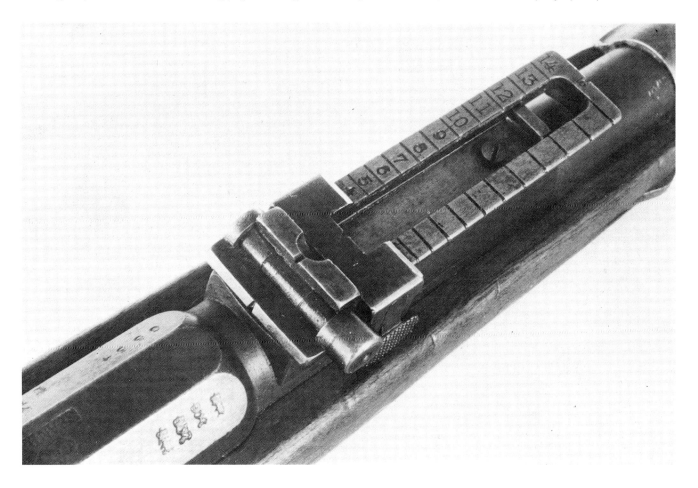

65

On August 31, 1886 the decision was finally made in favor of the "Jäger sight." All rifles, including those of the infantry, were equipped with it. At the suggestion of the Rifle Testing Commission, the side of the large flap turned toward the riflemanwas to be plain and polished so that, for the sake of better legibility, only the markings cut into it would be black. When these last changes were decided on, the rearmament — in Prussia, at least -was already underway.

But we are moving ahead of time. Back to the year of its introduction, 1884 — at the end of January the War Ministry in Berlin reported:

"Secret: His Majesty the Kaiser and King has most graciously deigned to order that the M/71 infantry rifles to be made in the future be made according to a sample instituted by the All-Highest personally on January 17, 1884 . . .

According to the All-Highest decision of His Majesty the Kaiser and King, the rifles made according to the new sample, in the interests of keeping the specifications as secret as possible, shall carry the designation M 71/84; the expression 'repeater rifle' may not be used."

In all royal rifle factories in Prussia, retooling for the new production began immediately. Since practically all the machines had to be rebuilt and numerous new ones created, the beginning of series production could not be expected until the summer of 1886.

The manufacture of the thin-walled steel magazine tube proved to be particularly complicated. It was to be "cold-rolled" and seamless, made by a process that was brand new at the time, which the Danzig factory director, Major von Flotow, had developed for the production of steel-

Muzzle of the barrel, upper barrel band with bayonet attachment lug and magazine cap of the tubular magazine with stacking rod.

tube cavalry lances. In order to spare the other factories, which as yet had no experience in the realm of cold-rolling, laborious experiments, the War Ministry in Berlin decided that all the magazine tubes would be produced in Danzig.

Money and Machines are Lacking

On May 8, 1884 the War Ministry in Munich received a test model of the new rifle, and later that same month King Ludwig II approved its introduction in Bavaria. But with one limitation: The new weapons should replace the M/71's already in use only gradually, when the latter became unusable. Obviously the Bavarian government was not convinced of the impending threat of war. In addition, the new rifles cost a lot of money, and money was in short supply in Bavaria then, because the King's urge to build castles had made great inroads on the state finances.

But finances caused problems in Prussia too. A military loan of 2.2 million Marks was supposed to assure the retooling of the three rifle factories in Spandau, Danzig and Erfurt. In the 1884/85 budget another 1.5 millions were provided for preparation of the rifles. But the money was not enough. When Prussia tried to add a retroactive sum to the 1886-87 budget, Reich Chancellor von Bismarck rejected the suggestion, though mainly for the sake of appearances. For Bismarck said confidentially that the rifle factories should keep on working at any cost, and exceed their budgets if necessary. "The leap forward into new armaments as opposed to France must be maintained as much as possible. But it is not practical to call attention to this situation again by adding retroactive funding."

It took a painfully long time until the royal rifle factories were ready for production. One of the reasons was that there was only one factory in the entire Reich that could provide the necessary machines: the firm of Ludwig Loewe in Berlin.

This company, which will be mentioned several times hereafter, had created a monopoly situation, and the four royal rifle factories had to wait in line with their orders.

Spandau, Danzig and Erfurt needed a total of 504 new machines, and Amberg needed another 160. Machine production alone took almost a year. The delivery dates that had been set in advance (some of which were exceeded) were: Spandau, March 1885; Erfurt, June 1885; Danzig, September 1885; Amberg, early 1886. But then the factory chimneys smoked day and night six days a week. The three Prussian factories increased production during that time to 400 rifles a day each. Amberg, despite the greatest efforts, could only manage 200. Since production in Bavaria actually started only at the end of 1886, the planned schedule for rearmament could not be kept. By April of 1887 only 16,000 Bavarian rifles had been finished.

Since it would not have made sense to start rearming the Bavarian army corps with this small number, they were originally gathered in the arsenal, and their issuing was postponed until a later time.

The Prussian factories had reached their quotas in July of 1887. After that, until September, they delivered another 99,000 rifles for Württemberg, Saxony and the Imperial Navy. In October and November of 1887 the factories in Spandau, Danzig and Erfurt produced another 10,000 rifles for Bavarian use. By the end of 1887, even the south German kingdom possessed the needed 96,368 new repeater rifles.

In Prussia the issuing of M 71/84 rifles had already begun in July of 1886. The border troops in the annexed "Imperial Territories" of Alsace and Lorraine were supplied with them first. Long before the rifles arrived, all the regiments in the Reich had already received "demonstration breeches", cutout M 71/84 mechanisms, with the help of which the soldiers could have arms training to prepare for their future rifles.

In all, 950,000 M 71/84 rifles were produced.

The Bavarian Military Commissioner in Berlin, Major General von Xylander, reported on his negotiations with the Prussian War Minister Bronsart von Schellendorf regarding delivery of M 71/84 rifles for Bavaria.

The License Contract with Mauser

Once again Paul Mauser had hoped in vain for a large order. Although his factory in Oberndorf was already set up for production of the tube-magazine repeater and thus could have begun series production much earlier than the state factories, the designer was at first not allowed to provide one single example for the armament of the Reich (other than the 2000 test pieces). Only in the summer of 1886 did Württemberg order 19,000 rifles. Paul Mauser had also hoped for a Bavarian order. But when L. Colin, a director of the Württemberg Union Bank, which was involved with Mauser in Oberndorf, made inquiries in Munich in December of 1885, he had no luck. Only in February of 1887, when Bavaria was in the process of rearmament, did the War Ministry in Munich take another look at Mauser's offer. But at that time the Oberndorf factory had its hands full with a large Turkish order.

In spite of that, Paul Mauser's situation at this time was not comparable with the one that prevailed after the introduction of his M/71 rifle. At that time he had to give the state the rights to his invention. This time he was able to retain his rights and do business. Mauser's rights were based on the 1878 Reich patent law. Since that year it was finally possible to attain patent protection for the entire Reich. Before that, the inventor had to negotiate independently with every state. There were Bavarian patents, Württembergish, Prussian, etc.

Since Mauser had taken a whole series of patents for his new rifle (for example, DRP 15 202 of January 23, 1880 for the fixed coupling of the cocking piece with the firing pin and its nut), the state had to negotiate with him.

Prussia, acting as the representative of the other states of the Reich, signed a patent use contract with Mauser on July 22, 1885. In brief, it included the following essential points:

#1: Mauser signed over all patent rights to the M 71/84, as long as the production of weapons for the German Reich was concerned, no matter where and by whom they were produced. Mauser also had to provide for

68

evaluation, free of charge, any improvements that might be developed by him in the future for the M 71/84.

#2: For the first 100,000 finished rifles Mauser was to receive a licensing fee of three Marks and for the rest one Mark each. Mauser had no right to confirm the production quantities calculated by Prussia (!).

#4: A guarantee sum of 300,000 Marks was agreed on. It was payable immediately after the contract was accepted.

The guarantee sum more or less covered the Prussian production of 1884-85. So Prussia alone paid the higher additional three-Mark fee.

It is interesting in this regard to look at the calculations of the state rifle factories and compare them with the price fixing of the private firm Mauser. Oberndorf had originally offered the M 71/84 rifles for 56 Marks. The three Prussian factories reckoned their own costs at 43 Marks, including the licensing fee. Amberg's calculation was 42 Marks. In a report to the War Ministry in Munich, the Director of the Rifle Factory nevertheless admitted that the actual costs, including the "costs of investment", would be about 55 Marks. In fact the lower price that the state factories calculated can be explained only in that the costs of retooling the factories and buying the many new machines did not need to be included in the calculations.

Faults of the M 71/84 Rifle

The new rifle showed one fault from the beginning that was based on its design, had been known of for years and thus would have been avoidable: the deviation of the line of fire to the right of the sight line. The cause was the one-sided bolting of the receiver, which had been retained from the M/71 rifle. In the old single-shot rifle the effects had, of course, not been so serious. Despite that, the Rifle Testing Commission in Spandau already had an eye on the matter.

In a report of November 29, 1886, which the Bavarian Captain Leichtenstern, who had been sent to the Rifle Testing Commission in Spandau, sent to Munich he stated:

"At the introduction of the M/71 rifle the right-side locking of the bolt, in regard to the receiver had already been regarded as a weakness, and the commission had expressed a wish for an (additional) structure on the left to help the situation.

When the cartridge is ignited, the recoil is taken up by the bolt head, carried over to the right-side structure of the bolt and its bolt guide, which is held by the cutout in the receiver. The first effect of this transmission of power from the bolt to the right side of the receiver bridge is a pulling of the weapon to the right, and the bullet also follows this, in that it leaves the barrel to the right of the original position . . ."

The pull to the right was considerable in the M 71/84 rifles. And knowledge of it had already reached the troops before the weapons could be delivered. To regain confidence in the new rifle, the Prussian War Ministry published, in December of 1886, a comparison of the year's firing results of four Jäger companies with the 71 Jäger rifle (1885) and M 71/84 (1886). The tables show a slightly superior accuracy for the new weapon and were supposed to be posted in all barracks to save the honor of the M 71/84. But that did not help much. For when the repeaters were delivered, the soldiers noticed soon enough what was wrong with the M 71/84. To help the situation, the foresight of all the newly made rifles had to be offset 0.6 mm to the right at the factories. In individual cases, with a strong deviation to the right, the battalion gunsmiths were even allowed to "drive" the foresight up to 1.2 mm to the right.

But the deviation from target increased in the summer, when warm cartridges were used. A similar phenomenon, the causes of which no one could explain definitively, had already been seen in the M/71. At that time, though, warm cartridges had resulted in shooting below the target. It was presumed that the high humidity of the air during the hot summer weather could have a negative effect on the performance of the powder.

Other faults of a minor nature, but which turned up more and more frequently, included swelling stocks, for the wood had been aged "only" three years on the average because of the rushed production. The magazine lever for the magazine often broke because many soldiers could not remember that the repeater mechanism could be turned off only with the bolt drawn back and the cartridge carrier raised. There were — though only a few — also cases of self-igniting cartridges in the magazine tube. These accidents fortunately never seriously injured a rifleman.

The Chamber With "Doubled Resistance"

Naturally Paul Mauser had also recognized the weakness in the one-sided breech. As early as the summer of 1886 he introduced a new breech with "doubled resistance" (double locking). Opposite the guiding rail, on the rear end of the breech cylinder, an attachment with an angled surface was to be attached that could be supported by a groove in the receiver at the left. It was not a fancy solution, but more of a makeshift arrangement. In the spring of 1887 Oberndorf delivered fifty test rifles to the Rifle testing Commission and the Military Gunnery School in Spandau. The test results were very good, but the changes to the bolt and case turned out to be too deep to be applied to the M 71/84 rifles being produced then. Thus the suggested improvement was filed away.

Only in December of 1887, when M 71/84 production was already finished, was the subject of the "Mauser breech" brought up again. The Prussian General War Department gave the rifle factory at Spandau the assignment on December 4, 1887: "... to set up tables for production of the Mauser bolt as well as the receivers to be changed thereby. The necessary machines ... will be ordered from the

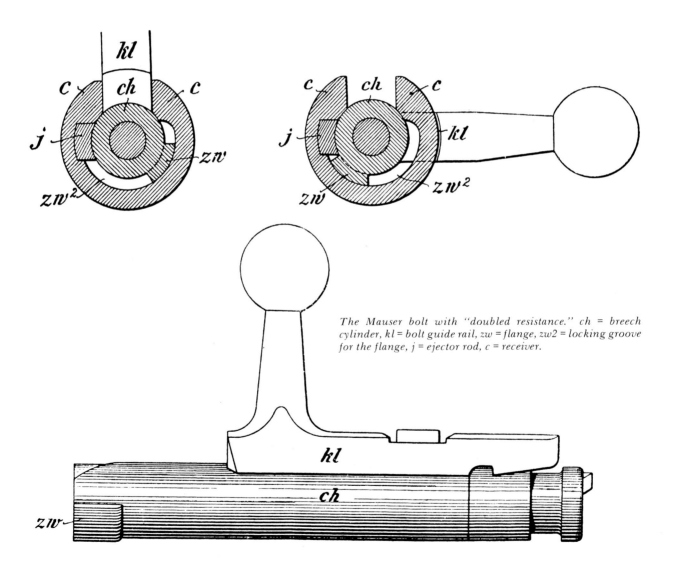

The Mauser bolt with "doubled resistance." ch = breech cylinder, kl = bolt guide rail, zw = flange, zw2 = locking groove for the flange, j = ejector rod, c = receiver.

firm of Ludwig Loewe in Berlin . . ."

Along with that there is a meaningful report from the aforementioned Bavarian Captain Leichtenstern. As an "insider" on the Rifle Testing Commission, he knew of all the tests of new small-caliber rifles that were going on at that time, which will be discussed in detail later. Leichtenstern wrote to Munich: "The changes to the M 71/84 infantry rifle (by the improved Mauser breech) are probably being introduced now because there is hope of turning the 11-mm M 71/84 rifle into a small-caliber rifle simply by inserting an 8-mm barrel with a jacket . . ."

They had thought it was that simple at first. But it turned out very differently. When the new small-caliber 88 rifle was accepted in the Reich the next year, after a very painful birth, it did indeed have a jacket on the barrel, but otherwise it had nothing at all in common with the M 71/84 rifle.

Repeaters with tubular magazines disappeared from military use after just a few years. As of about 1892, they were sold — still practically new — at a price of four Marks apiece. They still managed to achieve some significance later as the standard weapons of the native troops in the German colonies.

The German "Small-Caliber" Experiments

The tests of smokeless powder types, the development of jacketed bullets and, finally, the efforts to decrease military calibers from eleven to eight millimeters, taken as a whole, form one of the most exciting chapters in the history of German weapons. It began at the end of the Seventies and reached its dramatic high point in 1887 and 1888, when the Rifle Testing Commission in Spandau, under the pressure of time, had to conceptualize that new weapon in which the most modern technical and ballistic knowledge was to become reality: the 88 rifle. The reasons for this unseemly haste were once again — or more accurately, still — the tense situation with France, intensified by the expiration of the reinsurance treaty with Russia, which was not renewed in 1887. And just in the middle of this tense situation there burst the news of the new French "Lebel" 1886 rifle model, which was far superior to the German M 71/84.

A French deserter with the German name of Schnäbele had smuggled one of the first examples of the French 8-mm repeaters across the border early in 1887, along with a number of smokeless cartridges with jacketed bullets, and offered to sell them to the Germans. Schnäbele's asking price of 20,000 Marks shocked the interested parties. Only the Reich Chancellor, Prince Bismarck, whom the French deserter finally got to see, recognized the significance of the new weapon. He sounded the alarm and intervened subsequently and emphatically for a speedy solution to the "small-caliber question." The Chancellor himself — as he always admitted — did not know much about ballistics or armament technology. He regarded the new French rifle most of all as a threat of the psychological kind. In November of 1887 the Prince wrote to the Prussian War Minister Bronsart von Schellendorf: "The very situation in which we must admit to ourselves the inferiority (low value) of our armaments would be sufficient to encourage France or Russia to fall upon us."

The War Minister took the Chancellor's words to heart and made the urgency of the problem clear to the Rifle Testing Commission in Spandau. From then on, things happened in a rush: within a year a new rifle, a new cartridge and a new powder existed.

For a century, military historians have been dominated by the conception that everything was mainly the work of the Rifle Testing Commission and/or the ammunition factory in Spandau. Of the pioneering work contributed by the powder manufacturer Duttenhofer of Rottweil and the designer Armand Mieg at the time there has been little said. This seems to be the first attempt to portray the developmental history of the 88 rifle in an unbiased manner, with partially new, unpublished material.

Max Duttenhofer, gunpowder manufacturer from Rottweil on the Neckar, produced the first nitro-powder with little smoke in Germany.

The Rottweil Cellulose Powder (R.C.P.)

Max Duttenhofer (1843-1903), son of a Rottweil pharmacist, had already brought black powder to its highest stage of development in the laboratory of his powder mill on the Neckar by the early Eighties. Duttenhofer is the inventor of the brown prismatic "C 82" powder for naval artillery, world-famous in its day. The brown color of the powder was that of the only partly charred raw material, buckthorn wood, which gave the propellant considerably higher power, with moderate gas pressure, than the earlier types of black powder had achieved.

Building on his strictly guarded manufacturing secret, the partial charring of buckthorn wood, Duttenhofer proceeded in the autumn of 1883 to produce a nitro-powder. He was not the first to try it. Since the Basel chemistry professor Johann Christian Schönbein had produced guncotton in his laboratory in 1846, chemists and laymen in many lands had tried to create energy-rich propellants and explosives by treating cellulose with nitric acid. But the performance of the nitrocellulose was incalculable, it was dangerous to use and unstable when stored for a long time. The situation did not improve when the Prussian Artillery Captain Schultz in 1864 and the Austrian Volkmann in 1871 chose wood instead of cotton as the raw material. Volkmann, to be sure, succeeded in gelatinizing the nitrocellulose with alcohol and ether — an essential prerequisite for the success of the later experiments — but Volkmann's developments remained unfinished because the Austrian state, to protect its powder monopoly, forbade the inventor to continue his work.

When Max Duttenhofer started to experiment with nitrates in his little workshop laboratory in the autumn of 1883, he could not have known that at the same time the French chemist Vieille was working on the same problem.

From the very start, Duttenhofer was at a disadvantage compared to his French competitor, because he believed that the black-powder raw material of wood was also suitable for nitropowder. This mistake was only to be realized five years later, at least in Germany.

In the spring of 1884 Duttenhofer held the first sample of his nitrated, gelatinized and grained wooden material in his hands, and the firing tests with it seemed very promising from the beginning.

The inventor reported his success to Spandau and the Rifle Testing Commission showed an immediate interest.

In July of 1884 Duttenhofer received a shipment from the Rifle Testing Commission, of M/71 test rifles with 9-mm barrels, with which the Commission had been testing the performance of new bullet types and compressed black powder for years. Nine millimeters —that was now taken for proved — was the smallest caliber at which black-powder cartridges still gave satisfactory performance. Performance, moreover, that more or less equaled that of the 11-cm M/71 rifle.

With Duttenhofer's new powder, which was given the name of "R.C.P." (Rottweil Cellulose Powder), it was possible to exceed the results formerly attained at Spandau. The following table gives the performance of the 11-cm M/71 rifle with black powder and with R.C.P. as well as the statistics of the 9-mm rifle with R.C.P.

Caliber	Charge	Bullet	Muzzle Velocity	Gas Pressure
11mm	5g black	25g soft lead	430 m/sec	1500 atm.
11mm	3.5g RCP	25g soft lead	525 m/sec	1457 atm.
9mm	3g RCP	15.5g hard lead	607 m/sec	1937 atm.

Soon afterward, in October of 1884, Captain von Sack, an expert advisor of the Rifle Testing Commission, came to Rottweil with three non-commissioned officers to see for himself the performance of the new powder. On the firing range in Dietingen, near Rottweil, "R.C.P." was fired at distances up to 1200 meters. But the captain's final report to Spandau was not very encouraging. The Rottweil Cellulose Powder did indeed provide considerably more power than the black powder types, but at the same time also dangerously high gas pressure and irregular performance from shot to shot. Since it was still unknown how the new "white powder" — as it was called then to differentiate it from black powder —would stand up to long storage, the Prussian War Ministry at first halted all further tests (Memoranda No. 767 and 875 of December 19, 1884).

An Accident Almost Every Month

If one is familiar with the adventurous production methods that Duttenhofer used to make the first

A historic photographic document: The first firing tests with R.C.P. in October of 1884 at the Dietingen firing range near Rottweil. Captain von Sack (arrow) of the Rifle Testing Commission and Max Duttenhofer (X) observed the tests.

charges of R.C.P. at his mill, then one is not surprised at the limitations involved. The powder factory, shaken over and over by explosions, was still quite primitive at that time. In individual sheds in the Neckar valley, separated from each other by some distance, and sometimes under the open sky, material was roasted, nitrated, washed, dried and grained.

The R.C.P. production proceeded as follows:
Buckthorn branches as thick as one's thumb, delivered from the Black Forest, were first air-dried and then "roasted" in rotary iron retort ovens in the absence of air. In the process, wood vinegar flowed out of the retorts at first. When wood tar also appeared, the fire under the retorts was extinguished, as the roasted wood was only supposed to char up to 57%. After it had cooled, workers had to sort the contents of the retorts by hand. Pieces of wood that were too charred or not charred enough were sorted out; the rest was broken down in crushing mills.

The part of the work that could be dangerous to one's health began when the nitrates were added. Near the shore, in the shallow water of the Neckar, Duttenhofer had a large reaction vessel installed, with a stirring apparatus that could be activated with a long pole by a worker on the shore.

The nitrate vessel held the "corrosive", a mixture of concentrated sulfuric and nitric acid at a ratio of one to two. While the stirrer turned and the river water cooled the reaction vessel, a worker — standing in the water — had to shake grains of buckthorn charcoal into the acid by the spoonful. It was obvious that under such conditions the corrosive process could be neither controlled nor checked.

Often enough the charcoal disintegrated in the acid bath and a poisonous red plume of smoke rose over the Neckar valley to show that all the work has been in vain. But even when the nitration succeeded, the workers were exposed to the choking acid fumes, which in many cases eroded their incisors to

The Rottweil Powder Mill, circa 1885. In the shed in the center (arrow), Max Duttenhofer mixed the first sample of R.C.P.

the gums over the years. Old Rottweilers still remember these macabre identifying marks of the powder worker to this day.

The product of the corroding vessel — nitrocellulose — was then put in containers and soaked in the river until a litmus test showed no more reddening, which meant that the cellulose was free of acid. After drying came treatment with alcohol and ether, the "kneading." In the process the granules dissolved in gelatine which hardened with time into a solid mass.

The last work process was life-threatening: turning the highly explosive gelatine cake into grains. At the very beginning, young women employees had to grind the cake in coffee mills. Because of the constant danger of explosion, they worked in a big tent and wrapped their faces, arms and hands with damp cloths. There were small fires and explosions almost every day, major explosions could be expected every couple months during the mass production of R.C.P. They are recorded in the "Rottweil Hospital Chronicles":

January 26, 1885: Five dead, one badly wounded. The hospital administrator asserted: "None of the powder explosions here for 21 years was as bad as this one."

March 17 and 20, 1887: During chemical tests, five workers suffered severe burns.

May 8, 1887: "A small workshop in which chemical powder was prepared exploded; nobody was there; it went off by itself . . ."

February 4, 1888: Two men suffered severe burns.

February 19, 1888: ". . . in the evening four victims were brought out of the powder factory; it was terrible how they looked . . ."

July 10, 1888: Six hundredweight of powder exploded in the drying house. Three dead, three injured.

March 11, 1889: In the graining works, a cylinder of chemical powder exploded: two dead and five severely injured.

The "Consortium" Helps Duttenhofer Again

When the Rifle Testing Commission declined to make further tests with R.C.P., it was a severe blow for Duttenhofer the manufacturer, who had counted on a lot of business. But he believed firmly in the future of his product, for it had undeniable advantages over black powder despite its uncon-

trollable gas pressure and still unsatisfactory accuracy.

Its power was already talked of. There was also a remarkable decrease in smoke production and of deposits of combustion in the barrel. In addition, it could already be seen that the smaller charges of R.C.P. could result in the development of smaller, lighter cartridges. This consideration was just as significant for the concept of new repeating rifles as it was for the military supply system.

Further R.C.P. experiments were hindered by a fire in the cartridge laboratory of the powder factory in 1885, but Duttenhofer succeeded, with the help of his international connections, in interesting several countries (just which ones can no longer be determined for sure), in his powder. His contact with the designer Armand Mieg was even more important to the manufacturer.

The Bavarian Major Mieg had belonged to the Rifle Testing Commission in Spandau from 1873 to 1879 and had made a name for himself there as a ballistic specialist and designer. When he was sent to the reserves in 1880, he at first continued his experiments on his own. Along with a relative, the chemist Dr. Hugo Bischoff of Berlin, he developed a tungsten bullet that he patented inside and outside Germany in 1882. As of 1884 Mieg cooperated with the Frankfurt banking house of Weis-Beer & Co., and as of 1886 another contributor. Loewenberg & Co. of Berlin, joined the "Mieg Consortium." The business purpose of the Consortium, as expressed in a business contract of November 23, 1886, was: Realization of the Mieg patents for tungsten bullets and rifle mechanisms. Also, the founding of a tungsten factory.

The banks financed a testing facility for Mieg, in which he was the first in Germany to undertake systematic tests with small-caliber copper, brass, bronze and steel jacketed bullets. He invented new drawing systems, bullet-making processes and cartridge cases. Around the middle of the Eighties Armand Mieg was the best-qualified expert in the whole Reich to deal with the problems of new small-caliber rifle mechanisms. He was exactly the man Duttenhofer needed if he wanted to make a success of his nitro-powder.

The collaboration of Duttenhofer and the Consortium required that the powder factory be responsible for the Consortium's developmental costs in the event that the R.C.P. would not be accepted for military use after all. Duttenhofer also had to pledge to turn Mieg's test rifles over to the War Ministry in Berlin only on the condition that the Consortium would receive licensing fees in the event that one of the test rifles or parts thereof would be accepted for future military use. To make a long story short, when Duttenhofer finally thought he saw business ahead, he broke the agreement and left Mieg and the Consortium in the lurch.

At that time, though, in January of 1886, Duttenhofer was still far away from success. When Armand Mieg first came to Rottweil for testing, the test riflemen at the factory - as he reported later — had such a fear of R.C.P. that they were only brave enough to operate the shooting machine with a long string. At times the nitro-powder developed such high gas pressure that barrels ruptured. Today we know that the cause lay in the chemical properties of the raw material wood, which had not been researched to any great extent at that time, as well as the unfavorable granular form of the R.C.P.

Despite these inherent faults of the Rottweil nitro-powder, Duttenhofer was able, in collaboration with Mieg, to turn this uncooperative propellant into a halfway usable gunpowder in the course of two years.

In the beginning Mieg himself took part in the powder tests with an 8 mm caliber single-shot rifle of his own making. Only early in 1877 was his repeater finished; it had been made especially for the use of R.C.P. and was to be presented to the Rifle Testing Commission along with the new powder.

The following details of this test rifle and its ammunition are found in various sources, all of which agree:

Mieg's Experimental Rifle

The 8 mm caliber weapon had a symmetrically locked bolt and could be equipped optionally with a five- or eight-shot box magazine in the middle of the stock. For the barrel section of the test weapon, Mieg had a remarkable brainstorm: He delivered two interchangeable barrels with it, the one with riflings 24 centimeters long for copper-jacketed bullets, and the other with sharper 20-cm riflings for steel-jacketed bullets. The two bullet types were very much in competition with each other then. The changeable barrels had twelve trough-shaped

rifling grooves 0.12 mm deep. Trough-shaped riflings were then the most modern type used in gun barrels.

The actual barrel lay in a wider, thin-walled sheet-metal tube, the "barrel jacket", which reached from the mouth of the receiver to the muzzle. The barrel jacket that Mieg had already designed in 1879 did not seem to him alone to be the ideal solution. It allowed the barrel to swing freely when firing and expand unhindered when it was hot. Hindrances of barrel vibration by its attachment to the stock, as in the M/71, were ruled out. Even later, at a time when relations between Mieg and Spandau were no longer the best, the Rifle Testing Commission admitted: "Tests actually showed that the barrel jacket used by Mieg would guarantee the best results imaginable in terms of precision and evenness of shots . . ."

A second advantage of his jacketed barrel was stated by Mieg as "the ease with which conversion can be made to a new cartridge, to the extent that it needs a new barrel, as with rifles that have barrel jackets the installation of new barrels can be done easily and at comparatively low cost."

Efforts were actually made later to modify the just-delivered 11-mm M 71/84 rifles to "small caliber" by installing a thinner 8-mm barrel with a jacket. Mieg had presumably foreseen that and thus also used the M/71 case for his test cartridges. For the retention of the case length and the base diameter would have been a prerequisite for the rebuilding of the M 71/84 tube-magazine rifle.

The ammunition for the Mieg test rifle consisted of the following: The M/71 brass case, reduced from 11 to 8 mm in the bullet area, the 71 percussion cap. The charge consisted of 4.1 grams of R.C.P. with "15/20 graining", which meant a grain size of about one millimeter. Two cardboard sheets, each 0.5 mm thick, were used as intermediate material. The bullets (available with either copper or steel jackets, each type tested in nickel-plated form) weighed approximately 16 grams.

The test cartridge was 88 mm long, weighed 33.6 grams and achieved a muzzle velocity (V_{25}) of 577 meters per second. It proved to be strikingly superior in every way to the M/71 cartridge.

Bismarck Gets Into the Act

The Rifle Testing Committee experimented with

the Mieg test rifle during the summer of 1887, but apparently without enjoying it. Therefore the dynamic Duttenhofer, who wanted the tests to culminate in a state contract for "R.C.P." turned directly to Chancellor Bismarck. This move made use of a relationship that went back to 1876, when Max Duttenhofer had opened a branch of his Rottweil powder factory at Bismarck's ancestral estate of Friedrichsruh. Thus Max Duttenhofer's brother Carl, who directed the factory, became a neighbor of the prince. He made use of the opportunity to interest the Chancellor in "R.C.P."

After Carl Duttenhofer's first visit for this purpose, Bismarck wrote a long letter to the Prussian War Minister Bronsart von Schellendorf on December 24, 1886, in which he stressed the advantages of a new "small-caliber" rifle. The Chancellor was able to show a remarkably detailed knowledge, because he had been instructed thoroughly by Carl Duttenhofer. Bismarck wrote: ". . . to the extent that I as a layman can form an opinion, it seems to me that the troops that carry the smaller-caliber 8-millimeter rifles have a weapon whose effect is significantly superior to that of the 11-millimeter rifle . . . provided that the right powder is used in the smaller caliber.

According to Duttenhofer's information, which he provided to me orally, the bullet of the 8-millimeter rifle with the right powder carries 600 meters, against, if I am not mistaken, 480 meters for the 11-millimeter rifle, and is superior in the speed of the trajectory which in itself lends the smaller caliber a much greater and more exact effect; especially so for the magazine rifles, in which the possibility of firing at up to 600 meters without changing the sight carries more weight than with the single-shot rifles . . ."

Bismarck urged the War Minister to see to it that the tests and the acceptance of the Duttenhofer powder be hastened.

But the specialists in Berlin would not let themselves be rushed by anyone, not even the Reich Chancellor. When the deserter Schnäbele then smuggled the new small-caliber French Lebel M 1886 rifle over the border into the Reich in the spring of 1887, a very concerned Bismarck intervened in the powder competition a second time.

He invited Carl Duttenhofer to Friedrichsruh. Duttenhofer himself later described the discussion as follows:
"The Prince asked me whether it might be possible

for me to get a larger sample of the French low-smoke powder, so that Herr Schreiber (a state chemist) could examine it . . . I knew that my brother (Max Duttenhofer) had often obtained French-Russian powder from our Russian factory. French soldiers had stolen the cartridges and sold them to the Russians. A kilo cost 500 Francs . . . I telegraphed my brother that I would travel to Rottweil in the evening; he was to meet me and bring the sample, so that I could take the next train back. This happened, and I returned to Friedrichsruh two days later. The Prince was very happy . . ."

The Duttenhofers believed they were helping their own interests by providing the sample of French powder. But one may assume that it was not true. For the experts in Spandau recognized at once that the French powder, in flake form, was far superior to the Rottweil powder in terms of evenness and performance.

While the negotiations with Rottweil were still going on, extensive experiments were taking place at the Royal Prussian Ammunition Factory in Spandau with the aim of producing their own nitro-powder after the French model. But neither Bismarck nor the Duttenhofers knew that.

Duttenhofer is Shipped Out

At first it seemed as if the R.C.P. business would finally be settled after a long struggle.

On December 5, 1887, after the Reich Chancellor had intervened again, the Prussian War Ministry contracted with the Rottweil powder factory's Hamburg branch to deliver a total of 2500 tons of R.C.P. within fifteen years. The individual charges had to correspond to a sample that the Rifle Testing Commission had taken before the contract was signed. The contract stated:
"The decisive point for the acceptance requirement consisted of the powder to be delivered for use in 8-mm rifles, like those supplied by the Rottweil-Hamburg Powder Factory to the Rifle Testing Commission (Mieg rifles), shall show no less satisfactory accuracy at the distances of 300 and 600 meters than the normal powder when used in the same rifles with the same bullet types shows at these distances . . ."

Duttenhofer received an advance of two million Marks as well as a payment of 1.5 million Marks for providing his secret powder formula. For in the future all state powder factories were also to have the right to produce his "R.C.P." The contract included — and this is important for the events that followed - a right of withdrawal for the War Ministry in the event that R.C.P. should later prove to be unsuited for use by the troops.

This passage was necessary, of course, since there had been neither troop testing nor storage testing of the new powder before the contract was signed. At the same time, though, this right of withdrawal afforded the War Ministry the possibility of getting rid of Duttenhofer in case the state chemists at Spandau could create a superior propellant, which was expected. For Duttenhofer's "nitrate" or "white powder" was, at a price of 120 Marks per hundredweight, twice as expensive as the old black powder, but had a whole series of important weaknesses:

First came its high moisture content, which was necessary in order to decrease the danger of incalculable increases of pressure, but which simultaneously made storing the powder an unknown quantity. The smoke development of the R.C.P., which was still considerable, was also unsatisfactory, as was its complicated and risky production. Along with all that, the Rottweil powder did not perform well enough to make full use of the small caliber's advantages.

Nevertheless Duttenhofer's "R.C.P." was still the only nitro-powder available to the Prussian War Ministry when, in the spring of 1888, the Rifle Testing Commission set out to develop a new cartridge and a new infantry rifle in a small caliber. Without the Swabian entrepreneur and without the preparatory work that Armand Mieg's "Consortium" had performed, the development of the 88 weapon system within such a short time never would have been possible. The differences between the War Ministry and the Consortium will be dealt with later. At this point it must be noted that Duttenhofer, after military weapons had switched to the "Rifle Flake Powder 88" developed at Spandau, was given a replacement contract (dated 9/12/1888). At first he could continue to supply R.C.P. (to fill blank cartridges), and later, after he had converted his Rottweil factory, he also received contracts for flake powder.

The powder factory Rottweil during the mid-1890s. Instead of the old buildings, a new massive industrial complex stands in the Neckar Valley. In the foreground is the test target range, in the right rear the "corrosive" factory at the Fuchsloch.

Rifle Flake Powder (Gew.Bl.P.) 88

In making the flake rifle powder officially introduced in April of 1889, the chemists in Spandau had succeeded in copying the French Vieille powder, the sample of which the Duttenhofer brothers had supplied, to the last detail.

The question of why Max Duttenhofer had not gotten the idea of producing a cotton-based flake powder himself instead of wasting so much time and trouble on his grained wood powder remains unanswered.

We know now that wood, on account of its naturally irregular chemical composition, is less suitable for producing nitrocellulose than is cotton, which consists of nearly pure cellulose. Because of its fine fibrous structure it can also be worked more easily and evenly. The corroding, soaking and gelatinizing of cellulose followed the Rottweil process in principle. But in terms of forming the particles of powder, Spandau took another course.

The gelatine was now pressed through matrices and finally cut into thin square flakes with sides between 1.7 and 1.8 mm long. Their thickness was 0.35 to 0.40 mm.

Instead of the irregularly shaped and relatively coarse grains of the R.C.P., one now had uniformly shaped particles, the burning of which could be regulated exactly. The particles burn evenly from their large parallel surfaces to the middle, which means that the propellant gases given off grows proportionally to the increasing burning space behind the bullet in the barrel. The result is optimal utilization of relatively low gas pressure.

With the grainy R.C.P. powder, on the other hand, the highest gas pressure (as with the old types of black powder) developed at a time when the bullet either had not yet moved or had just moved a few millimeters in the barrel. After that, the pressure immediately falls off rapidly, since the burning space becomes greater and greater and the surface of the powder grains becomes smaller and smaller as they burn.

The superiority of flake powder despite a smaller charge is shown in the following comparison. The values apply to the 8-millimeter cartridge 88 with a jacketed bullet weighing 14.7 grams, fired from the 88 rifle:

Powder type	Charge	Shot velocity
R.C.P.	3.05 grams	584 meters/second
Gew.Bl.P.88	2.75 grams	620 meters/second

Armand Mieg

Armand Mieg, born in Ulm on December 20, 1834, was the son of a royal Württemberg First Lieutenant and entered Bavarian military service in 1853. In 1872 he became a directing member of the Bavarian Infantry Gunnery School at Augsburg, and on January 1, 1873 he was ordered to represent Bavaria at the Prussian Military Gunnery School in Spandau (Rifle Testing Commission). He stayed there until 1879.

During this time Mieg performed essential ballistic theoretical and practical design work. For his "secret service book" on "The Utility of the M/71 Infantry Rifle" he received the Prussian "Order of the Red Eagle 4th Class" in 1877, and a year later the Knight's Cross Second Class of the Bavarian Military Service Order. As a designer, Mieg looked for original solutions. He invented a device for quick determination of target hits, the "Mieg Target Controller", which was used in Augsburg and Spandau. In 1879 he presented two model weapons, constructed at his own expense, to the President of the Rifle Testing Commission in Spandau. One of the two rifles, which the Commission purchased for its collection, already had a bolt with symmetrical locking.

After his return from Spandau, Mieg became Commander of the 7th Bavarian Infantry Regiment "Prince Leopold" on January 1, 1880, but after his long absence from service with the troops, he did not feel at ease in this new position. He fell victim to a plot by his company chiefs and, after being judged by a court of honor in November of 1890, was pensioned off to the reserves and discharged on his own request in 1893. From 1880 on, Mieg worked, at first alone and later with the support of the "Consortium" (see pp. 75 ff), on the development of new bullet types and barrel profiles. Among others, he received a patent for a lance bullet of tungsten and lead in which the center of gravity was at the center of the bullet, so that the bullet, shot from a smooth barrel, maintained its direction without rifling.

Mieg's cooperation with the powder manufacturer Duttenhofer and his 8-mm test weapons were important contributions to the rapid solution of the "small caliber question" in the German Reich. A patent dispute concerning the barrel jacket of the 88 rifle, though, worsened Mieg's already shaky relationship with the state agencies to the point that he was closed out of further weapons development. A new Mieg prototype with a caliber of only 5 mm, which the designer offered in 1894, was not even tested in Spandau.

Armand Mieg had more success as a military author. His ballistic works of the Eighties and Nineties achieved great renown. He died in 1917 at Ahrweiler, near Koblenz.

The 88 Cartridge

Cartridge 88 (8 x 57)
Overall length: 82.5 mm
Gross weight: 27.3 grams
Case length: 57 mm
Case weight: 10.9 grams
Bullet length: 30.7 mm
Bullet weight: 14.7 grams
Bullet material: Copper-nickel plated steel-jacketed bullet
Bullet shape: Cylindrical with round head

Bullet caliber: 8.1 mm
Charge: 2.75 grams Gew.Bl.P. 88
Lateral pressure: 30 grams
Intermediate material: 1 cardboard sheet, 1.5 mm thick
Note: Five 88 cartridges were delivered in steel loading clips. The sheet-steel clips were reused. In order to avoid rust, the frames were given a coat of lacquer as of 1891. Every soldier originally received 150, later, as of 1897, only 120 cartridges.

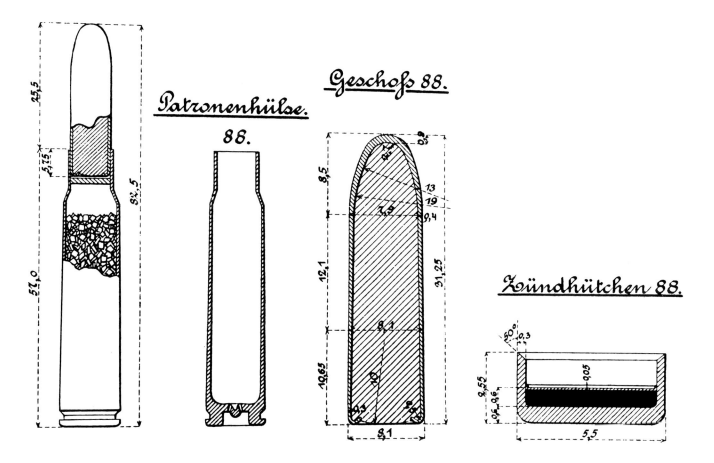

By the end of the Seventies the Rifle Testing Commission had already considered and experimented with the design of a new military cartridge. At first the purpose was merely to save weight but keep the same performance. Thus the soldiers' supply of ammunition could be increased without burdening them with a heavier load. This inevitably led to experiments with smaller calibers, because weight could be cut from the cartridge only in the heaviest part, the bullet.

At the end of the laborious tests with calibers of 10.5, 10, 9.5 and 9 mm it was found that when hard lead (93% lead, 7% tin) bullets were used, all the test cartridges gave the same performance as the 11-mm standard ammunition, but the dirt and lead deposits in the barrel became heavier and heavier. Nine millimeters — as the tests showed — was the smallest caliber at which black-powder shooting under military conditions still promised success.

The 9-mm test cartridge had a 15.6-gram hard lead bullet 26 millimeters long (2.9 caliber), with a charge of 4.4 grams of black powder. The case was like that of the 71 cartridge.

Using these 9-mm cartridges and M/71 rifles

with 9-mm barrels, the first tests with Rottweil powder were made later, in the summer of 1884. The possibility already appeared in the process that the Rifle Testing Commission could make its self-appointed task the creation of not only lighter but also higher-performance ammunition.

In the pause that followed the temporary end of Rottweil powder testing, the officers of the Rifle Testing Commission turned their attention to the development of new bullet types, with the hope of decreasing the lead deposits in the barrel. This task could not be accomplished satisfactorily with hard-lead bullets. Heavy copper and brass bullets worked well in the barrel, but in free flight they lost speed and energy too quickly, because the bullet material was too light. Armand Mieg's patented heavy tungsten bullets would have been a good solution, since tungsten's specific weight of 18.3 is con-siderably more than that of lead (11.3). But the large-scale manufacture of tungsten bullets was impossible for two decisive reasons: 1) the rare metal could be had at that time only in very small quantities at high prices, and 2) it could only be worked by the sifter process, being pressed into shape as a powder.

The Jacketed Bullet

The ensuing tests concentrated on a type of bullet whose invention in 1875 is attributed to the Prussian Major Bode: the jacketed bullet.

It consisted of a lead core and an outer skin of tough material that could take the form of the rifling grooves but was scarcely worn off on them. As jacket materials, copper, brass, steel and nickel

88 cartridges with loading clips and a box. The cardboard containers, each with three filled loading clips, would fit into the two leather cartridge pouches on a soldier's belt. Each cartridge pouch would hold three boxes, for a total of 45 cartridges.

were possible. Experiments were also made with hard lead cores, some pressed in, others with the jacket soldered on (as Kommerzienrat Lorenz of the Metal Cartridge Factory of Karlsruhe had introduced with his "compound" or "armored bullets").

The following comparison shows what high demands were made on the material of the new small-caliber, smokeless-powder bullets:

The 11-mm lead bullet of the M/71 cartridge, with a muzzle velocity of about 430 meters per second and a rifling length of 550 mm, made "only" 836 revolutions in the first second. In the later 88 rifle, at 630 meters per second and a rifling length of 240 mm, the 8-mm jacketed bullet rotated 2625 times.

The best jacket material in the Spandau tests at first proved to be nickel-plated sheet copper, but later a change was made to copper-nickel-plated sheet steel. The bullet core consisted of 95% lead and 5% antimony. It was not soldered to the jacket.

The final decision on the caliber of the rifle to be created was not made until the summer of 1888. Barrel widths from 7 and 8 millimeters were under discussion. It was thought that the black-powder M/71 rimmed case could be made suitable for the new rifle, bullets and powder by narrowing the mouth of the case to 8 millimeters. Mieg's test rifles, which Duttenhofer presented at Spandau, had such cartridges, and the feared enemy, France, had followed the exact same course in designing the 8-mm cartridge for the M/1886 Lebel rifle: there the case of the French M/1874 11-mm rimmed cartridge had simply been narrowed at its mouth.

There was still another argument for the retention of the rimmed case: the planned changing of the 11-mm M 71/84 rifles to 8 millimeters, which was already being discussed. Only when the further course of testing at Spandau led away from this idea was the cartridge-case question open again.

A Rimless Cartridge from Switzerland

The decision was finally made in favor of a slim, rimless 57-mm brass case with drawn-in shoulder, built almost exactly like the cartridge that the Swiss Major Rubin had introduced in August of 1887 at a comparison test in the Confederation Military Gunnery School at Wallenstadt.

A confidential report on this event in a neighboring country attracted the greatest attention in Berlin, and the Bavarian military representative, von Xylander, reported to Munich that the superiority of the Rubin rifling and cartridge over the competitors had been proved clearly.

The rimless Rubin cartridge with a shoulder had more favorable outer dimensions than the rimmed cartridges for rifle design and ammunition pocket construction, but was far from problem-free. In the *Handbook Concerning the Ammunition for Handguns*, published in 1900 by the Rifle Testing Commission, said:

"The absence of the rim . . . influences the durability of the case in various ways: on the one hand, the measurements of the case base are lessened by the groove (for the remover), but on the other hand the metal in the bullet chamber is also under much pressure, because the inward sweep (the shoulder) must be kept very steep if it is completely to fulfill its purpose of serving as a counterfoot (against the push of the striker). This steep inclination . . . also causes a less smooth forward flow of the powder gases, thus increasing the gas pressure . . ."

The first manufacturers of the 88 cartridges. The numbers stamped on the cartridge bases indicate the month and year of manufacture.

Frister & Roßmann, Berlin
Deutsche Metallpatronenfabrik **L**orenz, Karlsruhe
(**D**eutsche Waffen- und **M**unitionsfabriken)

Keller & Comp., Hirtenberg
Arthur Krupp, Berndorf
A. **P**olte, Magdeburg-Sudenburg

Rheinisch-Westfälische Sprengstoff-Aktiengesellschaft **T**roisdorf
Georg **R**oth, Wien Munitionsfabrik **S**pandau

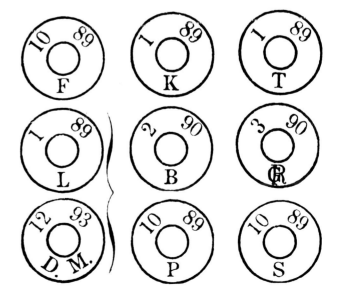

It may have been a result of this high strain that, with the introduction of the 88 cartridge, the cost-saving old custom of reloading old cases was given up.

As has been described already, a charge of 3.05 grams of R.C.P. was originally planned for the cartridge of the new rifle, which would move the bullet at 584 meters per second (V_{25}). Only in April of 1889 was the charge changed to 2.75 grams of Gew.Bl.P.88. The muzzle velocity (V_{25}) increased to 620 meters per second. The weights and measures of the new cartridge are given at the beginning of this chapter.

Changes to the 88 Cartridge

When the Rifle Testing Commission in Spandau decided on the rimless 8-mm cartridge in the summer of 1888, the participating designers had highly overestimated the know-how of the German ammunition industry. There were difficulties for years, especially in mass-producing the cases with their sharply sloping shoulders. Small modifications and time-consuming reworking at the state ammunition laboratories had to be resorted to until new manufacturing processes and more favorable alloys had been invented.

In a period of fifteen years, all the components of the cartridge, from the percussion cap to the bullet, had been changed, some of them several times. But then, in 1903, the cartridge had attained a quality that met all demands for half a century and can still be seen in our own day.

The following overview lists the most important modifications to the 88 cartridge prior to the introduction of the S cartridge in 1903.

Cartridges 88 · * · and 88* (1891-1894)

The first 88 cartridge cases that were manufactured developed tears in the cartridge neck after long storage. The causes were the conical form and the too-small interior dimensions of the cartridge neck. The pressed-in bullet broke the case metal. The result was that the bullets no longer stayed firmly in place, and some of them fell out of the cases. In addition, the cardboard discs slid down and sank into the powder.

Cartridges thus damaged had six indentations, in two rows, pressed into them from outside, and were also fitted with a crimp around the mouth of the case. Cartridges made new after 1891 had the cartridge necks of the cases slightly enlarged in order to avoid tearing. But at first the indentations and crimping could not be dispensed with if the bullet and cardboard were to stay firmly in place for a long time.

The designation · * · on cartridge boxes means that new cases with enlarged cartridge necks have been used. The "Cartridge 88*" type, on the other hand, has old cases from mobilization storage with subsequently expanded bullet chambers.

Cartridge 88 n/A
(November 1893-January 1895)

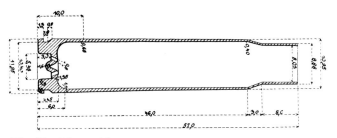

The 88 n/A cartridge case

Torn cases at the base of the cartridge and percussion caps that fell out when fired had led to accidents in the summer of 1892. These faults, along with those described above, finally led to a new design of the 88 case. The walls became heavier, the two ignition channels in the cap chamber were no longer stamped but bored, and the percussion cap was riveted to three points on the rim of the cap chamber. Thickening the case walls decreased the space inside. Thus the charge had to be cut down by 0.08 g to 2.67 grams of Gew.Bl.P. The velocity thus sank by about 10 m/sec to 610 meters per second.

Cartridge 88 n/A ●

After fine hairline cracks had appeared at the indentations in the cartridge necks of n/A cartridges that had been stored for some time, the case material and pressing process were reviewed again. The Lorenz Ammunition Factory in Karlsruhe suggested that the bullet chamber of the cartridge be heated after drawing, so as to remove the tension in the metal. This new procedure even allowed the width of the bullet chamber to be decreased again and the bullet to be pressed into the case chamber without damage. The indentations and thickening became superfluous. The 88 n/A • cartridges were the first to guarantee an airtight closure at the mouth of the case. The crimp at the mouth was retained, and the cardboard disc was thickened from 1.5 to 1.8 millimeters.

Cartridge 88 n/A • with 436 Powder

The Spandau Rifle Flake Powder 88, which had shown itself to be so clearly superior to the Rottweil Cellulose Powder from the start, also showed several faults right after its first troop tests. The main cause was the relatively high ethyl acetate content, which was used to gelatinize the guncotton and could at first be removed from the finished powder only to an unsatisfactory degree. During storage, the ethyl acetate disappeared from the powder, it became "sharper" and the gas pressure in firing increased. After years of experimentation with new gelatinizing agents and production methods, in which the Rottweil-Hamburg Powder Factory was again involved along with other private firms, the choice went eventually to a propellant that the Royal Prussian Powder Factory in Spandau had developed. This "Powder 436" was a flake powder, in the production of which sulfuric ether was used for gelatinizing, and which was also treated with camphor.

The "Powder 436" (the number indicates the testing sequence) was introduced by order of the Royal Prussian General War Department on April 24, 1899.

Cartridge Case 88/E

In the tests that preceded the introduction of the first German machine gun (Maxim system) it had been seen that the normal 88 cartridge could not be used in the new weapon without modification. The cases were too weak and too brittle, the cartridge bases tore off, and this resulted in jammed machine guns.

Therefore the Rifle Testing Commission in Spandau was given the assignment in September of 1899 to develop a uniform case for the 88 cartridge that could be used in both the repeater and the machine gun. With a softer brass material ("Alloy 72/28"), slightly strengthened walls at the base of the cartridge case, and a more precisely turned groove in the base for the remover, they succeeded in solving the problem. The uniform case "88 E" was introduced on October 17, 1901. The new cartridge cases were identified by the letter "E" stamped on the base.

Blank Cartridge 88

The 88 blank cartridge had the same case as the live cartridge. Unlike it, though, the blank had a hollow red-painted wooden bullet that splintered when fired and could do no harm at any distance beyond ten meters.

Until 1891 the blank cartridges were loaded with Rottweil Cellulose Powder and had a cardboard separator disc. After that it was replaced by a new Spandau Blank Cartridge Powder (Pl.P.P.). This was very fine-grained (0.15-0.5 mm) and colored a pale yellow. The charge weighed only eight tenths of a gram, thus part of the empty space in the case had to be filled with paper plugs.

In the beginning, the blank cartridges were remarkably expensive because, for reasons of durability, only new cases could be used. Only after the introduction of the "Karlsruhe heating process" was it then possible to use the spent cases of live cartridges to make blank cartridges. Cartridges of this kind reached the troops as of October 1893. The price was about 23 Marks per thousand. The blank cartridge powder was modified in 1895 and again in 1898.

Holzgeschoß 88.

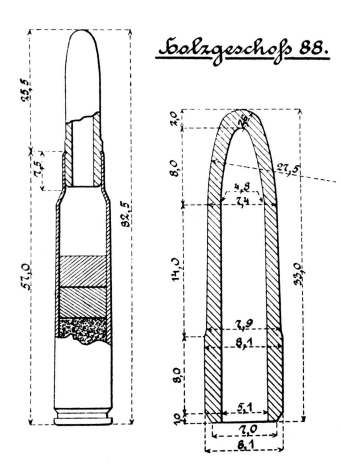

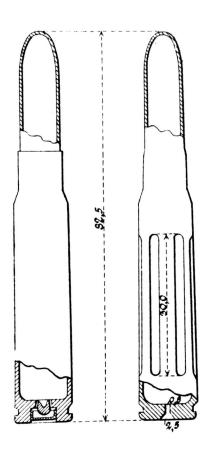

Left: Cutaway drawing of a blank cartridge with 88 wooden bullet. The small charge of powder is held down by paper plugs. Right: Comparison of the live cartridge with the 88 dummy type (far right). The latter is differentiated by a grooved case.

Infantry Rifle 88

Type: *Infanteriegewehr 88*
Number: 5334
Year made: 1891
Manufacturer: Royal Bavarian Rifle Factory, Amberg
Function: Repeater
Overall length: 1240 mm
Gross weight: 3.9 kg
Barrel length: 740 mm
Barrel caliber: 7.9 mm
Number of riflings: 4
Rifling direction: Right
Rifling depth: 0.1 mm (as of 7/7/1896: 0.15 mm)
Rifling width: 4.5 mm
Rifling length: 240 mm
Action: Bolt action with symmetrical lug locking and cocking on opening
Safety: Mauser leaf safety
Magazine: Box in mid-stock, Mannlicher system, 5-cartridge clip
Sight: Standing sight, small flap and frame (250-2050 meters)

Standard Ammunition: Cartridge 88 (8 x 57)
Disassembly: Press bolt release (left on receiver) and trigger, release bolt and draw it out the back of the receiver. Turn cocking piece to left until it rests in extension of bolt. Pull bolt head with extractor forward out of chamber. Put firing pin point horizontally on wood underneath and push bolt down toward firing pin spring until firing pin nut can be unscrewed. Carefully release firing pin chamber and cocking piece, take cocking piece and safety from firing pin, pull firing pin and spring forward out of chamber.
Reassembly: In opposite order. Note that the flattening of the firing pin lines up with the small threaded bolt in the cocking piece hole. **Screw the firing pin nut in all the way!** Otherwise the bolt action will be ineffective.
Loading: Push cartridge clip with five cartridges from above into the magazine well until the clip rests in the clip holder. Then move the bolt forward and lock it. The weapon is ready to fire.

When the rearming of the German armies with the 11-mm M 71/84 rifle could finally be finished at the end of 1887, preparations were already underway in Spandau to introduce a small-caliber successor model. The requirements for it, nitro-powder and jacketed bullets, were available, though not just in the German Reich. At almost the same time, all the great military powers were working secretly on the same problem, which the renowned *Viennese Military Journal* publicly called by name for the first time early in October of 1887: "The Solution of the Rifle Problem."

This newspaper article, with a wealth of precise information about the stages of development in the other European countries, inspired unexpected reactions in the German press and in public opinion. It even caused hectic activity in the War Ministry in Berlin. The halted attempts to arrive at a favorable caliber and the best ammunition were resumed; suddenly time was of the essence.

The Rifle Testing Commission still had Armand Mieg's two test rifles, which Kommerzienrat Duttenhofer had provided along with samples of his smokeless powder (R.C.P.), at their disposal at that time. Both rifles — as already described — had jacketed barrels. One had a box magazine in midstock and a cylinder breech with a symmetrical bolt. But this modern rifle design found no favor with the Rifle Testing Commission. It was, according to the report of the Bavarian delegate to the Rifle Testing Commission stated, "regarded as unusable in war because of its breech design and construction otherwise . . ."

Only the Mieg barrel jacket seemed useful to the testers, and the 8-millimeter caliber was also accepted for the time being. Beyond that, though, there was not even the outline of a plan for the new rifle in the autumn of 1887. So the gentlemen in the Prussian War Ministry finally got the idea of inspiring the creativity of their colleagues through a secret competition.

The announcement of November 1887 was sent by the Rifle Testing Committee in Spandau to "particularly capable officers and officials" of the Prussian rifle factories. The tasks were:

1. Modifying the M 71/84 infantry rifle into an 8-millimeter rifle usable in war, with and without a barrel jacket.

2. Making an 8-mm (repeater) rifle, usable in war, with and without a jacket, with any suitable bolt and repeating construction.

The modification of the M 71/84 tube-magazine rifle, still brand new at the time, was regarded as very promising. The installation of new barrels with jackets and new sights would have been the only necessary changes if the cases of the 71 cartridges had been retained and they had simply been narrowed to a diameter of 8 millimeters at the bullet chamber. The "adaptation" would have cost about twenty Marks per rifle.

In November of 1887 the Prussian War Minister, von Schellendorf, inquired of his colleagues in Munich, Stuttgart and Dresden whether they were in agreement with this suggestion. At the same time the plan was made to equip all M 71/84 rifles yet to be made with the "Mauser chamber with doubled resistance" (see page 70) in 8 mm caliber. Machines for the purpose were ordered from the firm of Ludwig Loewe in Berlin in December of 1887. But things were to turn out very differently.

A Bastard is Born

The officers of the Rifle Testing Commission, who were less inclined toward a cheap solution of the rifle question than to an optimal one in technical terms, concentrated more and more at the beginning of 1888 on designing a new weapon, in other words, on assignment 2 of the competition announced in November of 1887. Meanwhile the entries had arrived.

To the judges, a bolt design with two symmetrical locking notches behind the bolt head on the bolt seemed usable; it had been submitted by the Royal Prussian Senior Gunsmith Schlegelmilch of the Spandau rifle factory. It was a modification of the Mauser M/71 bolt body mechanism. The rear section of the bolt body with cocking piece, cocking piece, firing pin screw and wing safety remained essentially unchanged. The bolt guide rib was gone, and the bolt head was removable.

Schlegelmilch did away with bolt guide rib and its screw, using a spring loaded bolt stop (likewise an old Mauser idea) on the left side of the receiver

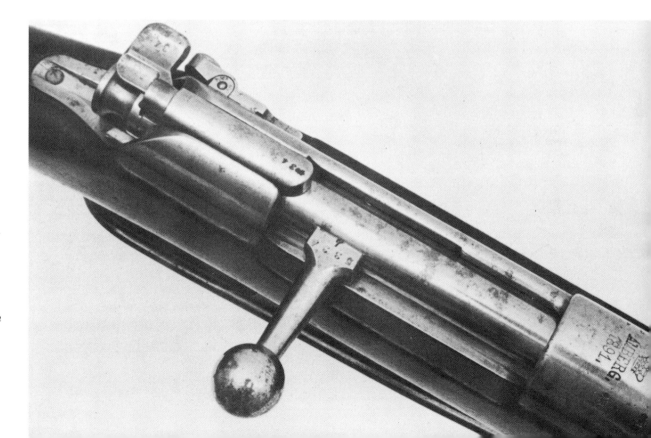

The 88 rifle, with bbreech locked, and uncocked.

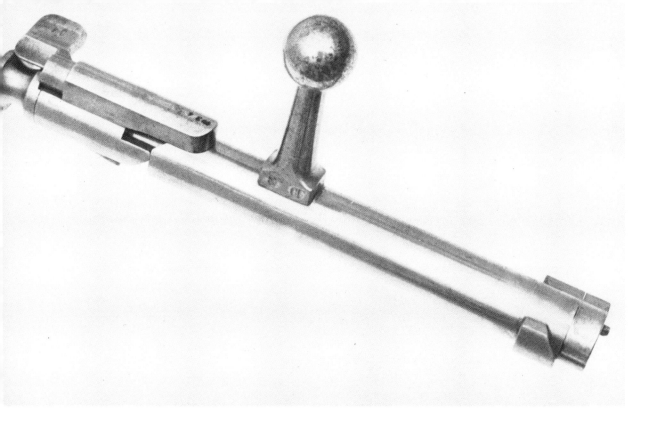

The complete bolt of the 88 mechanism.

instead, with its point projecting into the groove of the left lock, limiting its way back. At the same time, this point controlled a small, adjustable ejector, likewise built into the left-side projection of the bolt head. When the bolt body was driven back during repeating until it made contact, the ejector rod pushed against the rim of the cartridge base from the left, and the case — still held only by the extractor claw at the right — flew out of the receiver at the right.

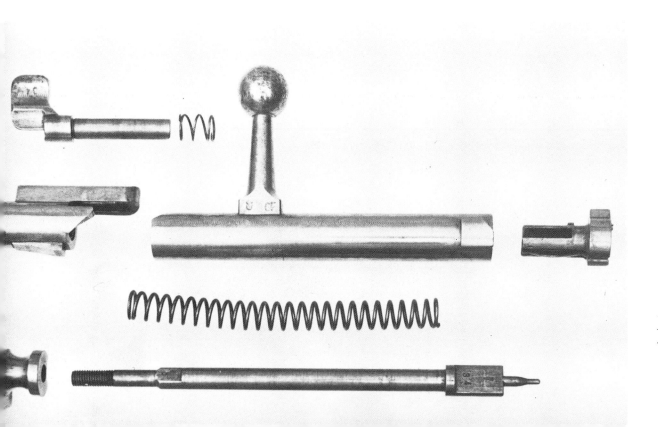

The disassembled 88 breech. From top to bottom: Safety with spring, cocking piece, bolt body, bolt head, firing pin spring, firing pin and firing pin nut.

To the Schlegelmilch-Mauser breech the designers of the Rifle Testing Commission added other parts which they believed would prove themselves: a barrel with a rifling length of 240-millimeter, borrowed from the French Lebel rifle, Mieg's barrel jacket, and a midstock magazine that the Austrian designer Ferdinand Mannlicher had created.

Mannlicher's magazine, used worldwide until a few years ago, is filled from above, through a slot in the receiver, with up to five cartridges held in clips. A spring loaded lever in the magazine well moves the cartridges up toward the lips of the cartridge clip. The uppermost cartridge is taken by the rim of the bolt head when the bolt is moved forward, and pushed out of the clip and into the chamber. Only when the cartridge is pushed all the way in does the extractor snap into its channel bed in the case head.

It is imaginable, even probable, that the first prototype with the Schlegelmilch bolt and Mannlicher magazine was still set up for the M/71 (rimmed) cartridge case drawn in to 8 millimeters, for the decision in favor of the new rimless cartridge in the Swiss style came only later, in the early summer of 1888.

From the files of the War Ministry it appears that the first test rifle must have been available in March of 1888. The Bavarian military representative in Berlin, General von Xylander, reported to Munich on March 23, 1888 that a "special commission" in Spandau had made the new rifle, "which takes the Mannlicher receiver (presumably meaning the Mannlicher magazine mechanism) with slight modifications. Moreover, it is thought in the Prussian War Ministry that the acceptance of this model is not yet assured, since it makes the use of the weapon as a single-shot rifle very difficult, and a lot of importance is still placed on the dual usability of the weapon in single-shot and repeater form, out of consideration for ammunition conservation and for easier firing discipline."

The Dogma of Combined Loading Possibility

The dual use of the rifles, as single-shot or repeater types, a dogma from the early Eighties, was still sacred to some of the Prussian generals. Thus it must have been regarded as a major weakness that

Mauser's suggestion for a rifle with an insertion magazine whose function could be switched off. The locking of the bolt body is effected here under the receiver bridge. This suggestion, made in the spring of 1888, found no favor with the Rifle Testing Commission.

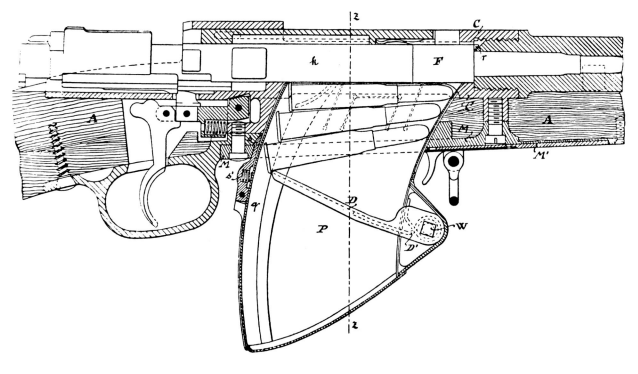

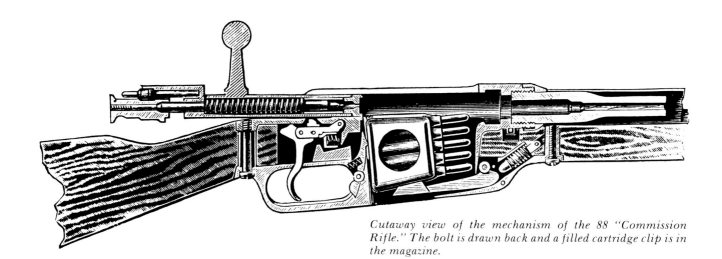

Cutaway view of the mechanism of the 88 "Commission Rifle." The bolt is drawn back and a filled cartridge clip is in the magazine.

loading single cartridges in the test rifle with the Mannlicher magazine was impossible.

Paul Mauser, who had been completely ignored in the preliminary work on the new small-caliber rifle, was now allowed, at the last minute, to present a design of his own in Spandau.

On April 3, 1888 General von Xylander wrote of it: "Recently the Mauser loading mechanism has been tested; it has more chance than Mannlicher's, because it can be set for single or multiple loading."

This description applies to a new, insertable mid-stock magazine (D.R.P. 45 561), for which Paul Mauser obtained a patent on April 18, 1888. It could be loaded with single cartridges in and out of the weapon. The supply could be switched off when the weapon was to be used in single-shot form. It was a fairly complicated mechanism.

In comparing the Mauser repeater with their own rifle model, the members of the Rifle Testing Commission reached a point at the end of April 1888 which they believed went beyond their own possible choices. They asked the War Ministry in Berlin to explain precisely whether the basis of the optional dual single- or multiple-shot functions was still binding. The Rifle Testing Commission, it was stated, considered that to be a decision of principle, tactics and discipline, which they themselves could not answer.

The text of the War Ministry's answer has not been recorded. But the further course of events allows only one conclusion: the generals sacrificed the "sacred cow" of combined loading possibilities for the infantry rifle in favor of magazine firing.

With that, the decision was made for the Mannlicher magazine with clip loading, and simultaneously for the Spandau Commission's model rifle.

At first twenty test models were made by hand and delivered in mid-May. But suddenly new doubts

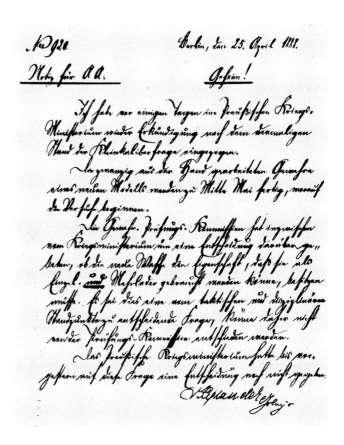

A secret report of the Bavarian military representative in Berlin on the state of testing at the end of April, 1888.

surfaced. General von Xylander reported to Munich on June 4, 1888: ". . . in the course of the tests (with the new rifle) up to now, results have appeared that have made the testers think of reducing the caliber from 8 mm down to 7.5 or even 7 mm . . .''

The decision on this question took a painfully long time. By mid-July the new rifle still had not been definitely designed. Despite that, mass production was to begin in October. Meanwhile it had become clear that large-scale troop testing would not be possible under these conditions.

The machines for the three Prussian rifle factories were —according to "the tables of measurements and dimensions in effect at the time" — already ordered from the firm of Ludwig Loewe, and in Spandau the walls of a gigantic new ammunition factory were rising, although the final form of the cartridge and powder had not yet been decided on either.

On June 2 the directors of the Prussian and Bavarian rifle factories had already met at Spandau and worked out a joint production schedule. They agreed that the seamless barrel-jacket tubes should be made only of Mannesmann steel. The raw barrels should be provided for all the factories by the firm of Marcoty. Marcoty steel had proved to be even better than Krupp material in testing. Another essential point made in the directors' meeting was that of planning production in case mobilization should be ordered during rearming.

It was clear that the German armies would have to go through any sudden war with the old 11-millimeter rifle. To complete the supply of rifles, the Danzig and Erfurt factories were to be "readapted" to M 71/84 production, while the new rifle model was to go into series production at Spandau and Amberg. On November 20, 1888 the Rifle Testing Commission's greatest hour finally struck. Kaiser Wilhelm approved the 7.9-millimeter Commission rifle and ordered its introduction into Prussian military use. The new weapon was given the official designation "Rifle 88"; the added "Model", "Mod." or just "M" was to be dropped in the future.

The introduction took place "subject to a troop test", a very unusual procedure that can be explained only in view of the pressure of time that the Prussian War Ministry believed existed at the time. The results of this rushed acceptance of a model that was nowhere near ready for series production was to grow into a source of constant annoyance.

Production Plans and Manufacturers

Today, more than a century later, one can only chuckle at the naiveté with which the Prussian War Ministry tried to keep production of the 88 rifle a secret. It was ordered that a rumor be spread that the Prussian rifle factories had stopped working after completing M 71/84 production and were being overhauled.

Actually, though, the factories at Spandau, Danzig and Erfurt were being rebuilt completely and expanded considerably. The new machines, ordered from Ludwig Loewe, were to be partially delivered and set up in the autumn of 1888, at first

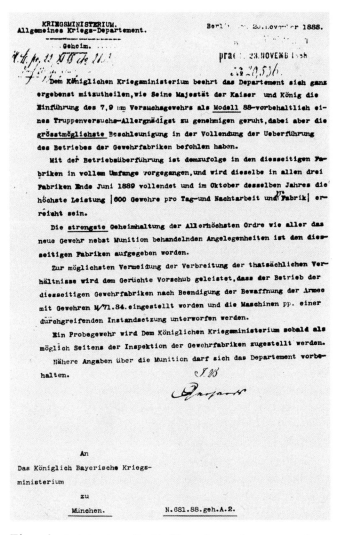

The order to introduce the 88 rifle and spread a rumor to keep the rearmament secret.

in Spandau, later in Danzig and finally in Erfurt. After all, on July 1, 1889, the Bavarian factory in Amberg was on the schedule. At this time the Prussian factories, it was hoped, would already be finishing the first rifles. In October of 1889 the machines were to be running around the clock in Spandau, Danzig and Erfurt. A maximum production of 600 rifles a day was expected of each of the three factories. The smaller Bavarian factory was to produce 400 a day.

Prince Regent Luitpold (who had taken over the regency after the death of Ludwig II), ordered the introduction of the 88 rifle in Bavaria in an "All-Highest Decree" of February 19, 1889. And shortly thereafter, the kingdom joined the "agreement on the uniform armament of all German states." In this agreement, the order of the army corps to be rearmed was established by tactical requirements for the first time. That meant that the Prussian factories, Amberg, and private manufacturers who also produced 88 rifles, were to deliver jointly to a pool from which the individual army corps could be supplied. The corps on the western border came first, then those in the east, and finally the troops in the heart of the Reich.

That could mean that, for example, the Prussian regiments in Königsberg received Bavarian rifles from Amberg and, on the other hand, the Bavarian Jäger in Kempten got their rifles from Spandau. For that reason it seemed necessary to introduce controls to assure that the rifles from the different factories had the same standard of quality.

The state factories agreed to exchange sample rifles from current production as well as inspection personnel. This was a process that was to work out very well in practice.

Even before mass production began in the state factories, the planners at the War Ministry in Berlin had come to the conclusion that in spite of the high daily production in the royal rifle factories, rearming with the 88 rifle would take too long. For that reason the Berliners looked for capable private firms that could produce 88 rifles in the required quality and quantity.

Mauser had to decline, since their capacity at Oberndorf was filled for years to come by a large-scale Turkish order. In their place, the machine works of Ludwig Loewe in Berlin, which since 1886 owned all the shares of Mauser stock, sprang into the breach.

Isidor Loewe, the boss of the company, had already made known by his entry into the "Mieg Consortium" that he wanted not only to provide the machine tools for the new rifles but also take a direct part in their manufacture. A contract was signed. In January of 1889 Loewe received his first order for 300,000 of the 88 rifles for the Prussian state, and later — despite the "Jews' Rifles Affair" — another order for an additional 125,000 rifles.

These large rifle contracts were given to the Loewe firm imprudently, as soon became obvious. For the factory could no longer maintain its machine delivery dates for the state factories. The Bavarians in particular suffered from the results. When by the end of August 1889, not one of the 200 machine tools that had been ordered had arrived, the Director of the Amberg Rifle Factory, Lieutenant Colonel Baron von Brandt, wrote to Munich: "The specified factory (Loewe) for its part would have been able to keep its accepted . . . commitments, if a rifle order had not been given to them by the Royal Prussian War Ministry, which led first of all to an overburdening of the factory and secondly to awakening their self-interest in producing machines and equipment mainly for their own use."

In fact, the rifle contract for Loewe was a tremendously profitable business for Loewe. The firm charged 49 Marks for every rifle they delivered. The height of the profit can be imagined when one knows that the state factories had calculated their own costs (without investment expenses) at 35 to 36 Marks.

The "Consortium" Obstruction

In view of the All-Highest order of strictest secrecy for the design of the 88 rifle, it is surprising indeed that, in the end, orders were even given to foreign firms. The private "Austrian Weapon Factory Society" in Steyr received an order for 300,000 88 rifles for Prussia early in 1889. Production was already running at full speed when, on October 31, 1889, a command of police appeared at the factory and forced the works manager to stop the machines. An Austrian judge had issued an order banning the further production of 88 rifles. The reason: violation of a secret patent on the rifle's barrel jacket.

To make any sense of this mess, we must look back to 1887, when Armand Mieg and the bank consortium had tried to make capital with their small-caliber test rifles.

Armand Mieg, the designer, had signed over all rights to his inventions, thus also to the barrel jacket, to his financiers. The Consortium applied for German and foreign patents. This was in vain in Germany, as the Reich Patent Office in Berlin obviously had been given a signal by the Prussian War Ministry. Since the use of the jacketed barrel in the future infantry rifle was already fairly certain at that time, the state hoped to save licensing fees by refusing the patent. Such a plot would have resulted in a scandal of giant proportions in our day.

When the 88 rifle was finally introduced, the Consortium requested at least compensation for their expenses of 300,000 Marks that had been spent on Mieg's years-long small-caliber experiments. But the War Ministry refused the banks' request. Instead of that, Berlin approved a personal honorarium of 50,000 marks to designer Mieg on March 20, 1889 "in recognition of your contributions in the realm of weapons technology."

The bankers went home with empty pockets. They could only hope to do business with foreign patents. For Mieg's test rifles had meanwhile been protected from imitation in Belgium, Great Britain and Austria. In the last case there was even a secret patent that had been awarded in 1887 and not made public.

When the Prussian government — unknowingly — offered a rifle contract to the equally unknowing Joseph Werndl in Steyr, the directors of the German bank consortium could decide at what point they wanted to spring the trap.

When that happened on October 31, the Consortium knew it had a superb bargaining position. For the factory in Steyr was under double pressure. On the one hand, the factory had to fill the Prussian contract on time in order to avoid a fine; on the other hand, a new Austrian government order was

The muzzle area of the 88 infantry rifle. The upper band is fastened by a screw to a projection of the barrel jacket. The bayonet lug, cleaning rod can be seen. The foresight sits on the barrel jacket, which becomes smaller at the muzzle.

on hand. The factory management could not afford any work stoppage and negotiated its own agreement with the Consortium, at its own expense. The "Weapons Factory Society" agreed to the following licensing regulations with the German banks: One Mark for each of the first 100,000 88 rifles, 50 Pfennig for the second 100,000 and 25 Pfennig for the third 100,000.

An Expensive Armament Record — The New Guns Fail

Rearming with the M 71 rifle had taken four years in Prussia, its successor the M 71/84 had taken three, and the introduction of the 88 rifle had now taken two. This was a record achievement that was very much admired outside Germany. A few statistics: At the end of 1899 the Prussian state factories alone had delivered 270,000 rifles, and in 1890 they increased production to 660,000. Added to this were the deliveries from Amberg as well as those from Loewe and Steyr, in total: 1.9 million guns. The issuing of the new rifles according to the uniform rearmament schedule of the German states began with the troops in Alsace-Lorraine in the autumn of 1889 and ended with the Bavarian field troops at the end of July 1890. On August 1, 1890 all the active regiments in the Reich were equipped with the small-caliber infantry rifle. It was the beginning of a bad time, for the 88 rifle proved from the start to have catastrophic faults.

On August 6, even before the first rifles were fired in Bavaria, the War Ministry in Munich received a warning from Berlin: in Prussia there had been repeated severe accidents with exploding rifles. The warning came too late. On the very same day the first rifle exploded among the 11th Infantry Regiment in Regensburg. The cause: Destruction of the cartridge chamber from too-high gas pressure.

The next Bavarian accidents followed shortly: on August 13 in the 2nd Jäger Battalion in Aschaffenburg and on August 21 in the 9th Infantry Regiment in Augsburg: two men were injured. And so it went; in Bavaria alone there were 33 "barrel explosions and distortions of a dangerous kind" within two years. The statistics did not include the equally dangerous explosions in magazines and the "gas outpourings to the rear" resulting from ripped cartridges.

Note: this only concerns *serious* accidents in *Bavaria*. There were many more in big Prussia. Only as of about 1896 (when rifling depths were

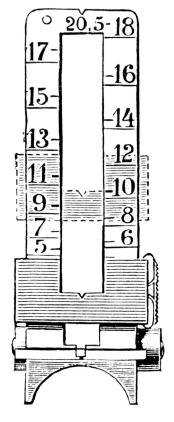

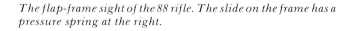

The flap-frame sight of the 88 rifle. The slide on the frame has a pressure spring at the right.

changed!) did the number of accidents with 88 rifles decline noticeably. In spite of that, Prussian regiments still reported to Spandau 947 cases of barrel damage in the 88 rifles between March 1900 and March 1901.

The situation among the troops is reflected in the following reports from Prussian soldiers: ". . . in shooting practice at Brandenburg on the Havel in 1890 the rifles were so bad that it became a stereotype in the officers' way of speaking to ask the men for defective rifles after every shooting drill. There were also regularly some among them that had to go to the gunsmith's shop, and we were always allowed to fire only five live cartridges . . ."

And: "Not long ago I went on a drill with the railroad regiment. Two rifles blew up. One tore the man's thumb off, the other injured the soldier severly, almost killing him . . ."

These reports and a number of similarly shocking ones on the dangers of the 88 rifle were published by the Berlin school principal Hermann Ahlwardt in 1891 in a pamphlet with the title *New Revelations — Jews' Rifles*, which stirred up a tremendous storm throughout the Reich.

The "Jews' Rifles" Affair

Hermann Ahlwardt, who started the ball rolling, already had a certain reputation as a "scandal-monger of letters" at the time. He was a pathological nationalist and zealously sought the enemy in those circles that he and his kind had seen as "un-German": Jesuits, Freemasons and Jews.

When the first news of serious accidents with the new 88 rifles became known, the guilty party was already clear in Ahlwardt's mind: the Jewish firm of "Ludwig Loewe & Co." in Berlin-Martiniken-felde, which had been given a large contract by the War Ministry. Ahlwardt researched madly in order to reinforce his preconceived opinion, which he expressed in the following words: "The international Jewry (has) neglected nothing that can contribute to a German defeat in the next war, and has finally made the unspeakable attempt to put a rifle in the German soldier's hands that must be . . . almost less dangerous to the enemy in the war than to the user."

Since the Loewe firm had not designed the rifle and had manufactured only a total of 425,000 rifles, just a part of the total production of 1.9 million

Landsturm men before World War I, armed with 88 rifles. (Photo: Bavarian War Archives)

guns, this theory was ridiculous. Nevertheless, Ahlwardt's revelations, which were printed in vast quantities, and to which he added a second section in 1892, contained a lot of inflammatory material. From conversations with former Loewe workmen the unbelievable conditions under which the state contract had been handled by Loewe & Co. came to light.

To be able to keep to the delivery schedule and decrease the cost of replacing defective parts, several members of the state control commission were bribed.

Rifles that were rejected at the final examination were given the stamp of approval in the dark of night and were smuggled into the freight cars with the regularly accepted rifles by breaking the lead state seals.

When the guns were fired, Loewe workmen secretly attached two targets one over the other, so that each bull's-eye shot produced two scorecards. The extra cards then had the numbers of badly shooting rifles that had not passed the test written on them.

What Ahlwardt brought to light was unbelievable. But all his accusations, though confirmed in lieu of oath, did less damage to the head of the firm, Isidor Loewe, than to his manager, Kühn, a Christian who had become the director of the Royal Rifle Factory at Spandau before he had entered Loewe's service. Ahlwardt's revelations also hurt a number of minor inspection officials, who were soon tried and punished.

Nothing was done to the Loewe firm. At that time it already held a market-controlling position in the arms sector and, because of its quality products, an outstanding international reputation. And in fact, the faults of the 88 rifle, which did not turn up only in those made by Loewe, were due less to its manufacture than to its design.

Design Faults of the 88 Rifle

According to an old regulation, all rifles damaged during firing had to be sent to Spandau for inspection. When the shooting accidents with the 88 rifle kept increasing from 1890 to 1892, the officers of the Rifle Testing Commission stated three main causes:

Explosions with opened breech: The receiver mechanism had no safeguard against two cartridges being pushed into it at once. When the first one was already in the chamber but the extractor hook had not reached into the channel of the cartridge case, then the shooter could load a second time. Then a second cartridge was driven out of the magazine into the rear of the first one in the chamber. The result: the roundheaded bullet of the second cartridge hit the percussion cap of the first cartridge and ignited it with the bolt open. The shock wave and splinters hit the shooter, and the rifle was damaged.

No way to prevent this design fault of the 88 rifle was ever found. A Prussian troop test in 1891 with a changed bolt head, which was supposed to make it impossible to put in two cartridges, brought no good results. The originally numerous accidents did decrease in number when the soldiers were especially warned of the danger of double loading during weapons training.

Gas emission to the rear; The first series of new 88 brass cartridge cases still showed numerous manufacturing defects. The cartridges often ripped. While cracks in the jacket of the case usually had no serious effects, cracks in the base of the case almost always led to injuries, because then the high-pressure, 1000-degree hot combustion gases could escape out the rear of the receiver and hit the shooter's face. The hot gases made their way through the leading groove of the left locking lug into the receiver. In the first version of the 88 rifle, this groove (with the breech locked) ran like a channel from the chamber to the rear end of the receiver without anything to stop the gas. But this fault was easy to do away with. In a troop test in the autumn of 1892, Prussian regiments tested the functioning of a new firing pin nut and a reinforced bolt release. The firing pin nut had a small gas shield at the left side, which closed the exit from the groove. And the spring lever of the new bolt holder, on the left side of the case, now had a massive steel projection that fit into the groove and blocked the path of any gas that might flow out. This modification was added to ongoing production in 1894, and already existing rifles were modified. At about the same time, ways were found to eliminate the cause of ripping cases by improving manufacturing processes in the ammunition factories.

Barrel explosions and ruptures: The alarming increase in barrel explosions and ruptures in the new 88 rifle was at first unexplainable to the designers on the Rifle Testing Commission. At first they assumed that the thickness of the barrel walls was inadequate. At the suggestion of the Commission in Spandau, the Prussian War Ministry ordered on January 9, 1891 that the outward form of the barrels be changed. Instead of the curve by which the old-type barrel had narrowed before the cylindrical part of the chamber, the new barrels were made with a cone. Since this change could not be seen because of the barrel jacket, it was ordered that rifles with reinforced barrels be marked in the following way: An indentation had to be made in the middle of the receiver, about three millimeters before the threading.

But the reinforcement of the barrel did not eliminate the problem of frequent barrel explosions. The cause lay deeper, and it was to take five years before the fault, in bullet advance, could be recognized and eliminated.

Bullet & Rifling: A Delicate Relationship

The 88 bullet, with lead core and copper-nickel-plated steel jacket, had a diameter of 8.1 millimeters in its cylindrical section. The bore diameter of the barrel, though, was only 7.9 mm. The oversized bullet thus was forced to deform itself under the

pressure of combustion gases and fill the riflings before it could begin to move. This system was created especially for the qualities of the jacketed bullet.

In the days of lead bullets, such as for the M/71, the bore and bullet dimensions were the same. The soft bullet had compressed under the pressure of combustion gases and filled the riflings. The designers of the 88 rifle had worked on the assumption that this compression could no longer take place in a jacketed bullet. That was a mistake.

In fact, not only the usual gas pressure but additional compression effects as well occurred as the 88 bullet passed through the barrel. The results increased bullet friction, dangerous pressure on the barrel material and frequent barrel explosions.

Signs of danger, whose significance no one noticed for a long time, were heavy nickel deposits in the riflings (to remove which "unnickeling rods" with wire brushes were issued to the troops) and unbelievably fast wear to the riflings, only a small part of which could be attributed to overly vigorous cleaning.

To mention just one example, a weapon inspection in the 9th Bavarian Infantry Regiment at Würzburg in March of 1893 turned up 47 rifles which were set aside with the following notation: "The riflings in two-thirds of the barrels are no

Details of the bolt of the 88 rifle: Left: Firing pin nut with gas shield and safety. Right: Bolt head with extractor (left) and ejector (right), and the two locking lugs behind them.

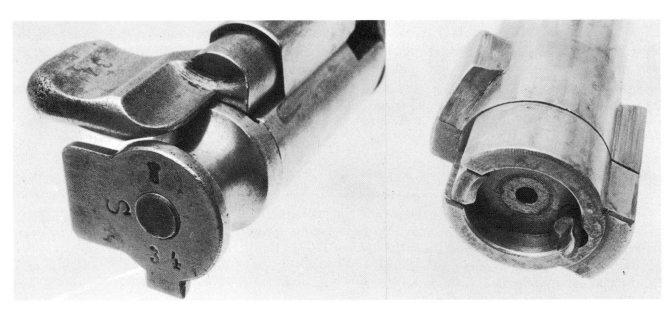

longer recognizable. Only at the muzzle can traces of them be found. The rifles produce ricochets and are fully useless."

The Würzburg case was not an isolated one. After only three years' service, all the 88 rifles and carbines in the whole Reich had to be returned to the artillery depots in the spring and summer of 1893 for repairs. More than half of the weapons received new barrels.

In this first process of exchanging, the peacetime army was completely equipped with new rifles from the mobilization supplies.

In 1897 and 1902 additional exchanges became necessary. In 1897 the alarming result was that more than 50% of the returned rifles needed new barrels.

Meanwhile, though, the fault in the bullet/rifling relations had finally been found and its elimination was in progress.

The "Z" Rifles

The first doubts about the bullet and rifling sizes had turned up in Spandau when an examination of bullets fired into a water tank showed projectiles with cracked jackets. But only six years after the 88 rifle was introduced did the commission decide to recalculate and retest bullet advance.

It was thought that the rifling depth of 0.1 mm was too shallow and thus responsible for the fast rifling wear and barrel explosions.

In the autumn of 1894 tests began in Spandau with deeper riflings of 0.125, 0.15, 0.175 and 0.2 mm. Gas pressure, velocity, target accuracy and durability of the barrels in steady use (5000 to 10,000 shots) were tested.

Success was instant. The best results came from barrels with a rifling depth of 0.15 mm. They gave the same values as the old 0.1 mm barrels plus the following advantages: fewer nickel deposits in the barrel, almost no more ripped jackets. In addition, thanks to decreased bullet friction, the lifetime of the barrels increased considerably. The test results led to Prussian "All-Highest Decree" No.10 345 of July 7, 1896. It stated:

"In agreement with the measures taken in the realm of the Royal Prussian Military Command it is hereby decreed that in new production of 88 barrels, instead of the former rifling depth of 0.1

mm, one of 0.15 mm shall be used. *The rifles equipped with such barrels are to be marked externally on the barrel and on the case by a Z.* These barrels are to have, instead of a refuse-cylinder of 8 mm, one of 8.05 mm."

Note: The refuse-cylinder in question is the measuring cylinder with which the barrel's suitability for use is determined. From then on a barrel was judged unusable if it was bored out so much that the 8.05 mm cylinder would fit into the muzzle.

The Introduction of Oil Cleaning

It is technically interesting that cleaning weapons with oil was introduced in Prussia and the entire Reich only at the end of 1897. Until that time, the 88 rifle had always been cleaned with water, as had the black-powder weapons before them. In a new "appendix" to the service regulations of October 1897 it was stated:

"Cleaning the interior of the barrel is done exclusively through the use of oiled wiping pads, in the garrison with cleaning rod and muzzle protector, outside the garrison with wiping cord and muzzle protector . . ." Oil cleaning and limitations on the use of the wiping cord (the predecessor of the metal chain) would, it was hoped, protect the barrel.

The 88 S Rifle

After the introduction of "S ammunition" (by order of 4/3/1903, No. 251.03), some of the Prussian supply of 88 rifles and carbines were adapted for the new cartridges with pointed ("S" for "Spitz") bullets (see page 134).

The S cartridge had a bullet caliber of 8.22 mm, larger than the 88 bullet. The "S cartridge case" thus had a somewhat enlarged bullet chamber. Aside from this change, the "S case" was exactly like the 88 case.

So as to be able to fire the new ammunition from 88 weapons, they had to have new barrels with riflings 0.15 mm deep ("Z" on the head of the case) and a widened chamber. It was also necessary to change the distance markings on the frame sight to suit the data of the more powerful new S cartridges.

The War Ministry ordered that only 88 rifles with new, unused barrels be adapted for the new S ammunition. The necessary small widening of the chamber was to be ground out with reamers. For identification, the adapted rifles were stamped with a 3-millimeter "S" on the head of the receiver.

Note: 88 S rifles were still loaded with the old big loading "frames" of five cartridges. The magazine mechanism remained unchanged. The S ammunition was delivered in loading frames to troop units that used the 88 rifle. During World War I, parts of the Prussian Landsturm and other troops in rear areas were armed with 88 rifles in their original form as well as 88 S rifles. For field use it was found that mud and sand could get into the weapons through the magazine shaft, which was open at the bottom, and cause damage. For that reason a magazine lid of thin sheet steel, which could held firmly over the shaft opening was introduced in December of 1914. The empty cartridge frame, which until then had fallen down out of the magazine, had to be removed in another way after the introduction of the magazine lid. The solution of the problem was simple and practical: On the inside of the magazine lid, at the back (outside the swing of the loading arm), a small coil spring with a plate was riveted on. It had the job of pushing the cartridge frame upward out of the magazine. That was impossible as long as there was still a cartridge in the frame. Only when the last cartridge had been fired and the cartridge ejected by drawing back the bolt, did the empty cartridge clip fly *upward* out of the rifle.

Magazine lids for the 88 and 88 S rifles were made only at the Spandau rifle factory. The factory produced a total of 75,000 pieces for the use of all German troops in World War I.

The head of the breech case of an 88 carbine with stamped ●ZS (arrow), indicating a barrel cone, deep riflings and S cartridge chamber.

The 88/05 and 88/14 Rifles

While the "88 S rifle" could take the new pointed cartridge but still had to be loaded with the old loading clip, the "05" and "14" transformations made it possible to set up the 88 rifle for loading with S cartridges and charger strips. For this purpose, the following changes in the 88 mechanism were necessary."

1.) On the open rear section of the receiver bridge a "charger strip holder" was created (held by two rivited on brackets in the 88/05, and simply welded onto the 88/14). In addition, a small cutout was made in the head of the receiver for the points of the bullets to pass through.

2.) A semicircular cutout, the "thumb slit", was reamed out of the left wall of the receiver for pushing the cartridges into the magazine (in the 88/05 it is farther forward than in the 88/14).

3.) The magazine well had to be made shorter and narrower, as the S cartridge was somewhat shorter than the old 88 cartridge. In addition the space that the loading clip had formerly occupied in the magazine now became superfluous, as did the clip

holder. Making the magazine space smaller was done with the help of a metal strip that was set into the rear wall of the magazine (and in the 88/05 also by an inset sheet-metal housing).

4.) On the upper edge of the magazine well an apparatus, the "cartridge holder", was created so that the cartridges could not spring up and out of the gun when the bolt was drawn back. The cartridge holder, with its spring and screw, was set in the left wall (horizontally in the 88/05, diagonally in the 88/14).

5.) The magazine well was closed at the bottom with a clipped-on sheet-metal lid (similar to that of the 88/S, but without a coil spring).

6.) The sight had to be given new distance markings or replaced by a new one. 88 guns modified in this way corresponded almost exactly to the 98 rifle in operation, functioning and performance. A typical 88 fault remained all the same: the possibility of seating two cartridges together. One may assume that the danger of ignition with an open bolt grew even greater with the use of the pointed cartridge.

The 88/05 rifle with riveted-on holding plates for the new Mauser charger strips (arrow).

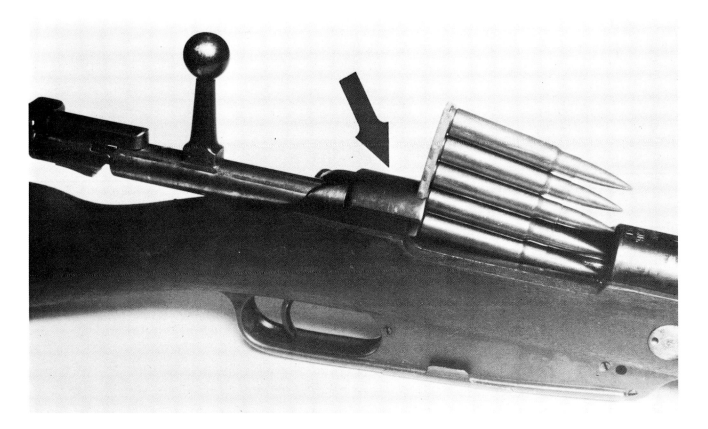

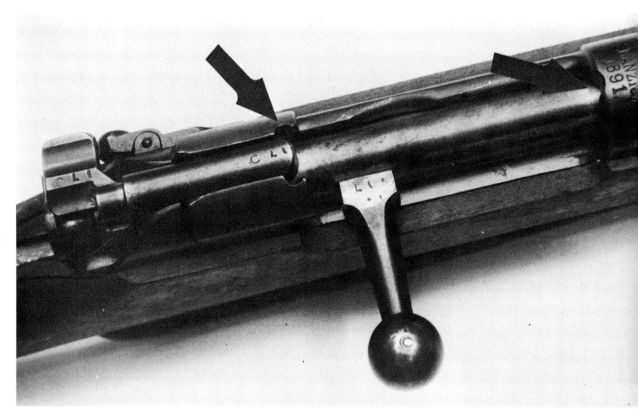

The 88/05 rifle from above. The arrows show the changes that were necessary for conversion to the S cartridge. Left: Machined lips for the charger clip. Right: cut out in the receiver face for passage of bullet points.

The 88/05 rifle: The new sheet-metal magazine lid closes the magazine well (arrow). Foreground: a single magazine lid.

The changed sight of the 88/05 rifle. The small flap is gone, the old markings on the surface of the frame are ground out and new numbers have been stamped in.

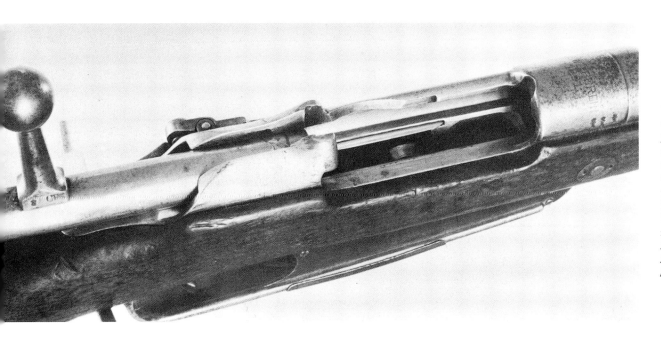

The 88/14 rifle: The lips for the Mauser charger clip have been welded roughly to the breech case. This rifle was made by Ludwig Loewe in Berlin (1891).

The differences between the 88/05 and 88/14 rifles derive from the times in which they were modified. The 88/05 type was made in 1906 and 1907, under peacetime conditions. The changes were made by experts and cost 8 Marks per rifle. At that time a total of some 200,000 88 rifles were made usable with S cartridges and charger strips at the rifle factories. They were intended for the reserve troops, as an interim solution, until new 98 rifles could be delivered. Later the 88/05 rifles were sent to the Landwehr depots.

The 88/14 model, on the other hand, originated only much later under the special conditions of wartime production in 1915 and 1916. The changes were made primitively.

The fact that the old 88 rifles still could play such a great role in World War I was a result of the unexpectedly high losses of war materials, which the weapons industry could scarcely replace. Thus lacking 98 rifles often had to be replaced by hastily modified 88's. Of course sales to private individuals had already begun in 1907 (officers paid two Marks for an 88 rifle), but when the war broke out, there were still large supplies of them on hand in the depots.

The modified 88 rifles became dispensable only in 1917, when the German weapons factories had increased production so much that larger supplies of 98 rifles could be gathered despite the high losses in battle. In April of 1918 the German states turned the greatest part of their remaining 88 rifles over to their needy Turkish allies.

Before that, there were still on hand:

State	88/05 rifles	88/14 rifles
Bavaria	2,394	34,944
Saxony	2,579	—
Württemberg	10,050	2,601
Prussia	55,309	10,885*

* The deliveries to Turkey are already subtracted from the Prussian statistics.

What happened to the 88 rifles that remained in Germany can be shown with Bavaria as an example: In October of 1919 the "Einwohnerwehr Bayern" (EWB) — a civilian militia for protection against the "red" revolutionary troops — was to be armed with the remaining 88 S, 88/05 and 88/14 rifles. But the dispersal office of the War Ministry in Munich no longer had the weapons at its disposal. All the rifles had already gone into the melting pots at the Luitpold Foundry at Amberg.

Bayonets for Model 88

Either the M/71 or the M 71/84 bayonet could be fixed to the 88 rifle, since the jacketed 7.9-mm barrel had the same diameter at the muzzle as the 11-mm barrel of the M/71 and M 71/84 rifles. The Bavarians made use of this possibility by reactivating their old supplies of 71 bayonets and issuing them for the new 88 rifles.

The upper arm of the crossguard of the bayonet for the 88 rifle had to be formed as a ring that encircled the muzzle of the barrel, since the "lug fastening" on the upper band of the stock did not offer enough stability to the bayonet. Later, in World War I, a new "makeshift bayonet" with the designation 88/98 was created. It had a steel handle painted field gray and blades measuring 25 to 31.5 cm long. The scabbard was also made of steel. This bayonet had a double diameter muzzle ring that fit over the barrel of the 88 rifle or the muzzle of the 98 rifle.

"Makeshift bayonet" 88/98 with steel scabbard. The handle is made of metal, the crossguard shaped as a fork.

Carbine 88 and Rifle 91

Type: *Karabiner 88* (identical in form to *Gewehr 91*)
Number: 7644
Year made: 1892
Manufacturer: V.C. Schilling, Suhl
Function: Repeater
Overall length: 955 mm
Gross weight: 3.15 kg
Barrel length: 435 mm
Barrel caliber: 7.9 mm
Number of riflings: 4

Rifling direction: Right
(Other barrel data same as Infantry Rifle 88)
Action: Cylinder with symmetrical locking lugs and open cocking
Safety: Mauser wing safety
Magazine: Mannlicher system with 5-cartridge clip loading
Sight: Standing sight, small flap and frame (250 to 1200 meters)
Standard ammunition: Cartridge 88 (8 x 57)
Disassembly: Same as Infantry Rifle 88

Like the 88 rifle, the carbine was also a creation of the Rifle Testing Commission in Spandau. The model of the small cavalry weapon grew out of the work on the rifle. Tests were again in progress early in 1889, but in March of 1890 every squadron of the cavalry regiments received a carbine for training purposes.

The magazine and breech of the carbine were exactly like those of the 88 rifle — aside from the bolt handle, which was flattened and bent downward on the carbine.

The barrel and stock were shortened. They ended together in a heavy steel muzzle cap that includes the foresight and sight protectors on top. The carbine also has a barrel jacket.

The sling is fastened on the left side in carbine style, at one end by a forged-on ring on the lower band, at the other by a snap on the right side of the butt. The sling also passed through an opening in the stock.

Except for the bolt and breech case, all the steel parts were blued.

The designers on the Rifle Testing Commission had shortened the cavalry weapon by some five centimeters from the length of its M/71 carbine predecessor, without regard for the soldiers who later had to stand the recoil of the powerful 88

The muzzle cap with foresight and sight protectors on the 88 carbine. The carbine also had a barrel jacket.

The flap-frame sight of the 88 carbine, made in 1892 by Schilling in Suhl, and later adapted for the S cartridge (and so stamped!).

The stacking hook that allowed several weapons to be hooked together is the only difference between the "Rifle 91" and the 88 carbine.

cartridge with the short weapon (the barrel measured only 43.5 cm). The fact that the frame sight of the carbine is marked for a longest shot of 1200 meters indicates the vast overestimation of its ballistic possibilities.

Along with the carbine, Prussia introduced an identical weapon on November 4, 1891, under the confusing designation of "Rifle 91." The only difference from the carbine was a steel hook with a baseplate set into the forestock, which allows several rifles to be stacked.

The foot artillery in Prussia, and later also in the other states of the Reich, were equipped with 91 rifles. Since the state rifle factories were fully occupied until 1891 with production of the 88 infantry rifle, the first carbine orders went to private industries. The firms of V.C. Schilling and C.G. Haenel in Suhl delivered some 200,000 carbines in

How the 91 rifle was carried. On the march the weapon could be stuck into the carrier on the rider's right thigh. (Photo: Bavarian War Archives)

all to Prussia, Saxony, Württemberg and Bavaria by 1892, at a price of 47.50 Marks apiece. The entire order was charged to the Prussian War Ministry.

When the high-speed production of the Royal Prussian Rifle Factories was gradually cut back toward the end of 1891, as the planned supply was finished, the factory in Erfurt was equipped for production of the short 88 weapon. In the ensuing years the German states received the rest of their 88 carbine needs and all their 91 rifles from the factory in Thuringia. Production in Erfurt continued until 1896.

An example of the state of rearmament with the short weapon: In May of 1893 Bavaria had only 18,574 91 rifles and 24,160 88 carbines.

Changes to Carbine 88 and Rifle 91

On account of the already described faults of the 88 mechanism, the 88 carbine and 91 rifle were given the same modifications as the 88 rifle. The cavalry and artillery also had life-threatening shooting accidents, and the carbine barrels wore out just as fast as those of the rifles. For these reasons the short weapons were also included in the great exchange actions of 1893, 1897 and 1902. They also received modified firing pin nuts with "gas shields", reinforced bolt releases and new barrels with deeper 0.15-mm riflings.

In 1904 and 1905 *all* 88 carbines and 91 rifles were modified for the S cartridge. The short weapons with the 88 mechanism stayed in active troop use markedly longer than the infantry rifles, because there were great difficulties in deciding on the successor model and its 98 mechanism. The 88 carbine and 91 rifle could only be taken back to the depots slowly starting in 1909-10, when the delivery of the new carbine 98 (a) began.

Paul Mauser on the Way to Model 98

The world-famous "98 mechanism", Paul Mauser's last contribution to the development of the repeater rifle, succeeded so perfectly that the designers have not thought of any essential way of improving it to this day. A century-old work, it stands completely alone in the technical world.

But the "98 mechanism" was no "stroke of genius", but rather the result of thirty years of tireless work on details. In it there were united all the improvements that Paul Mauser had invented for the military rifles of his time. And that is easy to prove. Mauser's patent documents since 1868 show an unbroken line of development. The "red line" of Mauser's conception is shown especially clearly in the foreign models made since 1889.

When the Prussian War Ministry gave preference to the design of the Rifle Testing Commission over Mauser's competing model in the spring of 1888, that was a great disappointment for the inventor in Oberndorf. In the years after 1888 Mauser depended fully on foreign business. The Turks were his biggest customers. In 1887 they had ordered half a million tube-magazine rifles in 9.5 mm caliber, which corresponded to the German M 71/84.

While mass production of the black-powder rifle, which was no longer exactly up to date, continued at the Oberndorf factory, Paul Mauser was already addressing himself to the needs of the new market for small-caliber weapons with smokeless powder. And with the very first model, which was introduced in Belgium in 1889, he began a series of successes. The 1893 Spanish rifle finally led directly to the German 1898 model.

Turkish Model 1887 Rifle

In 1886 Paul Mauser took part in an international competition that the Turkish government had instituted. Its goal was a new repeating rifle for the Turkish army. Mauser entered with a rifle that essentially resembled the German 71/84 model. The only differences were those of caliber, length and lock.

The Turkish rifle was made for a rimmed 9.5-mm cartridge which Mauser had developed from the German M/71 cartridge. The case form and length (60 mm) corresponded to the German cartridge, but the performance was considerably better, as a comparison of the muzzle velocities of 440 (M 71/84) and 536 meters per second (M/87) shows.

The 1887 model was four centimeters shorter than the M 71/84. In order to avoid the inclination of the bullet to the right, which had caused so much trouble in the German M 71/84, the Turkish model already had the lock with "doubled resistance" (see description, page 70) at the rear end of the bolt body.

In addition, the 1887 model had a cleaning and unloading rod carried in the side of the forestock between the barrel and the magazine tube. In German troop tests before the introduction of the M 71/84, the Rifle Testing Commission and the War Ministry in Berlin had decided against the cleaning rod.

The Turkish order was to include 500,000 rifles and 50,000 artillery carbines (a shortened version of the rifle), a gigantic order that would have overwhelmed the production facilities of the Oberndorf factory in 1886 by far. But since Paul Mauser could only accept the order if he could prove to the Turkish agents that he had the required production capacity, he looked for a potent partner: the firm of Ludwig Loewe in Berlin.

This company, which has already been mentioned in various contexts, was just trying at that time to convert from making traditional machine tools to weapon production. Isidor Loewe, who directed the firm alone since the death of his brother Ludwig in 1886, accepted Paul Mauser's offer. He wanted, if the contract were given, to produce half the Turkish rifles in his factories.

The Mauser-Loewe offer was accepted. On February 9, 1887 the contract with the Turkish government for 500,000 rifles and 50,000 carbines was signed. And since Mauser already had been equipped to build tube-magazine repeaters for years (test models for Prussia, artillery repeaters for

Serbia, M 71/84 for Württemberg), production in Oberndorf could begin in the same month. After a few extensions to the works, the daily production rose from an initial 200 to 500 rifles. At the end of 1887 the Turkish inspection commission, which lived in a house built for them in Oberndorf, had already accepted 70,000 rifles. On December 28, 1887 another decision, very significant for the Mauser firm, was made: The firm of Ludwig Loewe bought all 2000 shares of "Mauser Weapons Factory" stock and had the final say in Oberndorf. Paul Mauser, who had sold his own 334 shares, was suddenly nothing but the general manager. After the merger, Mauser was also assigned the Loewe part of the Turkish order. By that time only 60,000 M/87 rifles had been produced in Berlin. On the other hand, Oberndorf delivered 220,000 of them by 1890. Then a new 7.65-mm caliber model was designed, as the Turkish government was no longer satisfied with the black-powder rifle. In the 1887 contract they had included a clause that Mauser always had to deliver his most modern rifle to them. And this situation occurred when Paul Mauser made his new M/89 model public in Belgium.

Belgian Infantry Rifle M/89

Type: *Belgisches Infanteriegewehr M/89* (Mauser system)
Number: R 9332
Year built: No data
Manufacturer: Fabrique Nationale Herstal-Liège
Function: Repeater
Overall length: 1275 mm
Gross weight: 4 kg
Barrel length: 779 mm
Barrel caliber: 7.65
Number of riflings: 4
Rifling direction: Right
Rifling depth: 0.125 mm
Rifling width: 4.2 mm
Rifling length: 250 mm
Breech: Cylinder with linked cocking piece, cocked by closing the breech
Safety: Mauser wing safety, working also when bolt is uncocked
Magazine: One-row midstock type with five-cartridge strip

Sight: Step frame sight (100 to 2000 meters)
Standard ammunition: 7.65 x 53 Mauser
Cartridge:
Overall length: 78 mm
Total weight: 28 grams
Case length: 53.6 mm
Case weight: 11.6 grams
Bullet length: 30.3 mm
Bullet weight: 14 grams
Bullet material: Nickel-plated steel jacket, soft lead bullet
Bullet form: Cylindrical with round head
Bullet caliber: 7.9 mm
Weight of charge: 2.55 grams
Kind of powder: "Poudre de Wetteren"
Lateral pressure: 30.47 grams, V_0: 620 meters per second
Notes: The Belgian M/89 carbine differs from the M/89 rifle only in length and sight markings (100 to 1700 meters). Carbines were manufactured at the "Manufacture d'Armes de l'Etat."

When the Belgian government announced a competition for the best small-caliber repeating rifle for the Belgian Army in 1888, Paul Mauser was already well prepared for this new challenge. He had developed his own cartridge (7.65 x 53) with jacketed bullet for smokeless powder, and also a removable midstock magazine with a loading indicator. The cartridge advance could be switched off when the rifle was to be used in single-shot form.

The cylinder breech, with dual opposed locking under the receiver ring when it was closed, still resembled the earlier Mauser models in its cocking motion: the cocking piece with its cocking arc was still firmly attached to the firing pin and firing pin nut. His test rifle, called "C 88" at the factory, had been equipped by Mauser with a closed breech case for reasons of durability. Only on top was there a cutout for insertion of the cartridge (for single loading) and ejecting the case. With the breech locked, though, this opening was closed by a specially formed covering and guiding rail. In this way Mauser tried to moderate the effects of gas streaming out, as could happen with the faulty cartridge cases then available (see 88 Rifle).

The Mauser Charger

Even before the competition date in the autumn of 1888, Paul Mauser made an important invention that inspired him to design a completely new mechanism in a hurry. This was the Mauser charger or "loading strip", which held a bundle of five cartridges together only at the base and was slid off when filling the magazine. This charger was the prerequisite for the development of new magazine types.

It is noteworthy that Paul Mauser held nine foreign patents on his charger but was rejected by the Reich Patent Office in Berlin. Mauser's patent

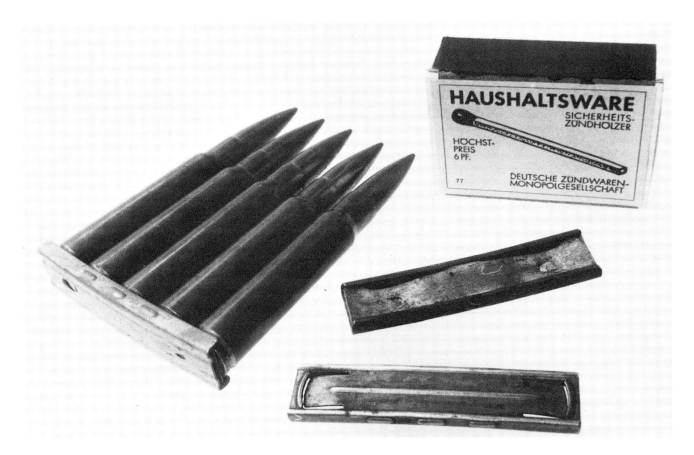

Pointed cartridges on a Mauser charger. At right are two different types, one with a built-in spring and tongue holder (above), and the original one-piece sheet-metal strip (below).

attorney, R. H. Korn, wrote in 1908 that the "omission of release from obligation" was the cause. The parallel to other cases already mentioned in this book allows one to conclude that in Berlin the significance of the invention for German military armament had been recognized and an attempt was being made to use the invention without paying licensing fees.

The new breech mechanism, which Paul Mauser built around his new charger, again had a breech case open at the top and the right side, so that the shooter could easily push the cartridges out of the charger and down into the magazine. The filled strip was inserted in a cutout in the front edge of the case bridge when the bolt was drawn back. It stayed there until the cartridges were stripped off it into the magazine. When the bolt was pushed forward, the front surface of the cylinder pressed the empty strip out of the fork and threw it out at the top.

Compared to the Mannlicher frame (of the 88

rifle), the Mauser charger had the advantage in that the magazine could be closed on the underside and loaded at any time with single cartridges.

In Mauser's first strip-loader magazine for the Belgian competition rifle, the five cartridges were still in a row, one above the other, under the pressure of two leaf springs, which acted on a Z-shaped supplier with two joints.

The positions of the cartridges in a row had the disadvantage that the magazine stuck out the bottom of the stock as in the German 88 rifle. The Belgian magazine could be taken out for cleaning, though. For that there was a spring snap inside the trigger guard.

Because of the large openings in the breech case, Paul Mauser considered it advisable to locate the two locking lugs forward, right at the front surface of the breech cylinder, to assure the stability of the mechanism. When the breech was locked, the two

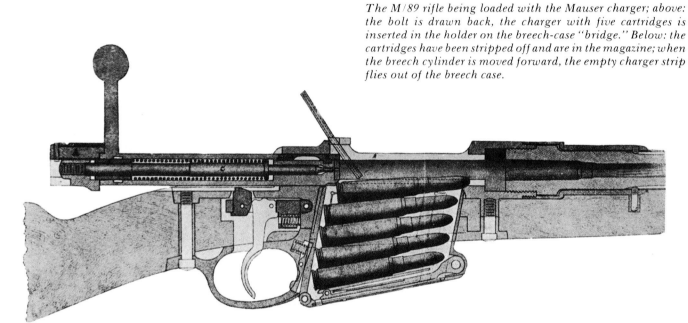

The M/89 rifle being loaded with the Mauser charger; above: the bolt is drawn back, the charger with five cartridges is inserted in the holder on the breech-case "bridge." Below: the cartridges have been stripped off and are in the magazine; when the breech cylinder is moved forward, the empty charger strip flies out of the breech case.

The Belgian M/89 carbine, made by the "Manufacture d'Armes de l'Etat."

lugs rested vertically, one above the other, in the ring groove of the case head.

The breech cylinder is made in one piece; there is no longer a removable bolt head as in the earlier Mauser models. The front surface of the cylinder has a reamed-out area into which the base of the cartridge fits. A small spring extractor reaches from above into the ring groove at the base of the cartridge. The surrounding rim of the front surface of the breech is filed away on the underside. Thus Paul Mauser wanted to be sure that the cartridge base was seized and held by the extractor as soon as possible, so as to avoid accidental loading of two cartridges. This was not yet a perfect solution, though.

The designer found a new solution for the arrangement of the rear parts of the breech. Unlike his earlier mechanisms, in this one he originally linked the bolt cocking piece guide by locking lug, and later by a simple thread to the breech cylinder. The coil-shaped striker spring works against the screw-neck of the cocking piece guide on the one hand, and on the other against the plate of the striker. The striker's movement is limited by the striker head, which is screwed onto the end of the striker and has a point that fits into a groove on the underside of the bolt. The point of the striker head presses against the trigger rod when the gun is cocked.

In the M/89 and all subsequent Mauser repeater mechanisms only the striker and its head move as a unit when the trigger rod frees the way for the striker. Unlike the previous Mauser models and the later Model 98, the bolt of the M/89 is cocked only on closing. For this the shooter must push the bolt lever forward against the resistance of the striker spring, and move it around the front contact point. The safety mechanism with the dependable Mauser wing is also noteworthy; in the M/89 it also acts on the cocked bolt and locks it to avoid unintentional opening. The combination of bolt stop and ejector, under a handy lever at the left side of the bolt case, is almost exactly like that of the later Model 98.

A look at the Model 89 mechanism.

Loewe is Involved with FN

It is noteworthy that the Belgian rifle has a jacketed barrel. It can no longer be proved today, but can be assumed, that the Loewe management in Berlin had "commanded" that the Mauser competition rifle have a jacket, which was in fashion then. In addition Loewe, as a member of the Mieg Consortium, could request additional licensing fees for the barrel jacket if the rifle was accepted.

The Mauser rifle did indeed win the international competition, but the Belgians insisted on producing the weapons themselves. The state-owned "Manufacture d'Armes de l'Etat" weapons factory in Liège was available for the job. But remarkably enough, the matter worked out quite differently:
In Herstal, near Liège, a completely new factory was built in 1889, in which the German firm of Loewe was allowed to be a 50% partner. The company later became world-famous under the name of "Fabrique Nationale d'Armes de Guerre" (FN). Only in 1919 did the German partnership fall victim to the Treaty of Versailles. By expropriation the Belgians became the masters of their own house.

Turkish Model 1890

After the success of the Belgian Mauser rifle, the Turkish government used the suitability clause in their 1887 contract with Mauser. The government asked that the 9.5-mm black-powder M/87 rifle be replaced by a rifle of equal value to the Belgian one.

They received an almost unchanged weapon, likewise set up for the 7.65 x 53 Mauser cartridge. Mauser had, though, made a few small improvements in the Turkish M/90, of which 280,000 were produced at Oberndorf until 1893, and these improvements are worth mentioning because they later reappeared on the Model 98.

The rifle was given buttress threads on the bolt sleeve for durability, as they lessened the tendancy for thread wear causing the bolt sleeve to shift to the rear. A breech action improvement was a one piece sear, and the rear sight had a ring-type base encircling the barrel, rather than the Model 89 sight base which was only soldered to the top of the barrel jacket.

But the most important modifications concerned the bedding of the barrel in the stock. The Turkish

The muzzle area of the M/89 rifle. The upper band with the bayonet lug on the underside and the cleaning rod are shown. The barrel jacket ends in a lug band that carries the foresight.

Model 90 no longer had a barrel jacket. Mauser had invented a simpler and less vulnerable solution, which also allowed a hot barrel unlimited expansion. He no longer made the barrel conical, but cylindrical with one step, which was covered by the lower band. Both the band and the barrel bed in the wood of the stock were widened by three millimeters at this point, corresponding to the diameter of the thicker barrel cylinder, so that the barrel had room to expand in length (German Reich Patent No. 54 694 of 3/26/1890).

In 1891 the Argentine government ordered 180,000 rifles, which were technically identical to the Turkish M/90. Since the Turkish order was still being filled at Oberndorf, the Loewe works in Berlin took over production.

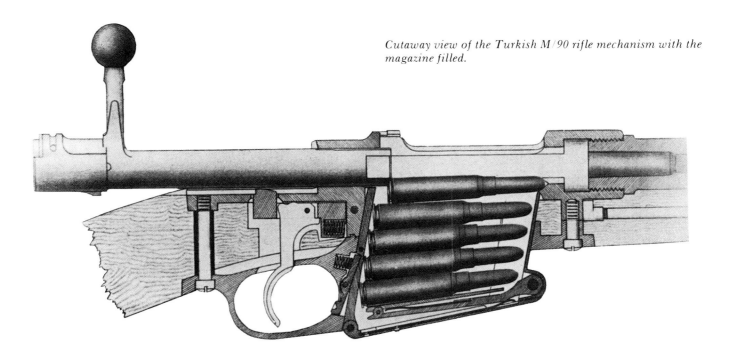

Cutaway view of the Turkish M/90 rifle mechanism with the magazine filled.

The Spanish M/93 Rifle

At the beginning of the Nineties the Spaniards also had the problem of equipping their armed forces with a "small-caliber rifle." In 1891 and 1892 they had Mauser send them a small number of test rifles and carbines, which basically equaled the Turkish M/90. But the final decision for a Mauser rifle came only after the designer had presented his consider- ably improved 7-mm caliber Model 93 in Madrid. The most important improvements to this weapon were the new midstock magazine with a staggered cartridge column and the wide sprung extractor with which Mauser had finally solved the problem of avoiding two cartridges being inserted one after the other.

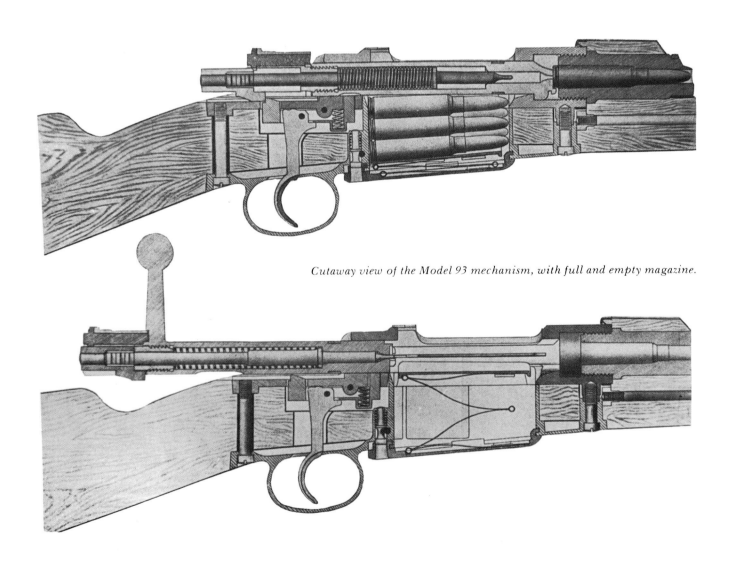

Cutaway view of the Model 93 mechanism, with full and empty magazine.

To take the magazine first, the magazine space could be kept so small, thanks to the space-saving zigzag position of the cartridges, that the magazine no longer projected from the stock, but fit smoothly into it. The stock was closed by a lid held by a hook at the front and a snap at the rear, and only to be removed for cleaning. On the inside of the magazine lid, an arm of the thin, W-shaped advancing spring was pushed into grooves. The second free arm was attached in the same way to the underside of the follower, a steel plate that pushed the cartridges upward toward the cutout in the breech case when the magazine was filled. On the upper side of the supplier, left of center, was a longitudinal rib which regulated the staggered column position of the cartridges. The two uppermost ribs mutually

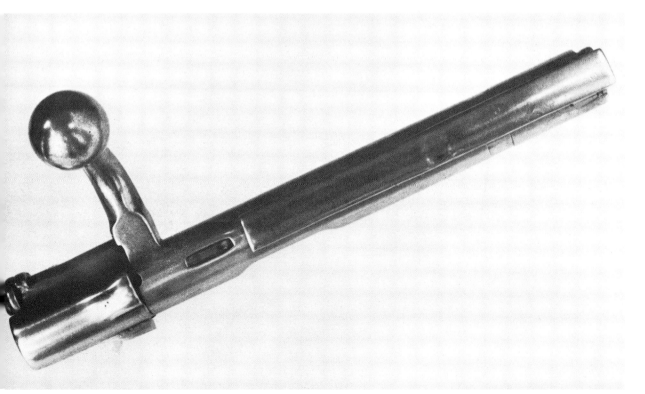

The complete M/93 breech.

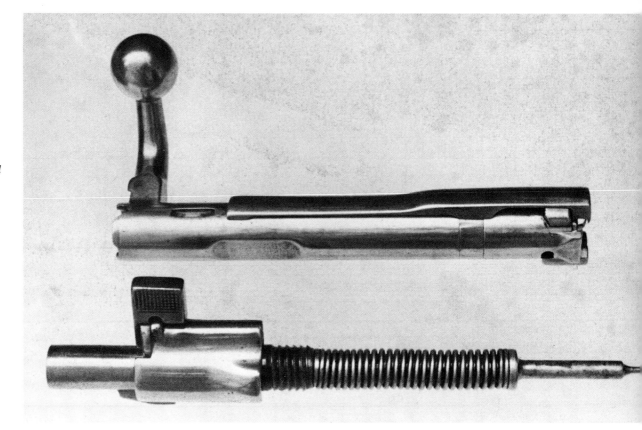

The bolt sleeve with firing pin and main spring, unscrewed from the bolt body.

prevented each other, when the bolt was opened and drawn back, from slipping out through the cutout into the breech case. The uppermost cartridge could only leave the magazine when it was

To take the magazine first, the magazine space could be kept so small, thanks to the space-saving zigzag position of the cartridges, that the magazine no longer projected from the stock, but fit smoothly

into it. The stock was closed by a lid held by a hook at the front and a snap at the rear, and only to be removed for cleaning. On the inside of the magazine lid, an arm of the thin, W-shaped advancing spring was pushed into grooves. The second free arm was attached in the same way to the underside of the follower, a steel plate that pushed the cartridges upward toward the cutout in the breech case when

Rear view of the M/93 bolt. The safety is raised to center position for bolt disassembly. At right in front of the bolt handle is the cutout for the trigger safety catch.

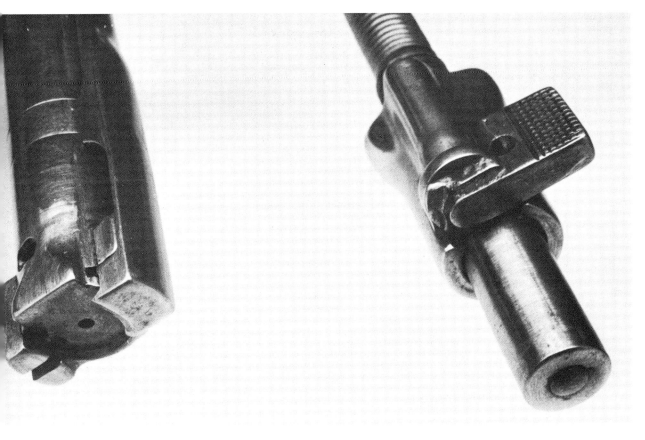

the magazine was filled. On the upper side of the supplier, left of center, was a longitudinal rib which regulated the staggered column position of the cartridges. The two uppermost ribs mutually prevented each other, when the bolt was opened and drawn back, from slipping out through the cutout into the breech case. The uppermost cartridge could only leave the magazine when it was pushed forward into the cartridge bed of the barrel by the front surface of the bolt (which in the M/93 still had a special angled attachment). When the last cartridge was taken from the magazine, the follower rib of the follower moved into the bolt way and blocked the bolt's movement — a warning sign for the shooter.

The extractor takes the form of a long, wide leaf spring that lies along the right side of the bolt, reaches over the right locking lug with a hook, and immediately hooks into the groove of the cartridge when contact between the bolt head of the bolt and the uppermost cartridge is made by moving the bolt forward. From this moment on, the extractor holds the cartridge fast. The connection is released only after firing, when the bolt is drawn back and the ejector reaches into the slit of the left locking lug from the left.

The cocking piece, as in the Turkish and Belgian predecessor models, is once again cocked by closing the breech. The cocking piece guide has gained two additions on its sides with which it slides onto the surfaces of the crosspiece of the case, and is thus better protected from turning. The safety mechanism has been simplified in the M/93 and acts only when the bolt is cocked. For disassembly, the bolt must be cocked and the safety wing positioned vertically. Then the unit of striker, striker head, mainspring and cocking piece guide can be unscrewed from the breech cylinder. Now the striker's point is placed on a firm foundation and the cocking piece guide is pushed down against the effect of the coil spring until the striker head is free. It can now be removed from the striker by a quarter turn (the "bayonet lock" of the M/93 is new!). Then the cocking piece guide, along with the safety wing, could be removed, as well as the coil spring of the striker.

Aside from the noticeably long path of the firing pin (it moves forward 2.5 centimeters), also the original trigger safety catch of the M/93 is worth mentioning. The sear in the trigger group is formed as a cradle with two projections that extend into the bolt guide. The rear projection serves as a sear, against which the point of the firing pin lies when the cocking piece is cocked.

When the trigger is pulled, the sear sinks, and at the same time the forward projection rises through an opening under the receiver bridge into the bolt guide and enters the cutout in the breech cylinder. But this is only possible when the breech is properly locked, which is when the bolt handle is completely turned down. When the action is only half locked, the trigger is blocked.

Spain ordered some 250,000 M/93 rifles and 30,000 carbines. The weapons were made almost exclusively by Loewe in Berlin. To even the score, Oberndorf received another large order from Turkey, for 200,000 M/93 rifles in 7.65-mm caliber.

The Mauser 7 x 57 cartridge

This cartridge, which Paul Mauser had developed for the Spanish M/93 rifle, was almost exactly like the German military 88 cartridge in its case form. For decades it was the standard cartridge of most Latin American armies and is still used today — with varying charges and bullets — for hunting. Here are the vital details of the 1893 military cartridge:

Cartridge: 7 x 57 Mauser.
Overall length: 78 mm
Total weight: 24.9 grams
Case length: 57 mm
Case weight: 11.1 grams
Bullet length: 30.8 mm
Bullet weight: 11.2 grams
Bullet material: Nickel-plated steel jacket with hard lead core
Bullet shape: Cylindrical-oval
Bullet caliber: 7.25 mm
Charge weight: 2.45 grams
Powder type: Rottweil flake powder 91/93
Lateral pressure: 29.1 grams
Muzzle energy: 280 m/kg
Muzzle velocity: ca. 700 meters per second

The 88/97 Rifle

Type: *Infanteriegewehr 88/97*
Number: 1729
Year made: 1895
Manufacturer: Mauser Weapons Factory, Oberndorf on the Neckar
Function: Repeater
Overall length: 1240 mm
Gross weight: 4 kg
Barrel length: 740 mm
Barrel caliber: 7.9 mm
Number of riflings: 4

Rifling direction: Right
(Other barrel data same as 88 rifle)
Breech: Cylinder breech, Mauser system, self-cocking when opened
Safety: Mauser wing safety
Magazine: Mauser magazine with strip charger
Sight: Clinometer, Lange system
Standard ammunition: 88 cartridge (8 x 57)
Disassembly: See text and "98 Rifle."

The Rifle Testing Commission's pride in its own design of the 88 rifle did not last long. As packages from all over the Reich arrived in Spandau practically every day, containing the ruins of exploded weapons to be examined, as the soldiers' trust in their weapons gradually sank to zero and the press, the public and even foreign countries became aware of the rifle's faults, the folks in Spandau were finally ready to talk to the expert Paul Mauser again.

It may have been his sensational success in foreign countries that brought the Swabian designer back into the picture in Prussia, and perhaps the influence of Loewe, the firm's owner in Berlin, played a role; in any case, the Kaiser ordered a troop test in November of 1894, with "two thousand 88 rifles, which are fitted with the Mauser bolt and magazine . . ."

The test weapon had a barrel jacket and corresponded to the 88 rifle in its stock form and fittings too. The only new feature was the Mauser bayonet attachment under the barrel, with a round rod onto which the hollow handle of the bayonet could be slid. Other new features for the German soldiers were the Mauser magazine (as on the Spanish M/93) and a bolt that had been developed further, with self-cocking when opened. Kaiser Wilhelm II had inspected the weapon himself and made two suggestions for modification, which presumably had the effect of orders. The Kaiser recommended the so-called "Lange" sight and also urged that the foresight and the deepest point on the backsight notch be marked with silver stripes. Wilhelm II had learned to know and appreciate this aid to aiming in semidarkness from his hunting rifles. The Lange sight was finally introduced, but the silver markings found no favor among military men.

The Rifle Factory in Spandau was thus chosen to produce 2000 test weapons, planning of troop tests began, but at first the smaller states of the Reich heard nothing of it all from Prussia.

Colonel Hoffmann, the Commander of the 6th Bavarian Infantry Regiment, reported on February 5, 1895 about his visit to Spandau: "In the gun room of the Rifle Testing Commission we were shown a Mauser model rifle, of which 2000 specimens were produced. It included two essential improvements over the 88 rifle, namely the clinometer sight and charger.

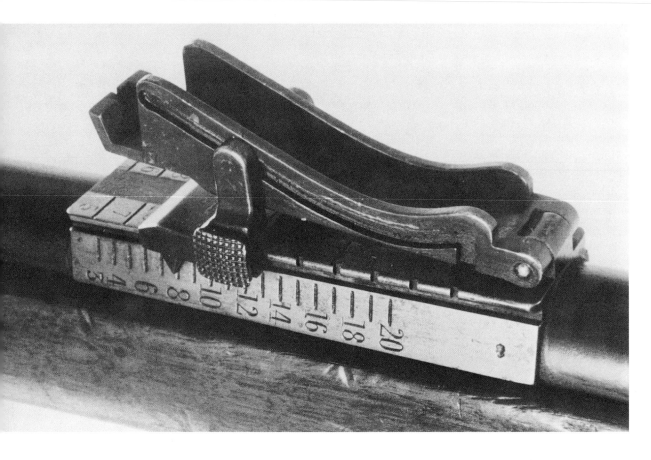

The "Lange" sight of the 88/97 rifle in its original form (300 to 2000 meters).

The first was named after its inventor, Lieutenant Colonel Lange, at that time the director of the ammunition factory in Spandau. An elevation flap, which moved forward and back, with arms on both sides of the sight running in a curved groove, allowed the various sight heights to be set and made only a single notch necessary. It showed only sighting settings in multiples of 100 meters.

Another modification concerned the clip which was replaced by a charger of thin sheet metal with a spring in the bottom; the clip was slightly curved, so that the five cartridges in the clip have the noses of their bullets leaning in toward each other.

Loading was done as with the 88 rifle, but now the pressure of the right thumb did not push the clip into the magazine any more; rather the five cartridges slid off the charger and lay free, one on top of another, in the magazine. The clip fell off to the front when the breech was closed. The advantage: was the box closed downwards; the disadvantage: when unloading, the rifleman had five individual cartridges in his hand."

On the basis of this report, the War Ministry in Munich requested further information from the Bavarian military representative in Berlin, Major General Haag. On March 8, Haag reported further

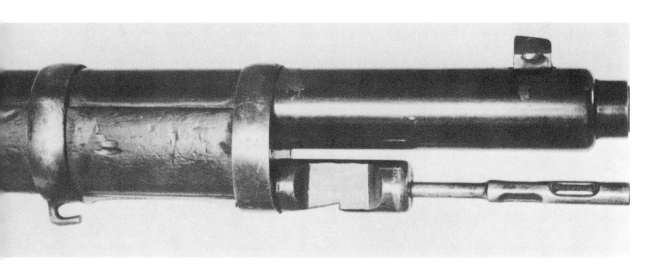

The bayonet attachment of the 88/97 rifle. The rod under the muzzle of the barrel was later, in the 98 model, revised as an angular lug.

advantages of the Mauser model: Loading two cartridges, firing without the bolt head, and danger to the rifleman from escaping powder gases, the best-known sources of danger in the 88 rifle, had been eliminated. In addition, new bayonets with Mauser attachments (see illustration) were to be tested. The test bayonet with 525-mm blade, broad back and point like that of the M/71, were made in Erfurt but not introduced in the end. In all, four blade types were tested.

The changes in the breech of the test model are noteworthy. Mauser had set up the bolt of the Spanish rifle to cock itself when opened by means of small modifications to the striker head and bolt, and added a third locking lug, which had a bed in a groove under the receiver bridge. The third lug was intended only for emergencies. It was to guarantee safety in case one of the two forward lugs fell off and also secure the groove of the sear against escaping gas. This security against hot streams of gas in case of ripped cartridges or penetration of the percussion cap was increased by other arrangements: gas escape openings, thumbhole and gas shield.

The two oval gas vents on the underside of the chamber were meant to conduct overly high pressure off into the magazine in case gas brought on by a penetrated percussion cap pushed through the firing pin opening into the interior of the breech cylinder.

The thumbhole, a semicircular cutout in the left wall of the breech case just ahead of the bridge, had two functions. In Mauser's German patent document, No. 56 068 of 8/9/1895, its only task is to conduct any exiting gas out of the leading groove of the left breech lug. (This groove is also blocked by the rod of the bolt release.) The thumbhole's second job is, in fact, almost more important. It eases that "thumb-grip" with which the cartridges are pushed from the clip into the magazine. The "gas shield", which was later copied by many other manufacturers, is nothing more than a type of flange on the front surface of the cocking piece guide which covers the gap in the receiver bridge.

Paul Mauser had not only thought of the shooter's safety; he was also able to make his new system easier to use and less likely to malfunction. These

Mauser patent drawings showing the bolt of the 88/97 test rifle.

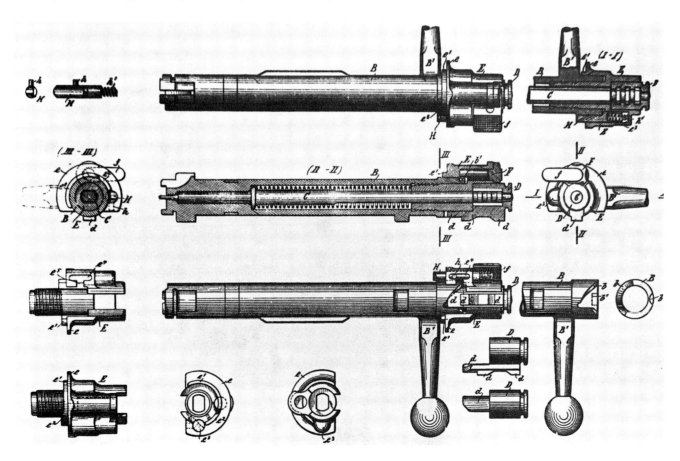

purposes are served by a small locking pin that projects from the gas shield at the left side of the cocking piece guide. It locks the cocking piece guide to the chamber. When the breech is opened and drawn back and the cocking piece guide and striker head are not guided by the groove of the receiver, the lock guarantees that the cocking piece guide cannot twist. The lock is automatically released when the spring pin strikes the wall of the receiver bridge and is pushed back during locking.

The 1895 Troop Test

Contrary to the original plans, it was not the Rifle Factory in Spandau, but Mauser in Oberndorf which received the contract for the test rifles in January of 1895. A thousand of them were to be made with the "88 trunnion bed." The second thousand were to be made, for testing purposes, without this screw attachment that increased the stability of the stock. The weapons were delivered early in the summer of 1895; troop tests began on August 1, with the following units taking part:
The Fusilier Battalion of the 1st Foot Guard Regiment, the Guard Jäger Battalion, the 3rd Battalion of the Fusilier Regiment "Queen" (Schleswig-Holstein No. 86), and the Infantry School at Spandau.
The troop tests ended on a positive note. Early in 1897 the War Ministry in Berlin reported to the state war ministries: "His Majesty the Kaiser and King has deigned to approve, on the 11th of March, 1897,

that in the 1897-98 budget year the rifles to be made in the rifle factories shall receive the bolt of the modified 88 rifle and carry the designation "Rifle 88/97." The rifles are not to be included in the budget amounts at first, but are to remain in the reserves. As for the ammunition for these rifles, there is only a change to the extent that the 88 cartridges (or 88 n/A and n/A●) are to be packed in charger strips instead of cartridge frames . . ."

Everything proceeded to what amounted to an extended troop test. It was apparently supposed to last another five to six years, as the Bavarian military representative in Berlin learned. As for an introduction of the 88/97 rifle on a large scale, he said, it was not considered for the time being, as money in the budget was lacking.

The Bavarian Prince Regent Luitpold originally followed the Prussian decision and accepted the 88/97 rifle for Bavaria on April 21, 1897. The Rifle Factory in Amberg was to be reequipped. But when it turned out at the end of the year that of the Prussian factories, only Erfurt was making 88/97 rifles and only at a "limited rate", with a daily production of only 130 rifles, the preparations for production at Amberg were cancelled.

Experiments with 5 and 6 Millimeter Calibers

The German decision in favor of the 8-millimeter rifle caliber in 1888 was made more or less by chance, since the Mieg test rifles had that caliber.

The 88/97 rifle: receiver face with Mauser lettering.

It could already be anticipated at that time that the jacketed bullets, along with the new smokeless powder types, would allow even more decreases in calibers. The ballistic experts dreamed of trajectories that were so extended that the zenith was still at a man's height at a distance of 1000 meters. For a weapon with such a powerful shot, a single fixed backsight notch would have been sufficient instead of a complicated frame sight.

The military practitioners, on the other hand, did not think much of such superfast bullets. They knew that this superior power could only be attained with very light, which meant extremely small-caliber, bullets. They feared that the "wounding capacity" of the small bullets would no longer suffice for military purposes.

This fear, which we now know was unfounded, lived on in the officer corps for decades. Even in 1935 the following could be read in F. W. Deutsch's *Theory of Weapons*:

"Cartridge length, powder evaluation, rifling difficulties in small-bore barrels, the danger of dirtying, poor economy (damage to barrels) . . . along with the limited wounding capacity of the bullet, set a lower limit which is reached by the rifle today at about 6.5 mm, if not exceeded by it . . ."

In spite of that, experiments with 5-millimeter rifles (!) had taken place at the Military Gunnery School in Spandau as early as 1892. Unfortunately, nothing has been recorded of the weapon, cartridge or performance. Presumably the ammunition was of the 5.2 x 67 or 5.2 x 68 type, which had been developed and manufactured by that time by the Polte Cartridge Factory in Magdeburg. These experimental cartridges with their shapeless cases were not suitable, though.

Prussian tests of 6-millimeter rifles a few years later were more significant. In October of 1896, Mauser of Oberndorf had received an order for 2185 test weapons. The breech and mechanism were to correspond to those of the 88/97 rifle. For the barrel, to be made in conical form without a step, no jacket was planned, but a wooden upper hand guard between the case head and the lower barrel band, as in the Spanish models. The "clinometer sight", a curved type with even scale markings and only one notch, was a Mauser design that was considerably simpler and more practical than the competing "Lange" sight of the 88/97 model. Mauser had equipped the base of the sight with curved panels on which the sight slide (moved by a leaf spring)

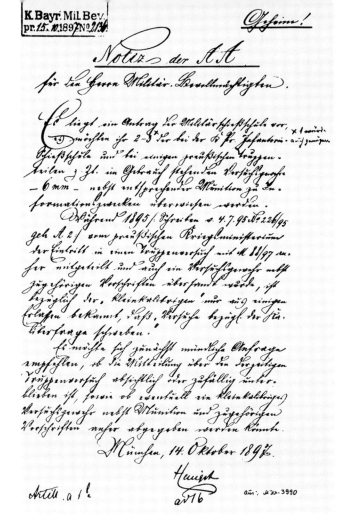

Bavaria asked its military representative in Berlin for information on the state of secret Prussian tests of 6-mm rifles, since Berlin had not informed the other states.

had to be set. Troop tests with this rifle began in 1897 and were to last until 1902. Thus the tests ran parallel to those of the 88/97 model.

The 6 x 59 cartridge, with a case that somewhat resembled the 88 cartridge in shape, was a Mauser development. It was loaded with a charge of 2.25 grams of Rottweil M. 91/93 flake powder, carried a jacketed 8.7-gram bullet 32 mm long, and gave an initial velocity of about 800 meters per second.

The superior performance of this cartridge, which was obvious since the tests began, may well explain the growing restraint in production of the 88/97 rifle in Prussia. Various references in the secret files of the Bavarian War Ministry suggest that the Prussian authorities were inclined to introduce the 6-millimeter Mauser rifle when the troop tests were ended. It was thought that the modest performance of the 88 cartridge was attributable solely to its "large" caliber and heavy bullet. Only the development of better types of powder and more streamlined pointed bullets from 1899 to 1902 were to create a new situation later.

The 98 Rifle

Type: *Infanteriegewehr 98*
Number: 2988
Year built: 1917
Manufacturer: Royal Bavarian Rifle Factory, Amberg
Function: Repeater
Overall length: 1250 mm
Gross weight: 4.1 kg
Barrel length: 740 mm
Barrel caliber: 7.9 mm
Number of riflings: 4
Rifling direction: Right
(Other barrel data same as the 88 rifle)
Breech: Cylinder breech, Mauser mechanism, self-cocking when opened
Safety: Mauser leaf safety
Magazine: Mauser staggered 5 round clip loaded magazine

Sight: Clinometer, Lange system (220 to 2000 meters); as of October 1, 1905: 400 to 1200 meters.
Standard ammunition: 88 cartridge (8 x 57) V_{25}: 640 m/sec, as of October 1, 1905, S cartridge; initial velocity: 895 m/sec
Disassembly: Cock the action and engage the safety in the vertical (middle) position. Pull out on the bolt stop and remove the bolt from receiver. Hold the bolt sleeve, lock in the depressed position and unscrew firing mechanism from the bolt. Put the firing pin in the disassembly hole in butt of rifle till flange rests on hole, push down on saftety thumbpiece until cocking piece is clear of bolt sleeve. Revolve cocking piece 90 degrees and remove from firing pin. Turn safety clockwise as far as possible and separate from bolt sleeve. Depress bolt sleeve lock until its stud aligns with disassebly cut in bottom of bolt sleeve; rotate bolt sleeve lock to left until it releases. Reassemble in opposite order.

In planning the successor model for the 88 rifle, the Prussian War Ministry proceeded with exemplary care. The two troop tests with 8-mm (88/97 rifles) and 6-mm caliber (Mauser) rifles were not enough. A third prototype was designated "Rifle 98" by the Kaiser on April 5, 1898 and was to be tested.

This new weapon combined reliable elements of the two previous test models, with scarcely anything new added. In consideration of the large quantities of 88 cartridges on hand, the 98 rifle was again given the 7.9-mm caliber. The interior design of the barrel, with 240-mm riflings and a depth of 0.15 mm, corresponded to the improved version of the 88 rifle.

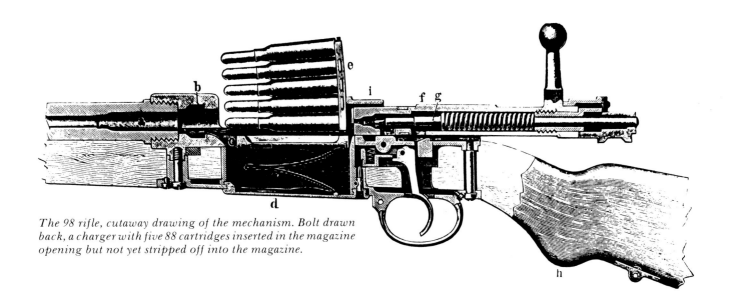

The 98 rifle, cutaway drawing of the mechanism. Bolt drawn back, a charger with five 88 cartridges inserted in the magazine opening but not yet stripped off into the magazine.

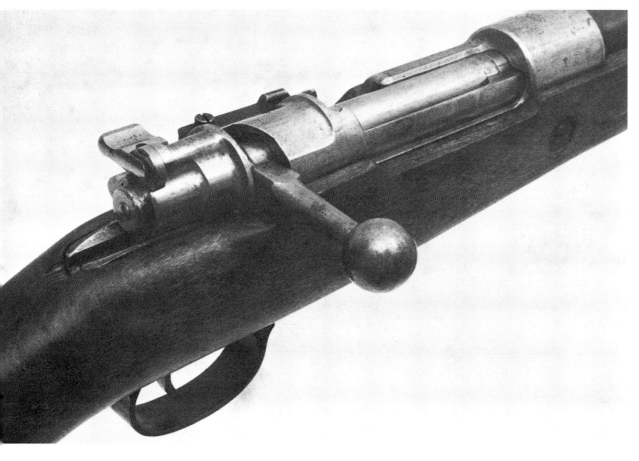

The 98 mechanism, seen from the right.

The barrel was made with steps and had no jacket, but rather a short upper hand guard of wood that reached from the front edge of the sight base to below the lower band. The "Lange" sight, with gradations from 200 to 2000 meters, was pushed over the barrel via two ring-shaped bands and soldered.

The stock once again had a trunnion bed and — more important — a "pistol grip" under the neck for the first time, which made it considerably easier to handle. On the right side of the butt, a round steel plate had been set and screwed in to bear the troop stamp.

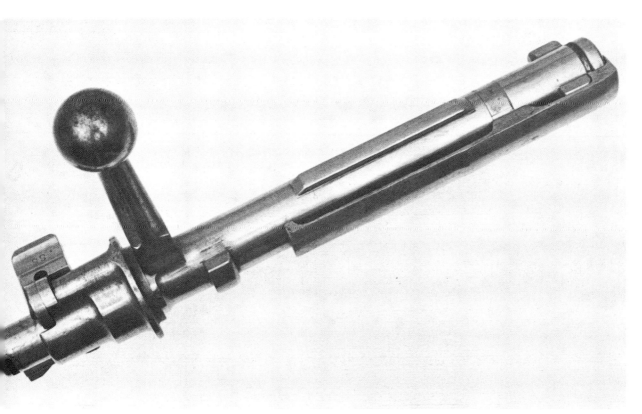

The complete Model 98 bolt.

Left: front surface of the chamber cylinder with locking lugs and extractor on the left. Right: The bolt with cocking piece guide raised safety wing and striker head.

The new type of bayonet attachment, using a heavy double T-shaped bar, independent of the barrel, was a further development of the Mauser attachment of the 88/97 and 6 mm test rifles. The bayonet lug under the nose was made integrally with the steel barrel cap.

The new bayonet of the 98 model series and modified older types gained a sure seat only from the lug that extended well into the hollow handle. The second attachment point at the muzzle of the barrel (with an encircling ring), customary in the older types, was now eliminated. The weight and leverage of the fixed bayonet would no longer influence the vibrations of the barrel in the future.

Below the bar, a short cleaning rod, only 395 mm long, protruded from the forestock, to be used only when, with the help of the threads cut into it, three such rods were screwed together.

Muzzle protector for the 98 rifle. The lid can be folded up as shown for use with the cleaning bed.

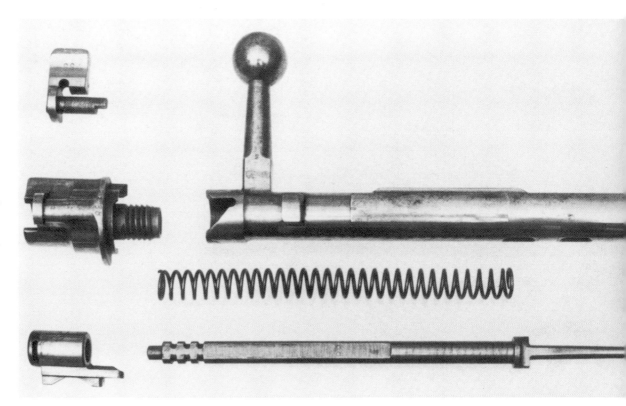

Parts of the 98 rifle. From top to bottom: safety, bolt with extractor, cocking piece guide, coil spring, striker and striker head.

Magazine assembly with lid removed, leaf spring and follower visible.

Since the 98 rifle (like the 88 rifle) should only be cleaned during peacetime with a "cleaning kit", a rack with a special vise, and with special cleaning rods, the short rod in the forestock was only intended for emergency use. The rod's most important use was in hooking several rifles together to form a pyramid.

A small modification to the Mauser system that the Rifle Testing Commission had requested is noteworthy: The bolt hol-open device has been eliminated from the magazine follower in the 98 rifle so that the head of the breech cylinder can slide over it even when the magazine is empty.

Paul Mauser's idea of equipping his mechanism with a warning device to prevent "empty loading" only gained respect in Germany at the end of World War I.

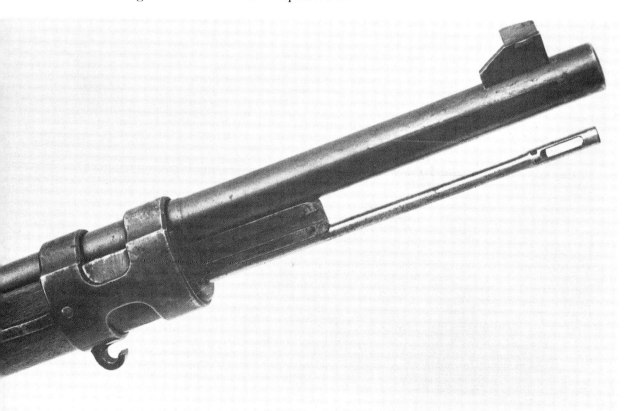

Upper band of the 98 rifle with bayonet attachment. The small hook is used to shorten the strap.

129

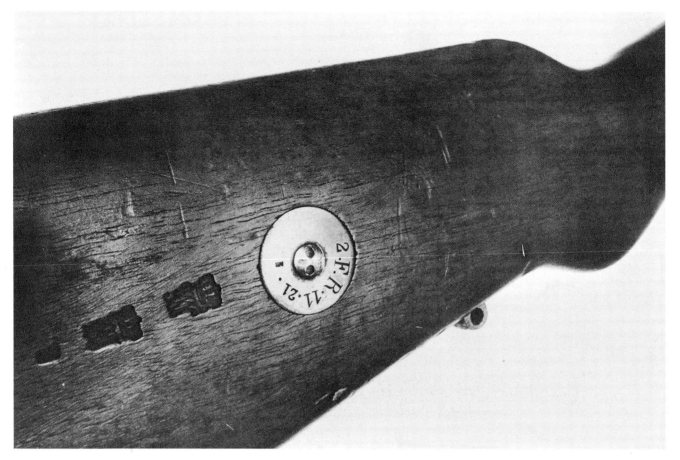

The stamp plate of the 98 rifle in its original form (before 1915). The mark signifies the rifle Nr. 21 issued to the eleventh company of "Füsilier-Regiment" Nr.2.

Mauser's License Contracts with Prussia and Bavaria

The Prussian Rifle Factory in Spandau had already made a use agreement with Paul Mauser, dated November 11, 1895 and in the name of the Prussian War Ministry. It concerned the following Mauser patents: A shrouded bolt head, full-depth thumb cut in left wall of receiver, bayonet attachment (later discarded), gas shield on bolt sleeve and bolt sleeve lock.

For the use of these individual patents, which were united in the 8-millimeter test rifle of 1894 (later called the 88/97), the Prussian state wanted to obtain a license for seven years, until 1902. For the first 100,000 rifles made it would pay one Mark each, for the rest 50 Pfennig each.

This contract, which originally applied only to the test rifles, later applied automatically to the Model 98 too.

On September 17, 1901 Bavaria also obtained the right for the Royal Rifle Factory at Amberg to manufacture Mauser rifles. For the first 20,000 rifles the Bavarians paid one Mark each, for the rest 50 Pfennig. The Bavarian contract was for four and a half years (through March 1905).

Even more important than the licensing fees for Paul Mauser was the fact that after his new rifle was accepted, he received large-scale contracts from Berlin for the first time. Until 1907, the year in which rearmament was completed, the Oberndorf factory delivered a total of 290,000 rifles.

In 1898 the new rifle had been regarded only as a test model at first. There was no thought of a general rearmament. When the War Ministry in Berlin ordered the first troop tests in the 1st Foot Guard Regiment, the Guard Jäger and Guard Rifle Battalions as well as the Infantry Gunnery School (beginning February 9, 1899), the War Minister put particular emphasis on the certainty "that neither from this nor from subsequent rearmament of individual troop units may the conclusion be drawn that a following general rearmament with new rifles was to take place. A careful retention of the present rifles (88), which — since the means to large-scale new production are not available — must still remain in the hands of the troops for a long time to come . . ." was therefore urgently required.

The Lifetime of a "Small-Caliber" Rifle: Five Years

Money really was lacking. Only when the Prussian War Ministry referred in a memorandum to the fact that, on account of the "fast wear of the small-caliber rifle", new rifles would have to be issued every five years, while the extent of funds in the budget formerly had been based on the ten-year life expectancy of the old black-powder rifles, was more money found.

The means "for creating replacements of small hand firearms" were estimated at 2.5 million Marks per year. But even with that, large increases were not to be made. Unlike the rearmament with the 88 rifle, which had been pushed through in two years without regard to cost or quality, the Prussian War Ministry now planned a long-term rearmament of the active troops with the 98 rifle, lasting until 1907. Only after 1912, in a second stage of production, would the reserve troops' turn come.

During 1900 the Prussian state factories (in addition to the Mauser works at Oberndorf) began to produce rifles at a "moderate rate." In February of 1901 Spandau delivered 107, Danzig 140 and Erfurt 54 rifles per day. By the end of the year the Prussian factories had produced a total of 90,000 rifles, costing 54 Marks apiece including the licensing fees.

The very first 98 rifles were intended for the Imperial Navy and the "East Asian Expeditionary Corps", which took part in the international punitive action against the Boxers in China at that time. In the autumn of 1901 the first three army corps in Prussia received new rifles, in the following year the next three corps had their turn, and so forth.

The Bavarians in particular gave themselves plenty of time. They were uneasy about the belated arrival of news from Berlin and waited until it was known whether the 98 rifle was going to be the long-awaited great solution or just another nine-day wonder.

On May 2, 1901 Prince Regent Luitpold accepted the Mauser rifle for Bavaria, in August the retooling of the Rifle Factory at Amberg to produce the new model began, but only in January of 1903 did production begin gradually. Seventy to eighty rifles a day was the goal. The Bavarians did not need to

The licensing contract between the "Reich Military Finances", represented by the Royal Prussian Rifle Factory at Spandau, and Kommerzienrat Paul Mauser, dated November 16, 1895, concerning the "Mauser bolt and magazine apparatus."

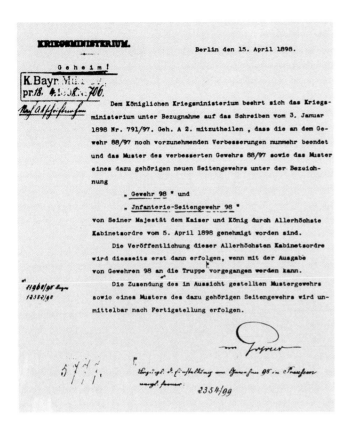

Bayonets for the 98 Rifle

Many bayonets from old stocks were modified for use on the 98 rifle during World War I. They include particularly the M 71/84 type with a 25-cm blade.

The most important new types made for the 98 rifle (and carbine) were:

Bayonet 98: 52 cm long, slim blade, wooden handle, black leather scabbard with steel trim;

Bayonet 98/02: 43 cm long, equally wide blade with saw teeth;

Bayonet 98/05: 37 cm long blade widening shortly before the point. 98/05 bayonets exist both with and without saw backs. Both versions have steel scabbards.

hurry, as the two army corps in the south were only scheduled for rearmament between October 1903 and October 1907. But scarcely had production begun in Amberg when the Prussians changed the model again. Of the minor modifications to the stock and breech, only the "firing pin", a 1901 Mauser patent, is worth mentioning.

Paul Mauser had planned this safety measure to avoid unwanted cartridge ignition with the breech unlocked in the rare case of a striker breaking. The brilliantly simple safety measure consisted of a safety firing pin with lugs that line up with shoulders in the bolt when the action is unlocked, thus preventing firing pin from moving forward into contact with cartridge primer unless bolt is fully locked.

The Spandau Tests with Pointed Bullets

The remarkably strong compression of the 88 bullet, which was responsible for the barrel damage and too-strong wear of the rifling in the 88 rifles, plus the modest performance of the 88 cartridge in comparison to the new cartridge types that came onto the market in the Nineties, inspired the members of the Rifle Testing Commission in Spandau to make new tests. A group under the leadership of Captain Thorbeck (who became President of the GPK during World War I) experimented with new bullet types which, mounted in 88 cartridges, could be fired from the 88 system weapons.

At the very beginning of 1898 the results of these tests crystallized into a new ideal form: the pointed bullet (Spitzgeschoss), later called the S bullet.

"The essence of the S cartridge," Captain Thorbeck explained, was "the invalidation of the principle of great lateral pressure hitherto prevailing in the design of bullets," as well as the "replacement of the long, heavy bullet with a rounded point and wide diameter with short, light bullets of slim form but equally large diameter . . ."

The Thorbeck group created a whole "family" of pointed bullets that differed in length, point shape and weight. Among them there were already streamlined typed similar to the later heavy pointed bullet (sS).

It was known in Germany that the French had already tested such "cigar bullets" (though of solid bronze) successfully. But in Prussia the first decision was made for a short, light, jacketed pointed bullet with its greatest diameter at its base.

The tests concentrated at first on a type that was designated "S 4" at Spandau, about which no data exist, but later the "S 2" type proved to be superior.

The "S 2" bullet weighed 10.3 grams and had a bottom diameter of 8.23 +/- 0.02 mm (later standardized to 8.22 mm). In Prussian-Bavarian parallel troop tests, carried out at the Spandau and Lechfeld military gunnery schools between October 1902 and June 1903, the S-2 bullet was tested and slightly changed again toward the end of the tests. Following a suggestion from Spandau, the point was made somewhat slimmer to save another half gram of weight.

A comparison of the weights and measures of the changed S bullet and the old 88 bullet is shown in this table:

Bullet	Overall Length	Length of Point	Length of Shank	Greatest Diameter	Bullet Weight
Pointed	28mm	19mm	9mm	8.22mm	9.8g
Type 88	31.25mm	8.5mm	22.75mm	8.1mm	14.7g

Although the pointed bullet's diameter of 8.22 mm was greater than that of the 88 bullet (8.1 mm), there was less barrel damage, because there were scarcely any compression effects with the new bullet. This was due chiefly to its slim form. The S bullet also had a stronger jacket of nickel-plated iron 0.5 mm thick. The 88 bullet jacket had been only 0.3 mm thick.

The (S) Powder 682 b

The first tests with the lightened pointed bullets had ended with a disappointment. Using the standard flake powder of Type 436, which had just been introduced, the pointed bullets did not even equal the performance of the 88 bullets. They were slower and strayed considerably off course. It turned out that the squarish flakes (1.6 to 1.8 mm long per side, 0.35 to 0.40 mm thick) were too big and thick and thus burned too slowly to accelerate the light bullet optimally.

The new "S" powder, or more precisely "Spandau Powder 682 b", introduced by a directive dated April 3, 1903 (No. 251.03, geh. A.2), was intended for the new light bullet. The flakes were smaller (1.2 to 1.5 mm) and thinner (0.25 to 0.35 mm), thus burned faster and, thanks to a new graphite treatment, progressively as well. The smaller flake dimensions also allowed more powder than before to be put into the cartridge.

Besides that, the chemists at the powder factory in Spandau had succeeded in eliminating a weakness in the old types of powder: the loss of power after long storage, especially in the tropical climate of the German colonies. A treatment with diphenylamine as a "disintegration delayer" finally made "S Powder 682b" able to withstand storage.

With this new propellant and a charge increased to 3.2 grams, the light pointed bullet attained a power considered sensational at that time. The initial velocity (V_{25}) was 870 meters per second. A comparison of the various German powder types up to the turn of the century follows:

Cartridge	Charge	Gas Pressure	Velocity	Powder Type
88	2.67 g Gew.Bl.P. (1890-91)	3350 atm.	610 m/sec	Ethyl acetate, made till 1899
88	2.63 g Powder 436 (as of 1898)	2700 atm.	620 m/sec	Ethyl alcohol powder
S	3.2 g S 682 b (1903)	3100 atm.	870 m/sec	Ethyl alcohol w/ diphenylamine

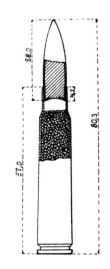
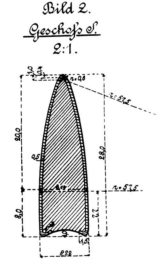

Bild 2.
Geschoß S.
2:1.

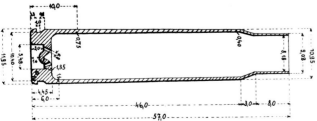

Cutaway drawings of the S cartridge, case and bullet.

The S Cartridge and its Introduction

S Cartridge (8 x 57)
Overall length: 80.3 mm
Total weight: 23.75 grams
Case length: 57 mm
Case weight: 11 grams
Bullet length: 28 mm
Bullet weight: 9.8 grams
Bullet material: Lead core, steel mantle
Bullet form: Short, pointed
Bullet caliber: 8.22 mm
Charge weight: 3.2 grams
Powder type: Spandau powder 682 b
Lateral pressure: 20.4 g/cc
Gas pressure: 3600 atm.
Muzzle energy: 375 m/kg
Muzzle velocity V25: 870 meters per second

Since the diameter of the S bullet was greater than that of the 88 bullet, the 88 E (for "Einheitshülse, uniform case, already described in an earlier chapter) cartridge case had to have its neck space increased somewhat. The diameter was now 8.18 +/-0.02 mm. For recognition a letter "S" instead of the former "E" was stamped on the base of the case.

The components of the S cartridge were: the S case with 88 percussion cap, the charge of 3.2 grams of "Spandau 682 b powder" and the pointed bullet (adapted S type) weighing 9.8 grams.

In 1904 the state factories delivered 1000 cartridges for 97 Marks; a single one cost 9.7 Pfennig. The superior power of the S ammunition in comparison to its forerunner, the 88 and 71 cartridges, is shown in this chart of their trajectories.

Zeniths of Trajectories

Cartridge	400m	600m	800m	1200m	1500m
71	+1.8m	+4.9m	+10.4m	+30.9m	+56.6m
88	0.8	2.5	5.4	17.4	34.1
S	0.25	1.0	3.0	11.9	25.5

Testing of the S cartridges at the Military Gunnery School in Spandau and the Lechfeld army base was scheduled to continue until June 30, 1903. In fact, though, the S ammunition was declared, and introduced as, the standard cartridge in Prussia by a secret directive on April 3, 1903.

An explanation of this action in advance of the troop test results is found in a report of the Bavarian military representative in Berlin, dated January 21, 1903. He stated: ". . . His Majesty the Kaiser, inspired by good hunting experiences with the new ammunition and by reports of very extensive and successful tests of a similar nature in France, is pushing" to introduce the S cartridge as quickly as possible. And so it happened. The troop tests continued pro forma, and yet they provided an important result in the end: the decrease of the pointed bullet from 10.3 to 9.8 grams, which was already mentioned.

In his final report on the troop tests at the Lechfeld base gunnery school, the Commander, Lieutenant Colonel Fasbender, reported to the War Ministry in Munich, adding a personal observation: "Great deformation of the bullet on hitting the target at long ranges, frequent loosening of the jacket from the lead core (by melting), and much splintering of the former. Considerably higher wounding capability than the 88 cartridge."

A ministerial functionary named Bucher noted in pencil on the margin of the secret document: "Thus unintentionally a similar effect to the infamous Dum-Dum bullet . . ."

As of October 1903, all ammunition factories that had state contracts were to convert to S cartridges, but the production of the new powder was particularly troublesome at first.

In the Bavarian Main Laboratory at Ingolstadt, for example, three sets of machines (built by the firm of Fritz Werner in Berlin) were working at cartridge production since May of 1904, but the powder was still being delivered from Spandau until well into 1905, since there were problems with vacuum drying at Ingolstadt.

Powder for Prussian use was also produced by the private Köln-Rottweil powder factories and the "Westphalian-Anhalt Explosive Corporation."

By the day when the S cartridge was to be added to the mobilization supplies, 23 million cartridges had to be produced in Bavaria alone.

The long-term Prussian schedule planned for the following quantities (in millions) for the next four years:

Date	88 Cartridge	S Cartridge (in millions)
10/1/1906	163	197
10/1/1907	132	228
10/1/1908	117	243
10/1/1909	110	250

The large supplies of 88 cartridges were to be phased out gradually. For that reason, no S cartridges were to be issued for shooting drill until 1907, but only 88 cartridges. They could also be fired from the weapons that had been adapted for S ammunition as long as the appropriate high sight was used.

Changes in Clips

Clips, introduced simultaneously with the 98 rifle in Prussia and the rest of the Reich, were not to be wasted in peacetime. Like the old cartridge frames of the 88 rifle, they had to be collected for reuse after firing drills.

The original Mauser clips of sheet steel were inclined to rust in extended use. For that reason the Rifle Testing Commission in Spandau suggested a brass clip, which should be nickel-plated along with the inset steel spring. This type was introduced in Prussia on February 7, 1900. Four years later the design of the clip was simplified. In October of 1904 a one-piece charger of brass (see the illustration on page 111) was accepted. Tongues were stamped from both ends and were stretched to give a spring effect and take over the function of the earlier separate steel leaf spring. The one-piece charger was not nickel-plated.

In later years, though, the two-piece sheet-steel clip was brought back into use.

Manufacturers who had already worked for foreign Mauser customers were the Lorenz/DWM Metal Factory in Karlsruhe, the "Spring Steel Industry Corporation" in Kassel, and the Polte Ammunition Factory in Magdeburg. The private firms delivered 1000 chargers for a price of 55 Marks. The state ammunition factories produced them only as of 1901 and calculated prices of only about 35 Marks per thousand.

Ammunition Lightening and Supply

The transition from the cartridge "frame" to the charger strip (1898) and the introduction of the lightened pointed bullet (1903-05) lightened the load of the individual soldier considerably. For the standard ammunition load of 120 cartridges suddenly weighed no more than three kilograms, as

Conclusion of drill at the (Bavarian) base in Lechfeld before World War I. The brand new 98 rifles are stacked. (Photo: Bavarian War Archives)

opposed to four kilos of the old 88 cartridges in their frames.

Thus there were questions asked in Berlin as to whether the supply should be increased from 120 to 150 cartridges. In the end, though, it remained at 120.

Every soldier carried three packs in each of the two roomy bullet pouches on his belt, and each pack held three chargers of five cartridges each: a total of 90 cartridges. The soldier had a reserve of thirty more cartridges in his pack.

Changes to the 98 Rifle for the S Cartridge

After the introduction of the S cartridge with its bullet, which was 0.12 mm thicker, the 98 rifle had to have the front part of its cartridge bed widened accordingly so the new ammunition would go in without jamming.

A second change was made to the sight, whose curves no longer agreed with the more powerful trajectory of the S cartridge.

Both changes (included in series production of the rifles as of 1903) had to be added to the older rifle supplies.

To enlarge the chamber, the Rifle Testing Commission at Spandau had developed a set of four special reamers that had to be used in the cartridge bed one after the other to bring it to the new width. Then a letter "S", 2.5 mm high, was stamped on the head of the breech case and again on the barrel 5 mm behind the base of the sight to mark the rifle as suitable for S cartridges.

Traveling commissions from the rifle factories in Spandau (for Prussia) and Amberg (for Bavaria) visited all the army bases in the Reich between November 1904 and August 1905 to prepare the old supplies of 98 rifles (as well as all the 88 rifles still in service!) for the new cartridges, as far as the barrel was concerned.

Reaming out the chamber, stamping and cleaning a rifle — as had been worked out at Spandau with Prussian thoroughness — was not to take longer than four minutes. Each commission was expected to modify 800 rifles per day.

In new production of rifles after 1903, the breech cases were no longer stamped. The "S" on the barrel, though, just behind the sight base, was retained.

Another stamping, which had been introduced uniformly in 1901, is of importance, as it indicates the exact barrel caliber of each weapon.

Since the barrels, despite improved manufacturing processes, had varying internal dimensions, a tolerance between 7.92 and 7.96 mm was established. Every barrel had to be tested with the well-known measuring instruments and the precise result, in hundredths of a millimeter, stamped on the "base" of the barrel just before the head of the receiver. Barrels with calibers of 7.95 and 7.96 mm could not be issued to troops in peacetime, because it could be expected that they would become unusable sooner.

Changes to the Sight of the 98 Rifle

By the day of the change to S cartridges, October 1, 1905, the sights were also to be changed. The troop gunsmiths took care of that. They had to remove the flaps of the "Lange" sights and send them to the appropriate rifle factory as soon as they were ordered to. Every unit had a different date for this, and for the time taken by the work of adaptation, the unit received spare weapons from depot supplies.

The "Lange" sight in its original form had a sight range from 200 to 2000 meters. Because of the more powerful trajectory of the S cartridge, it was believed that the lowest sight setting should be 400 meters.

Makeshift- and Aircraft-Sights in World War I

When Paul Mauser's great invention, the Model 98, had to pass its acid test in World War I, its creator was already dead. His rifle passed the test with honors.

The only weakness in the 98 rifle worth mentioning, which became apparent during the course of the war, was not attributable to Paul Mauser. For precision firing at small short range targets, the lowest sight setting of 400 meters proved to be useless. It had been introduced by the Rifle Testing Commission at a time when all the world still thought in terms of mobile war, and months of trench warfare at the shortest ranges, as at Verdun, were not even a bad dream.

When the enemy began to entrench himself behind steel breastworks and, behind the firing slits in their shooting shields, presented targets no bigger than a saucer, shooting had to be more exact than the military gunnery school programs had anticipated in peacetime. Using the 400-meter sight, the 98 rifle shot much too high. Since the sights could not be changed quickly, higher auxiliary foresights were issued, to be attached behind the original foresights for aiming at 100 meters. Another makeshift solution, the "aviator's foresight", was likewise attached at the front of the barrel. It simplified the choice of the right lead angle when firing at fighter and reconnaissance aircraft.

Changes to the sight of the 98 rifle: Above: The "Lange" sight for the 88 cartridge, with the original gradations starting at 200 meters. After conversion to the S cartridge, the slide could be pushed back only to the number 4. Below: A new S sight with its scale beginning with "4."

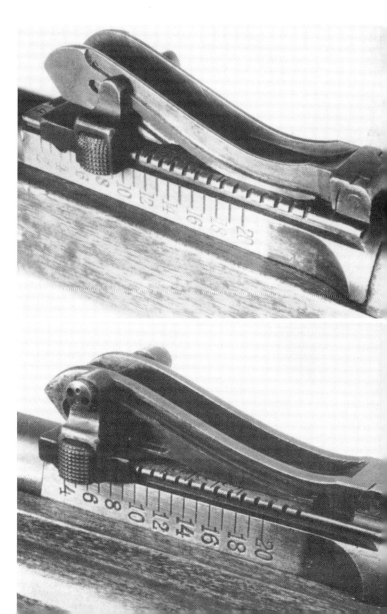

S.m.K. Ammunition

For use against air targets and shields, a special bullet with a hardened steel core was developed during the war. This "S.m.K." bullet (S with core) was longer than the normal S bullet. At its rear end (inside the cartridge case) it had a streamlined extension like that of the later "heavy S bullet" (sS). The steel core had a covering of lead, a so-called lead shirt. This soft sheath under the customary jacket of cast sheet iron allowed the necessary shaping to fit rifling.

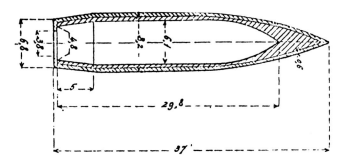

The S.m.K. bullet, cutaway drawing with dimensions.

At 11.5 grams, the S.m.K. bullet was heavier than the 9.8-gram S bullet, and it had a charge of only 2.9 grams of powder (instead of 3.2 grams), because the extension at the end of the bullet took up too much space inside the cartridge case. Thus the S.m.K. bullet was fired with a considerably decreased initial velocity of 815 meters per second, compared to the 895 m.sec of the S bullet. Thanks to its streamlined form, though, it did not lose speed as quickly, and passed the 400-meter mark at 583 meters per second (S: 578). As for shot energy, the heavier core bullet showed itself to be slightly superior even at the 100-meter mark. The comparison weights were 332 to 331 m/kg, and at 2000 meters the core bullet, with 24 m/kg, put exactly twice as much energy into a target as the S bullet.

Because of the higher power of the core bullet, which only became noticeable at longer ranges, the riflemen were instructed to use a 50-meter lower sight setting at ranges between 600 and 800 meters.

In a duplicated sheet of instructions issued during World War I it was stated: "The S.m.K. cartridge is used to fire on targets behind shields and penetrate metal parts (for example, machine guns, fuel tanks of aircraft). The S.m.K. bullets penetrate 4.5 mm

shields of the best chrome-nickel steel in a vertical position at up to 1400 meters, at a 70-degree angle at distances up to 900 meters . . ."

The final comment is noteworthy: "The use of the S.m.K. cartridge is to be limited to armored targets and aircraft, since large-scale production is not yet possible." Since the Germans had not only economical use but also the secrecy of the armor-piercing ammunition in mind, S.m.K. cartridges were issued only to especially good and reliable marksmen. These men were instructed to bury or destroy their core bullets in case of capture.

Along with the S.m.K. bullet, World War I also saw the origin of 7.9-mm incendiary bullets filled with phosphorus, and tracer bullets (for machine guns). And in August of 1918, shortly before the war ended, ammunition with 12.8-gram pointed bullets (sS) was issued for machine guns; in its form and ballistic properties it was similar to the S.m.K. bullets and better suited to use at longer ranges.

To save brass, cartridge cases for rifle ammunition were made of steel as of 1916. For protection against weather conditions, the steel cases were galvanized with a copper plating.

Bolt Protectors and Detachable Magazines

Under the rough conditions of trench warfare, in which rifles were exposed daily to mud and fountains of dirt from exploding shells, many weapons became unusable. When dirt got into the bolt way or locking grooves, the breech could no longer be closed. A simple accessory offered help: the "bolt protector" of sheet steel. It consisted of two parts: a clamp ring with an axle that was pushed over the stock and barrel in front of the case head and held there by a spring, and a protective lid that, when closed, extended from the bolt over the case head.

The cover can be both turned and pushed back and forth with the bolt on the rod of the clamp ring (on the left side of the stock). The movements of the lid are controlled by the bolt handle, which ran through a hole in the lid (on the right side) and was held in this position by a simple sprung flap.

But since the protector made loading the magazine with a clip much more difficult, large-volume 25-shot insertion magazines were developed and issued for the 98 rifle. These magazines could be inserted in the stock of the 98 rifle from below

Steel-core bullets cut open. Above: A short core with a tracer charge behind it. Below: A longer core of hardened steel.

when the normal magazine plate was removed. Its collar was made to fit into the snap apparatus of the old magazine and thus could not simply be removed again. These were not genuine replacement magazines, but only a makeshift solution. In decisive moments of battle, of course, the rifleman had 25 shots at hand, but after that the magazine had to be loaded very conventionally from above with clips.

War Causes Changes in Production

One can only be amazed at the precision with which 98 rifles were still being made even in the last years of World War I.

But there finally came a point at which the shortage of raw materials compelled economic measures: Walnut stocks that had to have been aged at least three years could no longer be obtained in sufficient quantities. During 1917 all the factories gradually changed to rifle stocks made of beech-wood.

Polishing materials were also in short supply. To save at least a portion of the costly emery (not to mention work time), breech cases were no longer polished to a high gloss as of the 1917-18 production year, but blued like barrels.

The third wartime change concerned the perforation of the stamp plate on the butt. This was, of course, not an economy measure but an actual improvement. When weapons were cleaned in the field at the beginning of the war, firing pins were often broken off; thus Prussia ordered that, as of 11/19/1915, only rifles with perforated stamp plates attached by a hollow rivet through the butt be made. The "eye" in the butts of 98 rifles and carbines held the tip of the firing pin during disassembly and assembly of the bolt. It was also handy when rifles were packed into packing cases

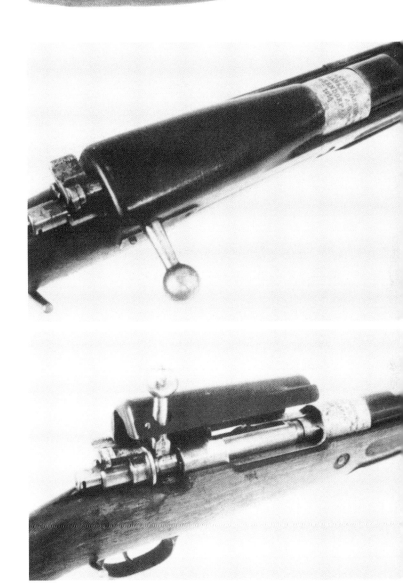

Bolt protectors: Above, with the breech locked; below, when opened.

or stored in warehouses, as the weapons could be secured with thin steel rods pushed through them.

The "Star" Rifles

When the state-owned and large private rifle factories in the Reich could no longer produce the required millions of 98 rifles without help, they gave outside contracts for individual components, bolts, safety, magazine and the like, to small and middle-sized firms. The rifles were assembled in their specific workshops, established especially in and around Suhl. 98 rifles made of parts supplied from outside were marked with a large five-pointed star on the receiver face.

The 98 rifle with "trench" magazine for 25 cartridges. The magazine cannot be changed. It was filled in the rifle.

Telescopic-Sight Rifles in World War I

Soon after the war began, in the autumn of 1914, the Rifle Testing Commission in Spandau began considerations as to how the troops at the front could best and most quickly be supplied with rifles that included telescopic sights. The changed nature of the war had taken the military by surprise; up to then, telescopic sights had been used only for precision tests in the gunnery schools (since about 1890), or individually for hunting.

When the war began, available models and production capacities in the optical industry were still meager; the development of optical aiming devices was still in its infancy.

Since the troops had to be equipped with telescopic-sight rifles in a short time, only requisitioning from appropriate privately-owned hunting rifles could be considered. But this was a delicate proposition. Unlike the peasantry, from whom the military could requisition horses and wagons without asking politely, well-to-do and often influential owners of telescopic-sight rifles had to be treated with consideration. The state did not demand, but rather asked for the weapons. In Prussia the Rifle Testing Commission passed on the request to the hunters; in Bavaria the ordnance office empowered Captain Otto von Feilitzsch to obtain the first rifles. At first he inquired of gunsmiths all over the country who had the names and addresses of hunters who owned telescopic-sight rifles. In agreement with the Rifle Testing Commission in Spandau, only rifles that had Mauser mechanisms and were able to take S cartridges, or 88 cartridges, could be sent to the front.

Captain von Feilitzsch mailed out patriotic appeals and, in most cases, received equally patriotic negative replies. Only a few dozen rifles were gathered. To meet the primary, urgent needs of the Bavarian front troops, Feilitzsch contracted with various capable gunsmithing firms for additional telescopic-sight rifles. The War Ministry paid 330 Marks for every rifle.

The chief suppliers were the firms of "Miller & Val. Greiss" of Munich (10 Mauser repeater rifles with S barrels, hair-triggers and "Gérard telescopic sights", tested at 200, 300 and 600 meters), the Goerz Optical Works of Berlin, which mounted its own lenses on 98 rifles from Amberg. Gunsmiths in Suhl also worked on Bavarian contracts.

The two most important types of telescopic sights at the beginning of the war were: "Gérard Model G", with fourfold magnification, field of vision to 100 meters: 110 meters, luminous intensity 45. Manufacturer: Dr. Walter Gérard's Optical Works, Berlin.

The other was the "Certar short" with fourfold magnification, made by the Goerz firm of Berlin. The "Certar" cost 70 Marks not including mounting.

On December 18, 1914 Captain von Feilitzsch made his way via Cologne to the Bavarian troops on the western front with his first varied assortment of 60 telescopic-sight rifles. By February of 1915 he had gathered another 120. Since there were also privately owned guns that could safely fire only the old 88 cartridges, these weapons were fitted with a stamped sheet-metal shield showing the outline of the 88 cartridge with its roundheaded bullet. Under it was lettered: "Only for 88 cartridges; use no S ammunition!" One might ask whether these weapons, for which special ammunition had to be kept on hand, were really suitable for use under front conditions.

The civilian S-type rifles too were only of limited use. In the first Bavarian reports of experiences at the front, the hunting rifles came off worse than the 98 rifles with telescopic sights. It was reported that the short barrels were less accurate, the muzzle blast was so strong that it betrayed their location, and even the hair-triggers turned out to be less than ideal under front conditions. Another problem mentioned was that the thin barrels of the hunting rifles could not handle S.m.K. ammunition. Numerous barrels had cracked.

In any case, though, the civilian rifles were regarded only as a temporary measure. From the start, all German war ministries agreed that only "telescopic-sight 98 rifles" were to be issued as soon as possible.

The first large-scale deliveries went to the front in

the spring of 1915. At this point Prussia already had contracted for 15,000 of them and reckoned on a total need of 18,421.

Bavaria had ordered 750 telescopic-sight rifles and estimated a total need of 1500. Throughout the Reich, each corps was to receive 120 telescopic-sight rifles, one for each company. But as the war went on, the importance of telescopic-sight rifles increased. By the autumn of 1918 Bavaria, for example, issued some 3000 telescopic-sight rifles to its 732 mobile companies. Every infantry and Jäger company had at least three of the rifles by August of 1916.

The best weapons from ongoing production were chosen from the start for conversion into telescopic-sight rifles. In Prussia the Rifle Testing Commission was responsible for the mounting and, if necessary, repair of telescopic sights. In Munich the firm of Miller and Val. Greiss handled the work.

For elevation (range) aiming, the telescopic sights had an upper frame panel with markings for 200, 400 and 600 meters (in Bavaria), as well as 100, 200, 300 etc. up to 1000 meters (Prussia).

There were also differences in the manner of mounting. The Bavarian telescopic-sight rifles had normal hunting-style hooking mounts with side support screws. The telescope was directly over the axis of the barrel. With the scope in place, the magazine thus could not be filled from clipss, but only with single cartridges. On the other hand, the scope was handily located right before the rifleman's eye and the "parallax error" remained small. The Prussian Rifle Testing Commission, on the other hand, mounted the telescopic sights offset to the left side of the barrel axis, so that it was possible to load with clips with the scope in place.

The 98/17 and Mauser "Assault" Rifles

From the experiences of Verdun the Rifle Testing Commission, then under the leadership of Colonel Thorbeck, the creator of the German pointed bullet, quickly drew conclusions. They developed a special weapon, based on the 98 rifle, for trench warfare, bearing the unofficial designation "Rifle 98/17." Early in 1917 the Prussian War Ministry ordered 5000 test weapons from the firm of Simson in Suhl for a front test that was scheduled for the summer and autumn of 1918.

The 98 rifle in the trenches of World War I. The soldiers have hand grenades, gas masks and gas goggles. (Photo: Bavarian War Archives)

According to a message from the Prussian War Ministry, production of the test weapons began late in March of 1917. Unfortunately, not a single example of this type seems to exist now in the Federal Republic of Germany.

The 98/17 rifle differed from the 98 rifle in the following details: The barrel, for the sake of low weight and material saving, was made not in conical but in cylindrical sections (as Paul Mauser had suggested twenty years before). The sight range began at 100 meters in order to make firing on short-range targets easier. A metal bolt protector in improved form, which also allowed quick reloading with clips, was built in. The follower of the normal five-shot magazine, with its vertical step, functioned as a bolt stop when there was no cartridge in the magazine. The trigger had a rippled surface, so as to prevent the trigger finger from slipping off in wet or muddy conditions.

Unlike the 98/17 rifle, which was created by the Rifle Testing Commission, the "Mauser 1918 rifle" was based on a private development from the Mauser factory. This weapon, which is described in the "History of the Mauser Works", features a few additional modifications from the standard 98 rifle, which were intended to be useful for trench warfare, of course, but may also have hindered practical mass production in wartime. Maybe that was the reason why the huge order of 800,000, which the Spandau Rifle Factory (representing the Prussian War Ministry) had given to the Mauser factory in 1915, was never filled.

The Mauser "Trench and Close Combat Rifle 18" was to have a genuinely replaceable magazine.

The magazine housings (for five, ten or twenty-five cartridges) had longitudinal ribs pressed into their sidewalls to make the cartridges slide more smoothly. The follower locked the breech with the magazine was empty. To change the magazine, a push-button in the trigger guard was used. Changing the magazine was only possible when the bolt was opened and drawn back (achieved by linking the bolt release with the trigger).

The Mauser 18 rifle likewise had a permanent, improve bolt protector as well as a new stock with a strengthened pistol grip.

The 98 Carbine

Among German army weapons there have been three "carbines" with the Mauser 98 system: Models "a", "b" and "k", and it must be noted that none of these weapons was a genuine carbine in the classic sense. The "a" and "k" carbines, with their 60-centimeter barrels, are more accurately "short rifles", and the "98b carbine" is not even that; its dimensions are exactly those of the rifle.

Not only in the German Reich but internationally as well, the very short, handy special weapons of the cavalry disappeared shortly after the turn of the century. The cause was the new development of high-performance cartridges with its strong charges, which absolutely demanded long barrels to keep recoil, muzzle flash within bearable limits.

Then too, the short weapons were no longer a privilege of the cavalry, meant to serve them only in times of need for self-defense in "fighting on foot" at short ranges, but were issued more and more often to newly organized special units. And for the machine-gun, airship and supply train units, for example, the performance of a carbine was doubtless more of an advantage than its small size.

The search for the best compromise, between handiness and performance, in the new German carbines, lasted more than a decade at Spandau. Between 1898 and 1908, when the 98(a) carbine was finally introduced, there were three test models in five versions, all of which are as good as forgotten today — their description follows.

"Cavalry and Artillery Carbine 98" (first model)

On April 20, 1900 the Prussian "General War Department" informed the united war ministries: "After the model of the 98 rifle, a cavalry and artillery carbine has been designed and presented to the department..." The Rifle Testing Commission had already received orders in the autumn of 1899 to start a small troop test, in which two (cavalry) squadrons and one foot artillery company were to take part. On May 18, 1900 it was stated: "The model (of the new carbine) has not yet been finalized..."

The first models of the cavalry and artillery carbine 98 corresponded exactly in their dimensions to those weapons that they were supposed to replace: the 88 carbine and 91 rifle. They were exactly the same, including the stacking hook of the 98 artillery carbine.

The carbines had the same mechanism as the 98 rifle; only the bolt handle was different. Bent down and flattened, it was snug to the stock.

The barrel was 43.5 cm long and covered from the sight to the muzzle with a complete wooden upper hand guard. The sight itself was an almost exact-scale miniature of the "Lange" rifle sight with an adjustment range from 200 to 1200 meters. The stock form of the carbine, with pistol grip and slim lower band, was likewise borrowed from the rifle.

"Artillery Carbine 98", No. 2710, made in Erfurt in 1901; barrel length: 42.5 cm, ammunition: 88 cartridge.

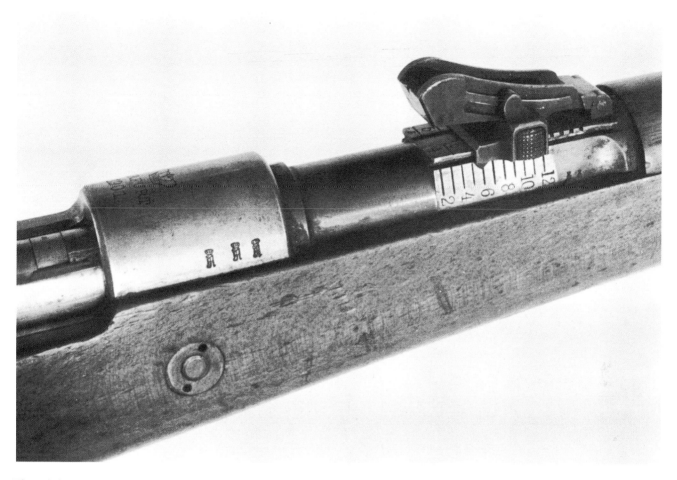

The miniature "Lange" sight of the test carbine. Sight range: 200 to 1200 meters.

The side sling passed through the butt in the rear and was held by a leather "frog" on the right side; in front it passed through the fixed eye on the lower barrel band.

The 98 artillery and cavalry carbines were both 96 centimeters long and — appropriately for their time — made for the 88 cartridge.

No report is found in the files of the Bavarian War Archives giving the results of the Prussian troop testing in 1899 and 1900. But the results must have been negative. There is no other explanation for the first models being withdrawn in 1902 and adapted into "target carbines" (for target practice with 5-mm rim fire target cartridge).

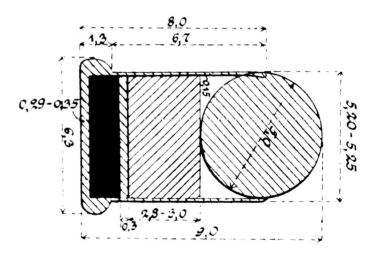

The target cartridge for practice shooting with the modified carbines at army bases.

The 98 carbine with bayonet attachment, No. 1834, made in Erfurt in 1904. The weapon is already set up for the S cartridge. (Sight to 1800 meters.)

"Carbine 98 with Attachment for Bayonet 98" (second model)

The final decision on the first carbine model had not yet been made, and several Prussian machine-gun units were already drilling with a new test weapon. This time the results appeared to be satisfactory, for the Kaiser approved the new short weapon on June 26, 1902 as "Carbine 98 with attachment for bayonet 98." There were no differentiations between cavalry and foot troops any more, and the new carbine was intended to be the uniform weapon for cavalry and special units.

The overall length, barrel length and the entire rear part of the new weapon, including the sight, were exactly those of the rejected predecessor models — only the front half was a new design.

The handguard no longer reached to the muzzle of the barrel; it ended under a broad band with two attachments, similar to the upper band of the 98 rifle and, as on the rifle, also enclosed the rod of the bayonet lug. Between this rod and the barrel the wood of the stock narrowed sharply and continued to the usual steel muzzle cap of a carbine, with foresight panels at the muzzle. A very unusual design, and a hard one to assemble.

Like the 98 rifle, the carbine too is provided with a short cleaning rod, which projects under the muzzle of the barrel and helps when hooking several carbines together. The sling attachments on the side of the ring and on the butt correspond to those of the earlier models.

The carbine had originally been planned for the 88 cartridge. But when the S cartridge with its

An unusual fore stock; the wood reaches all the way to the muzzle.

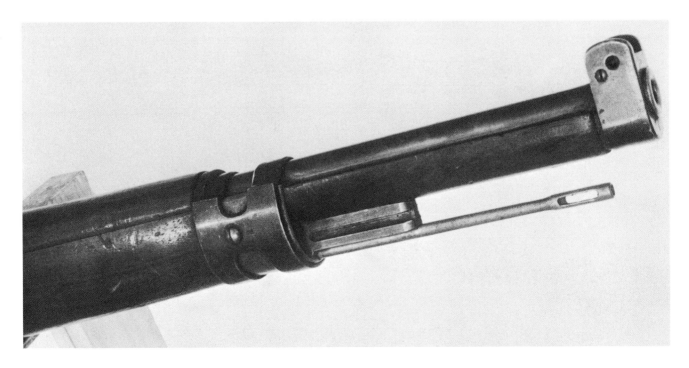

stronger charge of powder was introduced and the chamber of the carbine with its 435-mm barrel was reamed out and a new sight with markings from 300 to 1800 meters was soldered on, there was an unexpected displeasure.

On January 21, 1905 the Prussian War Ministry reported to Munich:

"In the attempts to fire 98 S ammunition from carbines, a louder blast and greater appearance of flash were observed (than with the 98 rifle), but these at first did not seem so significant that . . . a change would have to be made to the carbine. But now during the winter the appearance of flash has shown itself to a greater degree, so that with it and the loud blast of the short barrel, a problem for the men is to be expected, namely on the firing line. The unpleasantness has more effect on the shooter's neighbors than on himself, so that it would be advisable to give the short carbine to *those* troops who need the weapon only for self-defense . . . The Rifle Testing Commission has therefore been advised to produce models of a longer carbine and work out a program for troop testing."

Because of the difficulties described here, series production at Erfurt was halted at the beginning of 1905. The works, that had developed in a year and a half into a special factory for revolvers, pistols and carbines, took up the production of 98 rifles again for the time being.

How many 98 carbines with bayonet lugs had been produced by January of 1905 can no longer be determined. There could not have been very many of them, because the model for the Bavarian War Ministry, delivered on October 24, 1904, only bears the serial number 1834. The carbine, with the rather high production cost of about 68 Marks, was later withdrawn and likewise modified into a practice weapon for target cartridges.

Carbine 98 (lengthened third model)

As instructed by the War Ministry in Berlin, the Rifle Testing Commission in Spandau assembled the third (lengthened) test carbine. The barrel was now 59 centimeters, the whole weapon 109 centimeters long. A new type of sliding sight, on the Mauser pattern, with settings from 300 to 2000 meters, was in an aperture of the lengthened wooden handguard, which now extended from the receiver face to a slim barrel band held by a spring and similar to the lower band of the 98 rifle. The stock again extended almost to the muzzle and ended there in a steel carbine muzzle cap, which had a special half-moon attachment for a special muzzle protector (this is already found on the first model).

The bolt handle is no longer flat, but round as in the rifle, though bent downward. The underside of the handle knob is flat and rough. To make it easier

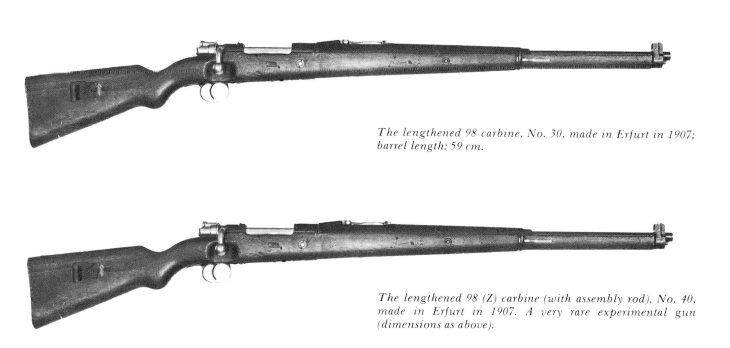

The lengthened 98 carbine, No. 30, made in Erfurt in 1907; barrel length: 59 cm.

The lengthened 98 (Z) carbine (with assembly rod), No. 40, made in Erfurt in 1907. A very rare experimental gun (dimensions as above).

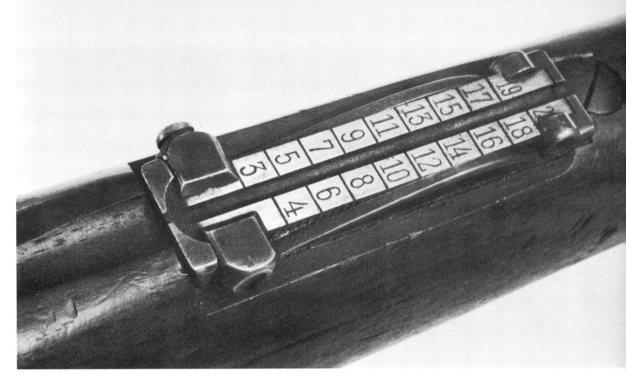

The curved sliding sight of the lengthened carbine (300 to 2000 meters).

to hold the bolt handle, the stock has a cut in it at this point.

To attach the strap at the front, there is a special swivel on the left side of the upper barrel band, which is screwed right through the stock.

In preparing the new carbine test models, there were once again differing opinions as to whether the short weapon should have a bayonet attachment at all, whether a uniform carbine was worth striving for or whether it was desirable to return to slightly different models for mounted and foot troops. A troop test was supposed to clear up these questions.

For the great test, which began on June 11, 1906, 706 lengthened 98 carbines with bayonet attachments and 100 without were issued. For the sake of comparison, seventy 98 carbines of the second prototype (with short barrels) were taken along.

The test ended in the summer of 1907, and the experiences of this great test resulted in the fourth carbine type, once again slightly modified and even equipped with attaching and stacking devices. It was the "Carbine 98 AZ" (with "Aufpflanz-und Zusammensetzvorrichtung"), which we now call the "Carbine 98(a)."

The nose cap with front sight protectors and half-moon under-cut lug for an experimental muzzle protector.

"Carbine 98 AZ" (Carbine 98 a)

Type: *Karabiner 98* (A)
Number: 5795, year made: 1910
Manufacturer: Royal Prussian Rifle Factory, Erfurt
Function: Repeater
Overall length: 109 mm, Weight: 3.57 kg
Barrel length: 590 mm, Caliber: 7.9 mm, Riflings: 4
Rifling direction: Right (other data same as 98 rifle)
Breech: Bolt action, 98 mechanism
Safety: Mauser leaf
Magazine: Same as 98 rifle
Sight: Curved sliding sight (300 to 2000 meters)
Standard ammunition: S cartridge (8 x 57)
Disassembly: Same as 98 rifle

In October of 1907 the Prussian Rifle Factory at Erfurt was ready to produce an experimental series of the new 98 AZ carbine (with receiver ring and stacking hook). It had a handguard that reached from the case head to an upper band just short of the barrel muzzle. The upper barrel ring could be detached for disassembly (by a snap), it holds the handguard and stock together and encircles the barrel, bayonet lug and baseplate of the stacking hook. The foresight is protected by sturdy sight protectors, the wide middle band, held by a screw in the stock, carries the sling loop on its left side.

The opening upper band, with bayonet lug and stacking hook, of the "Carbine 98 AZ" (later: Carbine 98 a).

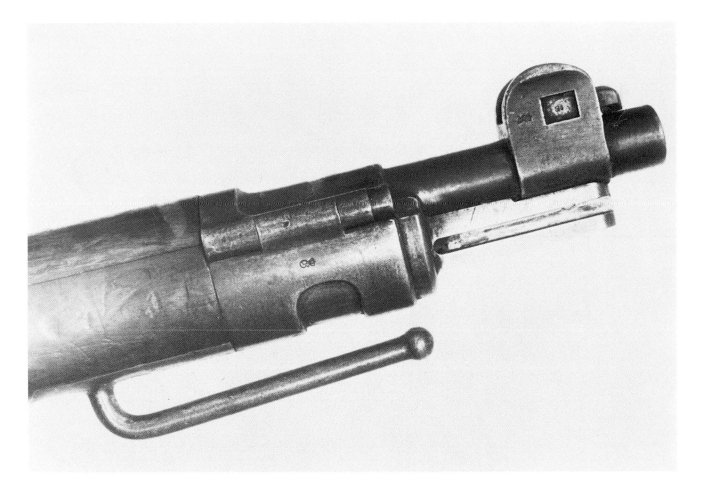

The lower stock, sight (300 to 2000 meters) and bolt handle with half-round head are exactly like those of the third prototype of 1906. Overall length: 110 cm, barrel: 59 cm.

For further troop testing, in which experience with the new weapon, especially with the bayonet lug, would be gained, the Prussians invited Bavarian troops.

A test report of the Bavarian 1st Light Horse Regiment (Nürnberg) shows that the new carbine did not suit everyone's wishes. It stated: "Essentially only the weapon's strong muzzle flash when firing, by which the rifleman's position is betrayed even at a long distance, the strong recoil, the folding sight and the strong heating of the sight after a number of shots are to be found fault with in the weapon . . ."

Muzzle flash, and strong recoil remained the particular characteristics of the carbine as long as the overly charged S cartridge was its standard ammunition. To avoid the unpleasant by-products, the carbines, already 110 cm long, would have had to be lengthened again (the rifle measured 125 cm), but that was impossible on account of its intended use.

On January 16, 1908 Kaiser Wilhelm II proclaimed: "The lengthened 98 carbine with attaching and stacking apparatus, whose model, having been presented to me, I hereby approve, is to take the place of the carbine introduced according to my order of February 6, 1902."

The 98 (a) carbine was to become the weapon of the cavalry, foot artillery, machine-gun units, technical services and supply units.

Prussia, Saxony and Württemberg fulfilled their needs from Erfurt. Bavaria had to have its share made in Amberg, although equipping the factory with new machines would not have paid in view of the small home needs. But Bavarian authorities were glad to keep the factory busy, since it had already produced all the needed 98 rifles and was without work. A greatly reduced staff of 540 workers, producing fifty carbines a day, produced the 30,000 weapons needed in Bavaria within two years. The cost (without amortization of machines or management costs) was between 51 and 55 Marks. The first Bavarian units were armed with the carbines in 1909.

A sentry with a 98 carbine and 98/05 bayonet during World War I.   (Photo: Bavarian War Archives)

150

German Gun and Ammunition Factories Before 1918

No private company could have afforded to work under conditions such as the state-owned rifle factories in Spandau, Danzig and Erfurt faced in the latter half of the 19th Century. Times of full production, such as from 1885 to 1887 and again from 1889 to 1891, alternated with periods in which all the machines were stopped and the staff, except for a small cadre of highly skilled specialists, had to be discharged (see chart).

Whenever a new rifle model was to be introduced, the war ministries in Berlin and Munich invested millions in expanded facilities and new machine tools. Overloads were created deliberately, and the fact that the facilities could be used only for a short time was accepted for the sake of rearming as fast as possible. Then, of course, the chimneys smoked around the clock six days of the week, the forging hammers thundered, the transmissions ran hot, and daily record outputs of 760 and more rifles were attained (Spandau, 1890).

Unlike the privately owned weapons factories in Oberndorf, Suhl and Steyr, which had to show a

Numbers of employees at the Prussian rifle factories up to 1900. The high peaks mark the points in time when rearmament with new models was in progress: 1875 (M/71), 1886-87 (M 71/84) and 1890-91 (88 rifle).

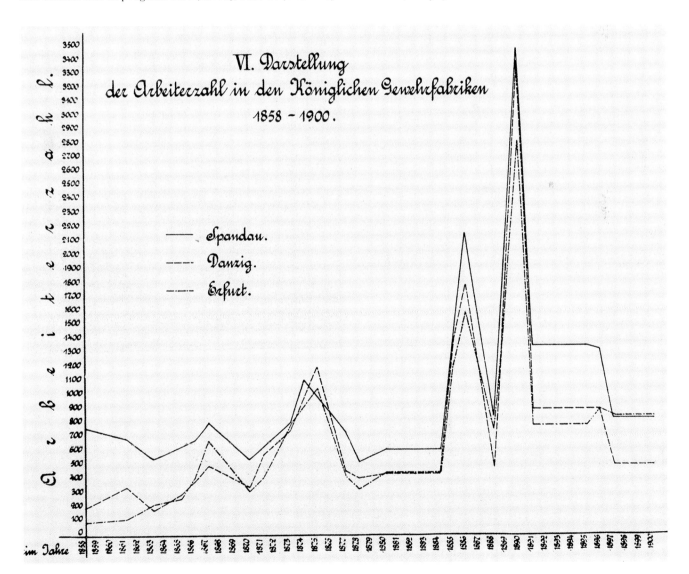

profit to stay alive, the economic aspects remained secondary to the standpoint of military-political effectiveness; Spandau, Danzig, Erfurt and Amberg delivered at net prices which did not include investment and management costs. By honest calculation, the state factories could never have broken even. An example: The cost of the M 71/84 rifle was reckoned by the Prussian factories at 43 Marks, by Amberg at 42 (the salaries were somewhat lower there). The Mauser firm in Oberndorf, of course, charged 56 Marks, but the Amberg factory director at that time, Ammon, admitted in a letter to the War Ministry in Munich that, including the investment costs for setting up the factory as well as the management costs, the cost per rifle would be 55 Marks.

The royal "weapons manufactories" had been founded in the 18th Century because at that time there were not enough private firms that would have been capable of satisfying the army's firearms needs in terms of quality and quantity. A hundred years later, when industrialization in the weapons industry had progressed to the point that the state could have had its weapons needs met by private entrepreneurs, there were both political and economic reasons not to do so.

How critical the granting of contracts to foreign firms could be had been shown when the Belgian government had declared an embargo on weapons at the beginning of the Franco-Prussian War, and Bavaria waited in vain for the critically needed M/69 carbines that had been ordered from Liège. Even orders in friendly Austria were not problem-free, as had transpired in 1889, when the weapons factory in Steyr had been put under great time pressure in filling an order for 88 rifles because the Austrian government wanted to have the factory do work to meet Austria's own needs.

In the Imperial and Royal Monarchy, the state had declared that it had priority over private weapons production capacities. The more liberal (at least economically) German Reich, on the other hand, did not intervene in the business of private companies. Thus it happened that the Mauser works in Oberndorf filled foreign contracts while rearmament with the 88 rifle went on in the Reich. Later the private weapons factories in the German Reich had to promise to switch production to fill military needs at least in the case of mobilization.

Ludwig Loewe & Co.

In the years before World War I, when the concept of "military economy" or "organization for total war" was still unknown, the military relied solely on the production capacities and constant availability of the four state rifle factories in Prussia and Bavaria. In the process, the responsible parties in Berlin and Munich overlooked the fact for a long time that the state factories in Spandau, Danzig, Erfurt and Amberg became more and more dependent on one private company: the firm of Ludwig Loewe in Berlin. By the early Seventies the Loewe machine works already had a monopoly in the realm of new machine tools in the American (Pratt & Whitney) manner. Loewe supplied some of the machines for the Model 71 and, later, all the machine tools for the M 71/84, 88 and 98 rifles.

On the basis of its monopoly position, this company could afford to dictate delivery dates to the royal rifle factories and fail to meet them if their own interests stood in the way of fulfilling their contracts on time. When the machines for the M 71/84 and 88 rifles were being made, the directors of the rifle factories at Danzig, Erfurt and Amberg found themselves begging for cooperation.

Loewe's lobby in Berlin, which established and maintained contact between the firm and the Prussian military officials, worked so effectively that there was always a suspicion of corruption in the air. Loewe engineers went in and out at the Rifle Testing Commission and the rifle factory in Spandau and were often informed of secret new developments sooner and better than the officials at the War Ministry.

How problematic the cooperation between the state rifle factories and the Loewe firm had become had to be clear to every observer when, in the mid-Eighties, the machine factory went into weapons production itself and became the nucleus of a gigantic concern, the German Weapons and Ammunition Factories (DWM)* within a few years, with even Mauser of Oberndorf joining it in 1887. The German Weapons and Ammunition Factories were not the only armaments company that arose in

* In 1915 the DWM factories produced some 1400 98 infantry rifles and two million cartridges per day.

the "Founding Years" before the turn of the century. The "Rheinish Metal Goods and Machine Factory" (founded in Düsseldorf in 1889 and later merged with Dreyse, Sömmerda), and shortly afterward the

Rheinmetall GmbH.

firms of Bergmann and Carl Walther in Zella-Mehlis, were, taken as a whole, capable of producing far more than the old royal rifle factories.

The fact that these ponderous giants no longer fit into the modern industrial scene was shown in all its clarity when the Spandau, Danzig and Amberg factories could scarcely be given work between 1907 and 1911 after delivering their quotas of 98 rifles. Of course World War I appeared to justify the existence of the state factories, but by Armistice Day in 1918 these factories had fulfilled their historic task. The terms of the Treaty of Versailles of 1919, which limited the Reich's armaments and simultaneously forced the closing of the state rifle factories, simply preceded the liquidation that was inevitable anyway.

There follows a brief outline of the development of the rifle and ammunition factories in Spandau, Danzig, Erfurt and Amberg, and of the fate of the factories after 1919.

Organization and Operation of the Royal Rifle Factories

The origins of the Royal Prussian Rifle Factories go back to the year 1722, when the King of Prussia at the time, Friedrich Wilhelm I (1688-1740), ordered

the founding of a weapon workshop at Potsdam. In 1733 a branch was opened at the fortress in Spandau. These weapons factories just outside the gates of Berlin, like the factories founded later in Saarn and Danzig, were run by private entrepreneurs.

Since the entrepreneurs constantly got into financial difficulties and often left much to be desired in terms of capability and desire to produce as well, the Prussian state took the rifle factories into its own hands in the early Forties of the 19th Century, subordinated them to the "Inspection of Rifle Factories" in 1857 and filled the management positions at the factories with army officers. The development of the Bavarian Rifle Factory at Amberg was very similar.

As a prerequisite for the mechanization of the rifle factories, Spandau and Danzig received their first steam engines, producing 3 to 16 horsepower, in 1843-44. Despite constantly improved boilers in all four state factories, the works suffered a permanent energy crisis. In times of full production, mobile agricultural traction engines, so-called "locomobiles", had to be rented to gain additional power for the many-branched power transmission systems in the machine shops. Electrical energy for lighting and operating the machines, of course, gained more and more importance in the early Nineties. But even the performance of the dynamos and storage batteries was dependent on steam power in the end.

After being taken over by the state, the Prussian rifle factories were equipped with their first modern machines. For the Dreyse breech-loading needle-gun, which was very complicated in comparison to the muzzle-loaders produced before that, boring, drawing and turning machines were needed in great numbers. The production figures and quality rose.

For example, in Spandau 777 workers using 272 machines produced about 12,000 needle guns during the year of 1857. It is especially noteworthy that at that time all the stocks still had to be made by hand.

Stock shaping machines, improved barrel-drawing frames and fully mechanized equipment were added to the Prussian factories and, shortly thereafter, to the Bavarian works, only between 1872 and 1874 for the production of the Mauser M/71 rifle. The Prussian machines came from the firm of Pratt & Whitney in Hartford, Connecticut; part of the Bavarian equipment came from Ludwig Loewe in Berlin. With the new machines, in considerably expanded factory buildings, staff and production numbers reached a first climax to date in 1875.

In each of the three Prussian factories, 1200 to 1300 workers produced some 60,000 rifles in that year. The smaller factory in Amberg attained only about half as much. The two subsequent rearmaments to the 71/84 and 88 models forced the factories to set new records. More and better machines, additional personnel and new buildings made 100% increases in production possible in 1886-87 and again in 1890-91 (see the graph), which were attained again and exceeded only later, during World War I.

Piecework System and Inspection

The employees of the rifle factories worked in teams according to the "master system." Each group, a so-called "Meisterschaft" or group of experts, specialized in producing one main component of the weapon, such as the barrel, stock or breech.

The factory provided machines and tools. The master, a sort of independent contractor within the

factory, bought the raw material from the factory management and ultimately sold it the parts made by his team, at predetermined prices per piece. Thus the workers were paid by their master, though the administration made sure the workers were not cheated. Since 1845 working hours, salaries and rights of employees in the state factories were regulated in Prussia. The only thing still lacking was protection from being discharged. Mass layoffs and mass hirings depended solely on what the factory was ordered to produce.

The old master system lasted, with small changes at times, until the beginning of the 20th Century.

For acceptance of parts and, above all, of finished rifles, the thorough Prussians had developed an inspection system as strict as it was effective. Official royal gunsmiths decided whether to accept the products; they were independent of the factory and therefore could have no personal interest in putting their stamp of approval on faulty weapons or those that did not fulfill the prescribed performance. Amberg operated on a similar system.

In order to guarantee the equal quality of Prussian and Bavarian rifles, Spandau and Amberg exchanged items from ongoing production as of about 1885, in order to inspect them mutually for standardization and quality.

Royal Rifle and Ammunition Factory, Spandau

Founded in 1722 at Potsdam, the Royal Rifle and Ammunition Factory was expanded by a branch in the fortress of Spandau in 1733. Until being taken over by the state in 1853, the works were run, in chronological order, by the businessmen Splittgerber, Schickler and Daum. In 1856, after the Potsdam factory was abolished, the focal point of the works moved to Spandau. In the ensuing years the center of Prussian state weapon production developed here, encouraged by its closeness to the Rifle Testing Commission in Spandau.

Because of the new technology demanded by production of the 88 cartridge, the ammunition factory at Spandau, until then a branch of the weapon factory, had to be run independently as of April 1889. In new buildings, with new machines for powder, case and bullet manufacturing, the capacity of the factory grew to the extent that Spandau, with 5000 to 6000 employees, could take over the work of the ammunition factories in Danzig and Erfurt.

After peace was made in 1919, the Spandau rifle factory, according to the terms of the Treaty of Versailles, was closed and partially razed. The equipment for the production of 98 rifles was sent partly to Brunn, Czechoslovakia and partly to Belgium. A new business, the "Deutsche Werke A.G.", utilized the trained work force, the buildings and the remaining facilities to manufacture machine tools. In the mid-Twenties the "Auto-Union" firm moved into the buildings of the former rifle factory. In 1945 the buildings were completely destroyed.

Royal Rifle and Ammunition Factory, Danzig

Friedrich Wilhelm III (1770-1840) founded the weapons factory in the eastern part of his kingdom in 1817, after the Wars of Liberation. The original workshops in the Danzig suburb of Neugarten, on the banks of the Radaune, received too little water power; therefore the mechanical part of the factory, the grinding, boring and hammering works, were moved to Günthershof near Oliva in 1820, but soon the power here was not sufficient either. In 1840 the two parts of the factory were reunited. The rifle factory moved into the three-story building of a former sugar refinery in the Danziger Weidengasse. After a lot of trouble with the businessman Apfelbaum, who had run the factory in the service of the state since its founding, the Prussian government took over the works in 1853 and equipped it to produce needle guns and bullets. (The ammunition factory, no longer needed after Spandau's expansion, was closed in 1889.) Until the end of World War I, Danzig produced mainly rifles, as well as steel-tube lances for the cavalry. After 1919 the factory passed to Poland. The machines were taken to Warsaw and formed the basis of the development of a Polish weapons industry.

Royal Rifle and Ammunition Factory, Erfurt — "ERMA"

The rifle factory in Erfurt was founded only in 1862, when the Prussian government decided to move two small weapons factories in Saarn and

Hattingen on the Ruhr, neither able to survive on its own, to a more favorable location. The factory in Saarn had been founded in a former monastery in 1814 and directed, until taken over by the state in 1840, by the Liège businessman Trenelle.

After moving to Thuringia, the factory flourished similarly to the works in Spandau and Danzig, though it lost its ammunition factory in 1889.

After the end of rearmament with the 88 rifle, the factory in Erfurt was specially equipped to produce 88 carbines and 91 rifles. In addition, the production of the M/83 "Reichs revolver" took place at the factory. Later a facility for the production of bayonets was added. From then on, Erfurt was involved chiefly in carbine and pistol production.

The results of the Treaty of Versailles hit the Thuringian works just as hard as the other state weapons factories, but despite that, the tradition of arms manufacturing in Erfurt could be kept alive. After the royal rifle factory was dissolved and the revolutionary troubles that followed World War I had abated somewhat, Berthold Geipel, one of the directors of the state factory, with the support of part of the old work force, established the "Erfurt Machine Factory" (ERMA) in 1922. Despite the ban on weapons production, development quietly continued there. By 1932 the firm's employees already numbered 1000 men again. Along with its machine-tool program, the factory put its first machine pistol on the market in the Thirties. Its great breakthrough came with the development of the MP 38-40 machine pistol in World War II.

When the victors marched into Erfurt in 1945, the factory had a staff of 5000 employees. The second liquidation was more thorough than the first, but even the Soviet occupying forces were not successful in abolishing the name of ERMA. In 1952 a handful of specialists reestablished the firm in the Bavarian city of Dachau. New machine pistols were developed, as well as sporting rifles and pistols. The old ERMA is not dead.

Royal Rifle factory, Amberg

Under the Bavarian Elector Maximilian II Emanuel (1662-1726), a small "armament factory" had been set up in Fortschau, in the Upper Palatinate, in which private gunsmiths from the area built or repaired rifles for the army. The works were poorly equipped and not even able to meet the needs of the

time, which were still modest. In 1800, Elector Maximilian IV Joseph ordered that the workshop be moved into the vacant mint building in Amberg, which was to be developed into a productive factory. In 1801 Amberg supplied only nineteen rifles; a year later production was already up to 773.

After very fluctuating experiences with private entrepreneurs at the factory, the War Ministry in Munich finally took the works back into state control. Under its director Philipp, Baron von Podewils, between 1853 and 1876, the small rifle factory developed into a productive industrial facility. The number of employees rose from 189 in 1845 to 460 in 1878. By 1872-73 — since the old "mint" no longer offered sufficient facilities — a new factory was built in open country outside the city, and had to be expanded several times in the future. During full production in 1889-90 the Amberg work force numbered 1500. The employees worked fourteen hours a day and produced about 100,000 88 rifles in twelve months.

A look at the factory's facilities in 1901 is very interesting: Four steam engines with a combined 782 horsepower, two dynamos with a total output of 82,500 watts, a storage battery with a capacity of 631 A/h, plus 1245 machine tools of all kinds.

After World War I the former Royal Bavarian Rifle Factory became a branch of the "Deutsche Werke A.G." of Spandau, which has already been mentioned. As of 1925 the firm operated as "German Precision Tool AG", and the Bavarian government was said to be a part owner. In 1932 the former manager, Otto Schulz, took over the works on his own and converted production to compressed-air devices. The "Deprag" firm of Amberg still exists.

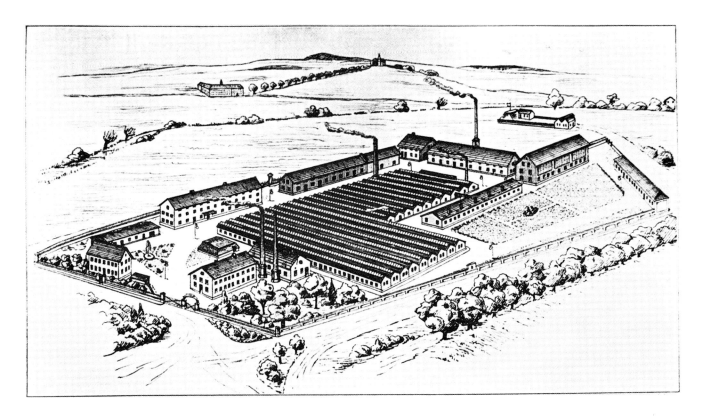

The Royal Bavarian Rifle Factory in Amberg (new factory) in 1901.

Philipp, Baron von Podewils. (Photo: Bavarian War Archives)

The Treaty of Versailles
and its Affects on German Arms Manufacturing

The peace treaty of June 28, 1919, in which the German Empire capitulated to the victors of World War I, included not only territorial losses and reparations payments but also the disassembly of the German military forces to a remnant of 100,000 men in the Army and 15,000 men in the Navy. Types and quantities of weapons were defined in Article 180: 84,000 rifles and 18,000 carbines of the 98 type, with 84/98 bayonets. Also 08 pistols, 1863 machine guns, 252 mortars and 288 heavy guns. All excessive equipment remaining from the war had to be handed over, and new military weapons could be neither developed nor built in Germany. The firm of Simson in Suhl, quite insignificant at the time, was to be, according to the will of the victors, the only German weapons factory that was allowed to produce rifles for the "hundred-thousand-man-army", the "Reichswehr."

This clause alone would have meant the end of the German weapons industry. In addition, the victors also demanded the disassembly of production facilities. The Mauser weapons factory alone (renamed "Mauser Works AG" in 1922) had to sell 1500 machines to Brunn, Czechoslovakia and 800 to Yugoslavia and convert their production, aside from limited hunting-rifle and pistol production, to machine tools and motor vehicles.

Other armaments industries were able to flee into neutral foreign countries. The Rheinmetall-Borsig

A.G., for example, smuggled some 2300 tons of tools, materials and secret production facilities into Holland in the dark just before the ordered disassembly was to begin. The material was stored for years, under false declarations, in rented warehouses in Rotterdam and Delfzyl. But since no cooperation with industries in The Netherlands developed, the Rheinmetall firm's management, through an Austrian "straw man" agency, gradually bought the majority of stock of the Solothurn Weapons Factory in Switzerland. As of 1929 the German firm

was again developing machine guns and machine pistols in Switzerland — work that would have been banned within Germany.

But the traveling "Interallied Control Commission" was not able to supervise obedience to the ban on weapon construction that closely. Since the "dictatorial" terms of Versailles were regarded by all Germans, regardless of their political inclination, as unreasonable, attempts were made to circumvent them quietly whenever possible.

Soon enough the old weapons manufacturers were working on new designs in carefully disguised offices. The secret developmental branch of "ERMA" (founded in 1922) had already been noted. In 1924 a group of Reichswehr officers decided to establish the groundwork for the development of a new armaments industry on their own. This enterprise naturally contravened the terms of the Treaty of Versailles and thus had to be concealed carefully, even from the government of the Reich. In January of 1926 they formed a false-front organization for this purpose, the "Statistical Corporation" (Stage), under the direction of the industrialist Dr. von Borsig.

Three years later Mauser of Oberndorf also opened a weapons development office. By the end of the Twenties the firm had already supplied military pistols of the C/96 type to China and South America.

The growth of the National Socialist Party allowed one to suspect that the days of the Treaty of Versailles and the limitations on German armaments were numbered. Weapon production promised to turn a profit in Germany again; the industry was just waiting for the starting gun. It came, audibly for the whole world, with the introduction of universal compulsory military service on March 16, 1935.

The 98 b Carbine

Type: *Karabiner 98 b*
Number: 6770 (without manufacturer or year)
Function: Repeater
Total length: 740 mm, weight: 4.1 kg
Barrel length: 740 mm, caliber: 7.9 mm, riflings: 4
Rifling direction: Right (other rifling data as 98 rifle)

Breech: as 98 rifle
Safety: as 98 rifle
Magazine: as 98 rifle
Sight: Curved sliding sight (100 to 2000 meters)
Standard ammunition: S cartridge (8 x 57); after 1934: sS cartridge
Disassembly: as 98 rifle

The terms of the Treaty of Versailles did not allow the "Reichswehr" founded in 1921 the possibility of choosing the type of its armaments. Only repeater rifles of the 98 type were allowed, and there were still huge quantities of them on hand after six million were turned over to the victors. Just how many weapons were taken home by German troops returning from the field could not be determined, as only a part of the army units could be demobilized officially, while the rest of the German front-line troops plunged directly into the confusion of the revolution. The free corps, the battalions of the communistic faction, and the civilian forces all made use of the supplies of weapons left over from World War I. And in the end there were still enough for the Reichswehr and the police.

98 rifles and 98 (a) carbines were at first used in their original form. Gradually (after about 1923) the rifles were equipped with new sights and the 98 (a) carbines were replaced by 98 (b) carbines, which were nothing more than slightly modified rifles.

The weights and measures of the 98 b carbine are no different from those of the rifle. The only new features are the tangent sight, the widened lower band, the sling attachment on the left side, the curved bolt handle and the bolt stop when the magazine was empty. In detail:

The new sight, with settings from 100 to 2000 meters in 50-meter stages, consists of a straight flap with a slide, a solid curved piece and a ring base that circles the barrel. In its construction, the sight is almost exactly like that of the old 98 (a) carbine except for the replaceable curved piece. This provision had been made in view of a possible later change of standard ammunition. The heavy S (sS) cartridge had still shown their advantages in the last phase of World War I.

At first the Reichswehr stuck with the S cartridge as standard ammunition for rifles but prepared for a change. When that day came, the curved pieces of the sights were to be exchanged.

The widening of the lower band had become necessary because the band now had a heavy loop attached on its left side for attaching the sling. The other end of the strap passed through a slot in the butt stock and was fastened with a clasp on the opposite side, just like that of the 98 (a) carbine and the short 88 and 91 weapons.

The curved bolt handle had a full-round bolt knob, while the stock was recessed for easy grasping of the knob.

The follower of the magazine (those of the German Mauser military weapons had hitherto been somewhat angled) now took on the form originally intended by Paul Mauser. The middle rib was no longer angled; with the magazine empty, the follower extended up into the receiver, causing the bolt to stop on its forward thrust and showing that the magazine was empty. There was also a slight change in the finish of the weapon. In the 98 b carbine, not only was the breech case blued, as was that of the 98 rifle in its last wartime form, but so were the bolt parts, with the exception of the extractor spring.

It is not known to what extent new 98 carbines were manufactured. Many of the existing ones bear dates and manufacturers' names that lead one to believe that these 98 b carbines were rebuilt from World War I 98 rifles.

The 98 b carbine was intended for mounted and technical troop units of the Reichswehr. The standby police also used them.

Transition from the S to the sS Cartridge

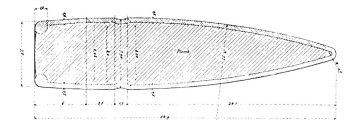

The heavy pointed bullet (sS bullet), weighing 12.8 grams.

The differences between the S and sS ammunition have already been mentioned in this book. To refresh the reader's memory, here are the most important details: Both types were developed at the beginning of the century by the Rifle Testing Commission at Spandau as alternatives chosen in 1903 because it was more powerful and also easier to

loaded S cartridge, sS ammunition was used. The Czech gunsmiths in Brunn were the first to put this experience to use. In 1924 they introduced a short rifle, with the Mauser action and a 59-centimeter barrel, for the sS cartridge, and even shortened their next short rifles' barrels to 45.5 centimeters (Model 98/29). But the best shooting performance with the sS cartridges with acceptable smoke, recoil and flash was given by the 60-centimeter barrels.

In 1934 production of S ammunition came to an end. The large quantities on hand were used by the Wehrmacht as training ammunition until 1939.

Opposite a short chart showing the differences between the S and sS cartridges.

	Case	Charge	Bullet Form	Bullet Weight	V_0	V_{100}	V_{300}	V_{700}
S Cartridge	88 case (S case)	3.2 grams	short, concave, arched base	10.2 grams	895	806	649	394
sS Cartridge	57mm long, rimless	2.85 grams	long, torpedo shaped	12.8 grams	785	737	642	481

produce. Toward the end of World War I, when the technical difficulties of bullet production had been overcome, the sS cartridge also reached the front as special ammunition for machine guns.

The streamlined heavy S bullet is slower at the start, but at long range it puts more energy into hitting the target than the light S bullet. The intersecting point of the speed curves is at 400 meters.

The Reichswehr retained both types of 7.9-mm caliber ammunition (S cartridge for the 98 rifle and sS for machine guns) at first, but even at the beginning of the Twenties it prepared to introduce the sS cartridge as the uniform ammunition for machine guns and repeater rifles. At that time the 98 rifle and 98 b carbine were fitted with new sliding sights with changeable curved pieces.

Tests had shown that the shortcomings of the 98 (a) carbine —heavy recoil, heavy flash and excessive smoke — disappeared when, instead of the over-

The greater volume of the sS bullet encouraged the development of numerous types of special ammunition. In addition to the SmK and tracer types already known from World War I, more than a dozen new explosive, core, incendiary, smoke and new tracer types, with the most varied combinations, were made before and during World War II. The most remarkable development was probably the screaming bullet, which had no other purpose than to demoralize the enemy.

During the war the cases were made of steel and originally copper-plated for protection against weather conditions, later just painted. (Cartridges with sheet-metal cases continued to be made for machine guns.)

To save lead, the normal bullets were made with iron cores set into the bullet jacket with a thin covering of lead. This "thrifty ammunition" was designated "S.m.E." (S with iron core).

The 98 Short Carbine - K 98 k

Type: *Karabiner 98 k*
Number: 10385 (no manufacturer or year)
Function: Repeater
Overall length: 1110 mm, weight: 3.8 kg
Barrel length: 600 mm, caliber: 7.9 mm, number of riflings: 4
Rifling direction: Right (other barrel data same as 98 rifle)

Breech: Same as 98 rifle
Safety: Same as 98 rifle
Magazine: Same as 98 rifle
Sight: Curved sliding sight (100 to 2000 meters)
Standard ammunition: sS cartridge (8 x 57)
Disassembly: Same as 98 rifle

The 98 k carbine with 39 telescopic sight.

At the end of the long developmental history of the 98 weapons there remains little to be said of the last, best-known and most widespread weapon in the series. This was the Carbine k (for "kurz": short), which was introduced in 1935 along with universal compulsory military service. The "K 98 k", intended to be the standard weapon of the German Wehrmacht that was just being formed then, was the first truly uniform weapon in German military history.

How many millions of them were made in the ten years from 1935 to 1945, and just who manufactured 98 k carbines, will probably never be determined exactly.

Of course the high points of production within the Reich and in the lands occupied during the war can be linked with the traditional centers of weapons production: Mauser in Oberndorf and Berlin (the branch there had been founded in 1934), factories in Suhl, the factory in Steyr and the weapons manufacturers in Brunn, Czechoslovakia and Herstal-Liège, Belgium, which were run under German leadership. But there were also a number of small and medium-sized machine shops that made carbine parts during the war.

The production statistics kept by the Ministry of Armaments includes the following numbers for the war years:

In February and March of 1945 Mauser of Oberndorf was still delivering 40,000 to 50,000 98 k carbines every week.

These vast numbers of 98 k carbines did not disappear without a trace after the German Wehrmacht surrendered. Some of them were taken by the victors (particularly France) for their own use, some were rebuilt into hunting rifles, and the rest were given to many third-world nations as "military aid." There weapons with German code markings ("byf" for Mauser, "660" for Steyr and "dot" for Brunn) still play a certain role today.

A few thousand of the many millions of 98 k carbines remained in Germany. The border patrols and reserve police carried World War II carbines until the mid-Fifties, and the Guard Regiment of the Bundeswehr still presents them when foreign chiefs of state are received.

A single sentence suffices to describe the 98 k carbine: It is a 98 b carbine with a 14-centimeter piece cut off between the upper and lower bands. The weights and measures correspond almost exactly to the World War I 98 (a) carbine: the barrel measures 600 mm and the whole weapon 1110 mm. The weight is 3.9 kg (weapons made during the war were 0.2 to 0.3 kg heavier).

Despite all this, performance comparisons with the 98 (a) carbine are not valid, because the K 98 k was used with different ammunition: the "heavy S cartridge" (sS).

	1940	1941	1942	1943	1944
K 98k	1,351,700	1,358,500	1,363,400	2,149,300	2,261,300

K 98 k: Signs of War Production

Compared to the model carbine of 1935, the last wartime products are inferior, practically trash. At about the beginning of the war, a deliberate lowering of quality began for all weapon components that were not absolutely necessary for shooting: the stock, trimmings, loading system, sight and finish.

At first this worsening of quality was not a sign of need. It was only planned to make carbine production easier and save material, work and machine time. The replacement of originally milled, polished and burnished parts of high-quality steel by those stamped out of cheap sheet metal, spot-welded and finally phosphated grew to ever-greater proportions from one war year to the next. At the same time, the concept of the carbine as a quality product was downgraded to that of utilitarian goods. At least the simplification of production had no influence on firing performance. In this respect

the last K 98 k of 1945 were just as good as those made in peacetime.

The changes in detail:
Stock: As of 1939 there were already no more walnut stocks. Walnut wood was scarce, had to be aged at least three years before use, and gave an average of 10% waste in the end. The cheapest and best substitute was beech plywood, which could be used for stocks without aging and almost without waste. "Plywood stocks" are, of course, 200 to 300 grams heavier than walnut stocks.
Trim and fittings: Instead of the milled flat butt plate that had originally been retained from the 98 rifle for the 98 k carbine in the first place, the plywood stocks had pressed sheet-metal caps that enclose the butt end and protect the wood there from breaking. The perforated stamp plate consists only of two sheet-metal discs held together by a hollow rivet. As of 1944 it disappeared altogether. In place of it, the stamped butt plate gained a hole

Training with the K 98 k at the Döberitz Infantry School in 1938. Bayonet fixed. (Photo: Gronefeld)

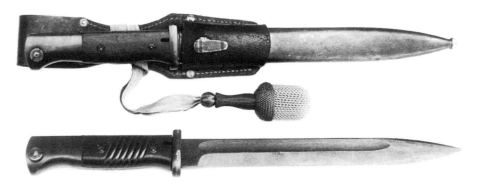

Bayonets for the 98 k carbine: Peacetime version with wooden handles and decoration in company colors, in a steel scabbard (above). Below: Wartime version with bakelite handles (shown here without the scabbard).

in the side to hold the striker point when the bolt was disassembled.

The lower and upper bands, originally milled, were replaced by stamped sheet-metal parts. In the process, the upper band lost its typical form with two attachments. The holding spring between the two bands, which did two jobs, disappeared. Toward the end of the war, the bands were even attached to the stock with wood screws. The bayonet lug (and with it the possibility of fixing a bayonet) was done away with, as was the short cleaning rod.
Loading system: All the parts of the multiple loading system were gradually replaced by sheet-metal parts, stamped and spot-welded. By the beginning of the war, the tiny guard screws that were supposed to secure both main screws had been eliminated.
Sight: The (actually superfluous) second scale on the underside of the sight piece was eliminated, and the fine securing pin through the eyes of the sight base disappeared.
Breech: The two gas exhaust ports on the underside of the bolt, formerly reamed out in an oval shape, were now simply bored out. Toward the end of the war even the guide rib on the breech cylinder, which fit into a groove on the receiver when the breech was opened to guarantee smooth closing of the breech, disappeared.

The 98 k Carbine with Telescopic Sight

Despite the experiences gained in World War I, the German Wehrmacht leaders originally undervalued the importance of the telescopic sight. Sharpshooters with telescopic sights on their weapons scarcely played a role at all in the Polish campaign. Only later on the eastern front, when Soviet sharpshooters made their presence known unpleasantly, was a German reaction forced. As of 1942 six per cent of all 98 k carbines made at the German factories were equipped with mounting rails for the 40 or 41 telescopic sight. (The standard 41 (W) and 43 automatic weapons were also made with mounts for a telescopic sight, and so were some of the assault rifles.)

For the 98 k carbine, two types of telescopic sights were used.

The 39 ("Zielvier") telescopic sight had fourfold magnification and could be adjusted from 100 to 800 meters by the upper milled disc. A locking screw held the disc. The focus was set on a half-round turning handle on the range disc (later on a lever before the rear ring). The mounting attachments were screwed onto the receiver bridge and receiver ring and (presumably) also soldered.

The front attachment was round and conically formed, the rear one as a dovetail. For assembly and

Carbine 98 k, "S/27", of 1938, No. 7118 with telescopic sight 41 (presumably added later).

disassembly the rear part of the telescopic sight had to be turned ninety degrees from the barrel axis. The 39 telescopic sights usually had a reticule in "T"-shape (picket post with crossbars).

The 40 and 41 telescopic sights had only 1.5-fold magnification. The ranges (100 to 800 meters) were marked on a milled ring in the middle of the tube. It was slid into a prismatic rail at the left of the sight base with a one-sided bridge mount, fitting into a spring lock. Reticule in "T"-shaped like the 39 type.

As to the development of the Wehrmacht telescopic sight, General Leeb, Chief of the Army Weapons Office, wrote: "Around 1938 a telescopic sight for the rifle was required. While the Army Weapons Office suggested fourfold magnification, the higher authorities requested one with 1.5-fold magnification and thus developed and introduced that. Here we see a case in which the industry, via very high party positions, forced a technically very good telescopic sight, but one that was militarily unusable, on the Army Weapons Office. During the war the request for a telescopic sight with fourfold magnification was made again; one was introduced around 1942 . . ."

The 39 telescopic sight, completely mounted (above). Below: the mounts on the receiver ring and bridge of the 98 k carbine.

The 41 telescopic sight complete with mounts (above), as well as the milled rail on the sight base to hold the mounts (below).

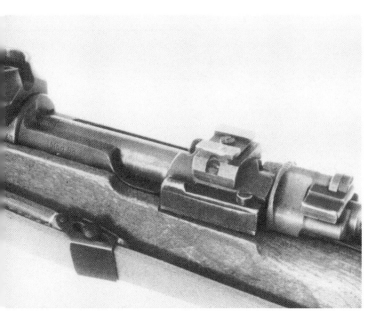

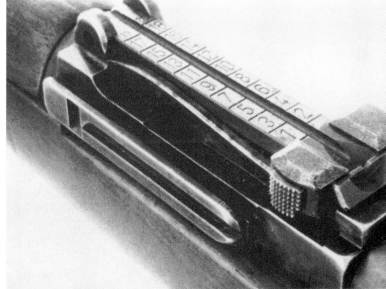

The Volkssturm Carbines

In the last weeks of the war, when everything was chaotic and finally a last sacrifice of children and old men was supposed to rescue the long-lost Third Reich, there arose those "shooting irons" that have become particular favorites of the weapon historian: the "people's" or "Volkssturm carbines." There was no officially accepted model for this weapon, and there were no standards of acceptance. They were usually made of spare parts from regular carbine production. In part, though, machine-gun barrels and box magazines of other weapon types, as well as newly made bolts, were used.

It is no longer possible to determine how many *Volkssturm* weapons were made, or which were made where. One of the few definite bits of information comes from the weapons factory at Steyr. Some 650 "people's carbines" were assembled there in 1945, corresponding to the 98 carbine in function and design. The forestock was simply shortened (as in a hunting rifle) and the upper handguard was left off.

Instead of a sliding sight, the Steyr people's carbine had a simple 100-meter fixed sight on the head of the breech case.

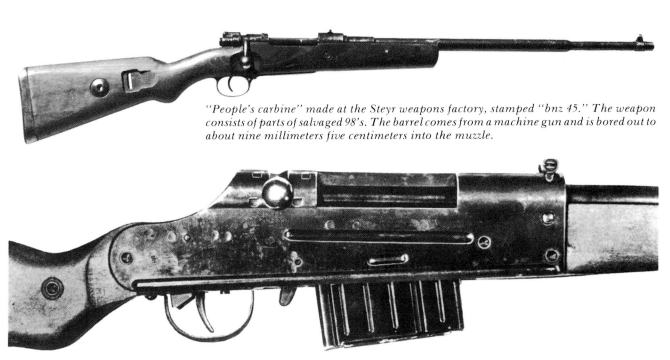

"People's carbine" made at the Steyr weapons factory, stamped "bnz 45." The weapon consists of parts of salvaged 98's. The barrel comes from a machine gun and is bored out to about nine millimeters five centimeters into the muzzle.

"People's carbine" with a primitive sheet-metal mechanism housing, a divided, crudely made stock and a ten-shot changeable magazine from a self-loading 43 rifle. The weapon is made to use sS cartridges. Manufacturer: "Deutsche Industrie Werke A.G.", Berlin. Code: chd.

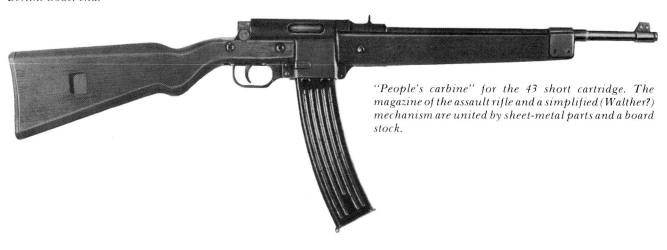

"People's carbine" for the 43 short cartridge. The magazine of the assault rifle and a simplified (Walther?) mechanism are united by sheet-metal parts and a board stock.

The 98/40 Rifle

Type: *Gewehr 98/40*, "jhv 41", No. 7363
Manufacturer: Metal Goods and Weapons Factory "Danuvia", Budapest
Function: Repeater
Overall length: 1105 mm, weight: 4 kg
Barrel length: 610 mm, caliber: 7.9 mm
Rifling direction: Right

Breech: Cylinder breech, Mannlicher mechanism with removable breech head
Safety: Wing, similar to Mauser type
Magazine: Midstock type, similar to Mauser, for five cartridges
Sight: Curved sliding type (100 to 2000 meters)
Standard ammunition: sS cartridge (8 x 57)
Disassembly: Essentially same as 88 rifle

When the limited German-Polish conflict began to grow into a big war during the course of 1940 and more and more new divisions had to be organized in the Reich, the needed supplies of handguns could no longer be met from government production. The conversion of the industry from peacetime to wartime conditions stumbled along in the wake of political events.

In this situation, the Weapons Office at first put captured Polish and Czech weapons into service, as they had Mauser mechanisms without exception and were suitable for use with German cartridges. They were used in the army under the general designation of "Shooting Weapon 98."

To meet further needs, the army leaders finally even dipped into the supplies of their ally Hungary, although the Hungarian Model 35 rifle could not be used without modification. This repeater was made for the Hungarian 8 x 56 rimmed cartridge, and its barrel diameter was only 7.87 mm (the German standard was 7.90). But the German sS cartridge could be fired safely from the narrow Hungarian barrel as long as the chamber was reamed out to fit it.

The Model 35 had a Mannlicher breech with guiding rib and closed cocking, a divided case bridge and a removable bolt head. The locking was threefold, by two lugs on the front end of the bolt and once by the chamber guiding rib. The firing pin head ended with a thumbpiece that made cocking possible after ammunition had malfunctioned. To save weight, the rib guide was hollowed out and the head of the bolt handle halved. In construction and function, the Mannlicher mechanism strongly resembles the old 88 system. While the breech could remain, except for a small modification to the bolt head, the original Mannlicher magazine of the M 35 with clip loading, which projected from the stock, had to be replaced by a loading system that resembled the Mauser type.

For this purpose the Hungarian rifle was given a new trigger guard whose forward extension included a cutout for the magazine base, which snapped into place. The walls of the magazine — unlike the Mauser type — were formed by a simple sheet-metal part. The follower and its spring, though, were like the Mauser model.

So that the improvised magazine could be loaded with chargers, appropriate cutouts were reamed out of the receiver clips bridge, plus a thumb hole in the left wall of the receiver. Further modifications: a new sight with 100- to 200-meter markings for the sS cartridge, a German bayonet lug and a relocation of the sling attachment (which was originally on the bottom) to the left side.

Only the walnut stock divided by a metal step on the neck of the butt and the two wide bands held by

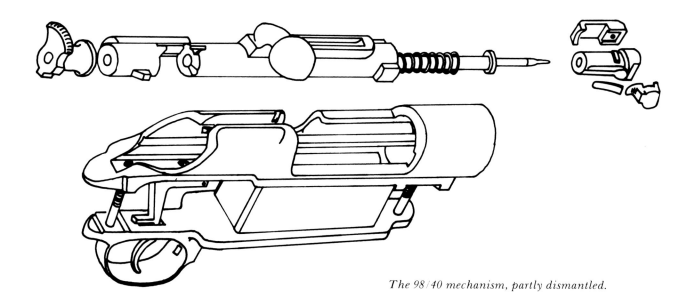

The 98/40 mechanism, partly dismantled.

screws in the stock remained of the old Model 35. The handguard reached from the sight to under the upper band.

After rebuilding, the Hungarian weapon was introduced in the Wehrmacht as "Rifle 98/40."

The Machine and Weapons Factory "Danuvia" in Budapest was occupied until 1943 with modifying the available supplies of M 35 rifles. In addition, though, new weapons on the 98/40 pattern were produced beginning in 1941; 20,000 of them in all are said to have been made. Unlike the modified weapons, they were made with normal German barrels of 7.9-mm caliber.

The 98/40 rifle, with bolt closed and uncocked.

The 33/40 Rifle

Type: *Gewehr 33/40*
Number: 2851, year made: 1942
Manufacturer: "dot" (Brunn Weapon Works, Czechoslovakia)
Function: Repeater
Overall length: 990 mm, weight: 3.8 kg
Barrel length: 490 mm, caliber: 7.88 mm
Rifling direction: Right
Rifling number: 4, width: 2.6 mm
Width of rifling fields: 3.6 mm
Depth of riflings: 0.2 mm
Rifling length: 240 mm

Breech: Model 98
Safety: Model 98
Magazine: Model 98
Sight: Curved sliding type (100 to 1000 meters)
Standard ammunition: sS cartridge (8 x 57)
Disassembly: Same as 98 rifle

For police use and special military services, the Brunn Weapon Works in Czechoslovakia had put their "Carbine 16/33" on the market in 1933. The weapon is 99 centimeters long and has a 49-cm barrel, extremely short for the 8 x 57 cartridge!

After the German advance into Czechoslovakia, the weapons factory at Brunn (Brno) produced both 98 k and 16/33 carbines for the Wehrmacht. In 1940 the Czech weapon with the German designation "Rifle 33/40" was regularly used by mountain troops.

This "rifle", which is actually a carbine, was given a cupped butt plate instead of a butt plate for this special purpose, to give the wood of the stock

Protective sheet-metal panel on the left side of the 33/40 rifle's butt.

better protection. In addition, a protective metal panel was screwed onto the left side of the butt. These changes were made for the special conditions of mountain warfare, in which the carbine often had to serve as a substitute for the "alpenstock."

Aside from the handguard, which extended from the receiver head to the upper band of the 33/40 rifle, the weapon corresponds fairly exactly to the 98 k carbine. To suit the shorter barrel, the sight is only marked for 100 to 1000 meters. The smoke and recoil are said to have been quite unpleasant. It is noteworthy that the Brunn 33/40 rifle had an inner barrel design differing from the German 98 model:

The barrel diameter is smaller (normally 7.88 instead of 7.92), and the riflings are clearly narrower, but deeper, than those of the 98 rifles and carbines. Wartime 33/40 rifles always bore the German code markings "945" or "dot" (Brunn Weapon Works) on the case head. Rifles stamped "945" (made up to 1940) usually still have walnut stocks. After that, from 1941 on (code: "dot"), the stocks were made of beech plywood and the knobs of the bolt handles hollowed out inside. That was probably done to compensate for part of the added weight of the heavy plywood.

The 33/40 rifle: the receiver ring with stamping, and the sight.

German Self-Loading Rifles

The first chapter in the developmental history of German self-loading infantry weapons again involves — how could it be otherwise? — the Oberndorf inventor and manufacturer Paul Mauser. When he, at the age of 58, introduced his new self-charging "C 96" pistol to the Kaiser at the Charlottenburg firing range on August 20, 1896, Wilhelm II was so impressed by the performance of the weapon that he particularly urged the inventor to build a self-loading infantry rifle. When the Kaiser wanted to know how soon the new weapon could be expected, Mauser replied: "Perhaps in five years, Your Majesty."

This scene at Katharinenholz has been recorded in correspondence. It shows that Paul Mauser had not yet thought seriously at that point of designing a self-loading weapon for infantry ammunition. For the problems that he was to meet in his last great task were so great that he was not able to solve them completely in five or, in fact, in the last eighteen years of his life.

It was not Paul Mauser alone who was stumped at that time by the task of building a light, simple, not overly sensitive self-loading rifle for military use. All the other designers, inside and outside Germany, who attempted it created test models of only limited usefulness.

Perhaps it was a mistake on Paul Mauser's part that from the beginning he settled on the principle of recoil operation that worked so well in his self-loading pistol. He avoided gas-operated systems, which were already known then. He had no desire to bore a hole in the barrel to obtain the gas pressure needed to unlock the breech. Paul Mauser — so it is recorded — is said to have feared that the vent in the barrel would burn out after long use and thus make the functioning and safety of the weapon questionable.

This — unfounded — fear on the part of the old master of German weapon designers stayed in other minds for four decades. Thus it happened that, in the mid-Thirties, the German Army Weapons Office in Berlin announced a competition for a gas-operated semi-automatic system working in other ways than by boring out the barrel.

The Mauser Recoil Operated Self-Loading Rifles to 1913

How eagerly Paul Mauser plunged into this assignment given him personally by the Kaiser is shown by his countless self-loader patents since 1898. In a straight line, as always in his life, he built on the tried and true, in this case on his C/96 pistol. From this design he originally took the combined recoil of the barrel and breech to an unlocking point at which the two parts separated, the barrel returning to its original position while the breech at first continued backward and then was brought forward by the closing spring. In the process, the bolt ejects the fired case and brings another cartridge in.

In sequence, Mauser concentrated between 1898 and 1908 on self-loading rifles with movable, "sliding" barrels. Then he recognized that he was on a dead-end course. Rifles with sliding barrels necessarily had to be heavy and unhandy. In 1909 the first prototype with a fixed barrel appeared, locked by two support levers behind the breech block, their positioning controlled by the inertia of the pusher on the breech lid. This model was later to play a modest role in World War I as the "Mauser self-loading carbine." Paul Mauser's last test model of 1913, with a fixed barrel and inertia-controlled turning-lug lock, on the other hand, gained no attention.

The problem that all Mauser recoil loaders had in common was unreliable cartridge ejection. The strong charge of the S cartridge developed such high gas pressure in the barrel (up to 3224 atmospheres) that the "inflated" cartridge cases stuck to the wall of the cartridge bed. Mauser recoil loaders worked only with greased ammunition and were thus of only limited use for military purposes.

The Mauser Self-Loading Carbine

Type: *Selbstlader-Karabiner Mauser*
Number: 486, year made: 1916
Manufacturer: Mauser Weapons Factory A.G., Oberndorf on the Neckar
Function: Semi-automatic, recoil operated
Overall length: 1140 mm, weight: 4.3 kg without magazine
Barrel length: 610 mm, caliber: 7.9 mm, number of riflings: 4
Rifling direction: Right (other data same as 98 rifle)
Breech: Recoil operated bolt carrier and bolt with firing pin and movable support lug locking
Safety: Lever on right side under breech
Magazine: Midstock removable type for 25 cartridges (each weapon had three magazines)

Sight: Curved sliding sight (200 to 2000 meters)
Standard ammunition: S cartridge (8 x 57) with core (S.m.K.)
Initial velocity (V_{25}): 830 meters per second
Disassembly: Swing trigger guard out, lift out magazine, pull cover latch (at left rear on the lid) out to left, take off cover. Remove locking supports. Draw bolt back to rearmost position. Unite cocking piece with recoil spring and breech block with "coupling wrench" (or other suitable tool) and lift out together.
Safety: Lever vertically downward. Release: Lever diagonally forward.

Paul Mauser's self-loader of 1909 probably would never have reached the hands of German soldiers if the airship and aircraft crews of World War I had not had such an urgent need of a faster-shooting weapon than the 98 carbine. The installation of machine guns still caused technical problems at first, and the Mauser self-loader seemed like a useful transitional solution. The fact that the weapon could only use greased ammunition was no problem for use in airships or airplanes, since filling the magazine on board was no problem, nor did the cartridges get dirty.

The half-stock with the unusual wooden hand-grip in front of the magazine was made for the particular conditions of firing on board. The weapon measured 1140 mm, just as long as the 98 (a) carbine, but somewhat heavier (4.3 kilograms without the magazine) because of its heavy receiver. The big, curved magazine for 25 cartridges had reinforcing ridges which also helped move the cartridges along.

The magazine is released by a magazine release button (at the front of the trigger guard). In the process, the trigger frame, along with the guard, swings downward. Only in this position can the weapon be loaded, unloaded or dismantled.

The top of the barrel is covered from the face of the receiver ring to the forward end of the stock by a full-length handguard that has an opening for the carbine sight (200 to 2000 meters). The angled bolt carrier has a cocking lever on its top, with two ridged wing grips. Farther back, under the flat receiver cover, is the movable lug activator. It has two curved guides by which the position of the support lugs is controlled. The roughened side surfaces of the lug activator project up from the breech housing at the left and right.

When the weapon pushes against the shooter's shoulder on firing, under the effect of the recoil, the movable lug activator remains in its old position on account of its inertia. For its position in the weapon, thrown backward by the recoil action, this means that the pusher is now one to one and a half centimeters further forward than before the shot. Guided by the curves of the activator, the front ends of the two support lugs swing out behind the bolt carrier and let it slide through between them.

The trigger guard, which swings out, has important tasks in the functioning of the weapon. Here the 25-shot magazine is being changed.

A Self-Loading carbine; right side: cocking grip (1), cutout for clip guide (2), lug activator (3), cover latch (4), safety lever (5).

Functioning of the locking flaps, shown here on an early Mauser prototype: Flaps support the bolt carrier (above). Flaps spread apart and let the carrier through them until it touches (below).

When it moves back against the recoil spring, the empty cartridge case is extracted and ejected. When it moves forward, the bolt carrier, under the pressure of the recoil spring, pushes a new cartridge out of the magazine and into the chamber with its bolt face, and the firing pin in the inside of the bolt is cocked.

At the end of its forward movement, the lug activator, under the pressure of a small coil spring in the lid, returns to its starting position, which means it turns the support lugs back to the locking position behind the bolt carrier. The weapon is again ready to fire.

Four actions are necessary for charging:

1. Swing out the trigger guard and take out the magazine.

2. Press the breech pusher forward by its side panels.

3. Draw back the bolt carrier by the cocking grip (it stays in the rear position only when the trigger guard is swung out).

4. Put in the full magazine and replace the trigger guard (the bolt carrier is thus released automatically. It goes forward and brings the first cartridge into the chamber).

The Mauser self-charging carbine can be fired only when the breech is properly locked. A bar to the right of the breech housing makes the connection between the activator and firing pin and acts as a kind of safety catch.

The regular safety is switched on and off by a turning lever at the right behind the trigger guard.

In the operator's manual for the Mauser self-charger it is said specifically: "The chamber and the receiver surfaces must always be lubricated with the grease that is provided. Likewise it is absolutely necessary that the cartridge cases be *lightly greased* in their entire extent."

This condition, as well as the complicated loading procedure, earned the Mauser self-charger its scarcely flattering sobriquet of "war-service-capable necessity-help-weapon."

How many self-charging carbines were made at Oberndorf in 1916 and 1917 can no longer be determined. Estimates range between 1000 and 2000.

The most important parts of the action: Pusher with guiding curves (22) for the guiding apparatus of the two locking flaps (31), receiver cover (24), bolt (32), bolt carrier (33), firing pin (42), recoil spring (46).

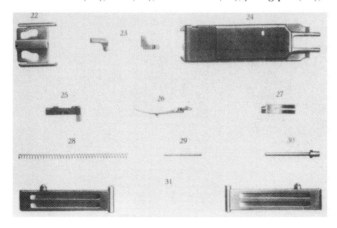

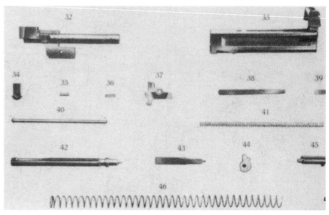

Self-Loading Aircraft Carbine 15 (Mondragon)

Type: *Flieger-Selbstlader-Karabiner* 15 (Mondragon)
Number: 806
Year made: No date
Manufacturer: Swiss Industrial Company (SIG), Neuhausen
Function: Semi-automatic gas-operated
Overall length: 1150 mm
Weight: 4.1 kg without magazine
Barrel length: 580 mm
Barrel caliber: 7 mm
Number of riflings: 4
Rifling direction: Right
Rifling depth: 0.11 mm
Rifling length: 220 mm
Breech: Turning cylinder, with seven lugs, with hammer lock

Safety: Lever ahead of trigger guard
Magazine: Built-in ten-shot midstock magazine can be replaced by inserted drum of 30 cartridges
Sight: Frame-leaf sight (300 to 2000 meters)
Standard ammunition: Cartridge 7 x 57 (Mauser). Initial velocity (V_{25}): 650 meters per second
Disassembly: Turn safety on (push lever ahead of trigger guard backward)! Turn holding screw for bottom section of breech case to the left, press holding spring, turn base to side and remove. Loosen handle lock, unhook coupling. Draw handle and turning cylinder breech out of the case to the rear.
Notes: Three drum magazines came with each weapon. The 7-mm special ammunition was made under German contract in the Belgian Ammunition Factory at Liège.

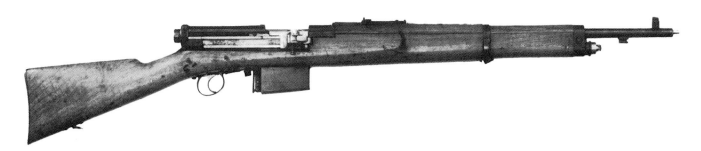

The "Self-Loading Aircraft Carbine 15", as it was called in German military use, or the "Mondragon Self-Loading Rifle 1908", as the weapon was originally called, is certainly a historically noteworthy design, though it, like the "Mauser Self-Loader", was usable only under certain conditions. In the service manual issued by the Prussian War Ministry in February of 1917, it was stated: "The Fl.-S.-K. 15" is . . . only a war-use-capable necessity-help weapon. It can only be used to advantage when the weapon can be carefully examined and maintained by technically trained hands before and after being used."

So one may well ask why the Ministry in Berlin ever introduced this weapon, which was made for special 7 mm ammunition too. It was probably because Mauser of Oberndorf, while its factory was operating at full capacity in 1915-16, could not produce enough self-loading carbines to equip the rapidly growing numbers of warplanes.

In this situation, someone in Berlin recalled an old offering of the Swiss Industrial Company (SIG) in Neuhausen, of a shipment of self-loading rifles of the Mondragon system, which had been ordered by the Mexican government years ago but had been neither paid for nor collected. Under the pressure of war circumstances, Berlin took them without testing them for long.

Having reached this point, we should look backward at the lively early history of this weapon. In begins at the beginning of the Nineties of the past century in Tacubaya, Mexico. There the artillery officer Manuel Mondragon had taken up what was then the most difficult of technical challenges on the world of weapons, that of building a self-loading rifle.

Mexico was a country without any tradition of weapon building, without industrial production capacities and without technical intelligence. In this agrarian state, filled with social tensions, the dictator Porfirio Diaz had ruled since 1876. He promoted the work of his officer Mondragon because he hoped to equip his army with self-loading rifles, the first in the world to be so armed, thus giving his regime security from within and without.

Thus the amateur designer Mondragon was already experimenting with self-loading rifles when the professionals in the USA and Europe were still fully occupied with eliminating the last faults of the repeating rifle.

General Manuel Mondragon (1855-1922)

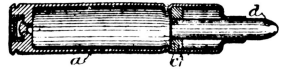

17,307. September 11, 1894. **Ammunition.** RUBIN, E., Thun, Switzerland.

Cartridges, small-arm &c.—To enable the size of the explosion chamber *a* to be increased at the instant of discharge, the bullet *d* carries a detachable collar *c¹* which moves forward a short distance with it when the cartridge is fired.

Patent application for the Rubin case with detachable collar (c1).

The Rifle Nobody Wanted

In 1893 Mondragon presented his first gas-operated rifle in 6.5-mm caliber. Fifty pieces were ordered from the Swiss Industrial Company in Neuhausen and tested in Mexico.

In 1894 a further order of 200 examples of an improved model followed. It had the then-sensational caliber of 5 millimeters. Manuel Mondragon had meanwhile made contact with the well-known Swiss ballistic expert, Colonel Rubin. Rubin, the director of the Swiss Weapons Testing Center in Thun, observed the Mexican's pioneering work with interest and helped him solve his ammunition problem. Whether Mondragon was well-advised to choose such an extreme cartridge as the 5.2 x 68 (Rubin) for his already troublesome rifle may well be asked. The high-speed bullet of the Rubin cartridge, weighing only six grams, needed a small detachable collar inside the cartridge case to be able to take up the energy of the powder charge.

In his next, improved prototypes, Mondragon returned to more practical types of ammunition. He experimented with the 30-30, 7.5 mm Swiss ordnance cartridge, and finally with the 7 x 57 Mauser military cartridge.

The Mondragon self-charger failed a British test in 1903. In the first test a part of the weapon broke. In the second test the weapon at least fired, but the testers complained that the rifle only fired when it was freshly cleaned. Besides, they found the weapon too complicated.

After further improvements, the Mexican Army finally accepted the Mondragon rifle with the 7 x 57 Mauser cartridge. It was designated the "Model 1908", and a first order of 4000 was to be built at the SIG. The contract of May 1908 agreed on a price of 160 Swiss Francs apiece, almost three times as much as a repeater rifle cost at that time.

When the first 400 Mondragon rifles arrived in Mexico in 1911, there were new complaints. In the centenary publication for the hundredth anniversary of the SIG it was said: "It transpired that the functioning of the self-charging rifle is so dependent on the quality of the ammunition, which plays a similar role in the self-charging weapon to that of the fuel in a combustion engine. Even when this knowledge was acted on, the weapon still remained sensitive, as it fired a long and powerful cartridge and its dimensions were limited . . ."

In short, the Mexicans wanted to cancel the rest of the order, the SIG halted production and now had the problem of getting their money.

The remainder of the Mondragon rifles — there could scarcely have been more than 1000 of them in

The drum magazine for the "Self-Loading Aircraft Carbine 15", complete (above) and disassembled.

all — now entered World War I, a few going to the USA and the greater part to the artillery depot in Spandau. As had the Mexicans and the Swiss, the Germans now tried to make the Mondragon rifle useful for warfare. The weapon was modified to take a German made 7 x 57 cartridge. It also was given an insertable drum magazine with a capacity of thirty cartridges, built basically like the special magazine of the 08 pistol.

This took almost two years. Only early in 1917 did the weapons reach the troops. For every airplane, to be on the safe side, two self-loading 15 carbines were provided simultaneously, as frequent failures were to be expected.

The Firing Process

The Mondragon carbine is a self-loading rifle with fixed barrel and vent (1), a gas operated turning bolt (2) that is connected detachably by an unusual coupling piece, or cocking handle (3), formed as a handgrip, to the gas piston (4).

165 millimeters in back of the muzzle, a small part of the combustion gases resulting from firing stream through a 1-mm hole bored in the barrel (5) into the gas cylinder below it (6). The gases push the piston (4) back, simultaneously pressing the recoil spring (8) that encircles the piston rod. The piston rod (4) expands into a right angle (7) in its last third, so that the holding pin (9) at its end can be held by the tooth (10) of the coupling piece (3).

The handle piece's oval lugs (12) fit into the corresponding screw-shaped grooves (13) of the bolt (2). The lugs give the breech cylinder the turn it

needs to be unlocked. It has already ended after the gas piston has moved back about 10 mm.

The locking piece (14), held back up to this point by a projecting, falling connection, now enters the corresponding hole (15) bored in the turning bolt (2) and prevents any turning motion in further backward movement. The turning bolt (2) and coupling piece (3) are thus locked together in any further backward motion (in the process, the fired cartridge case is drawn out of the bed and ejected). The recoil spring around the piston rod (8) brings about closing by working in the opposite order (as the bolt head takes a new cartridge out of the magazine and pushes it into the chamber).

To lock the turning bolt (2), the sprung locking bolt (14) is pushed back again through the raised guiding system. When the cocking handle moves

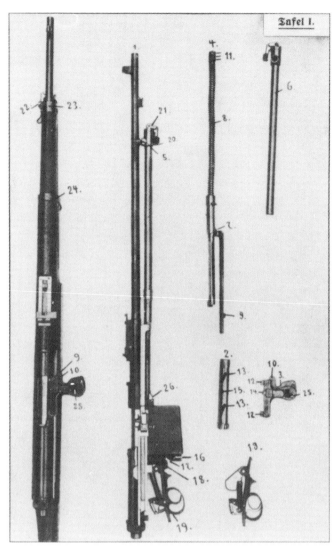

Self-Loading Carbine 15 partially disassembled. The numbers are explained in the text.

further forward, the oval lugs turn the turning bolt into its locked position. Then the weapon is ready to fire again.

The small slide under the stock, between the trigger guard and the magazine, is pushed backward to act as a safety catch, and pushed forward to release.

The Self-Loading Aircraft Carbine 15 has a built-in ten-shot box magazine with removable cover, follower and spring in the Mauser manner. It can be filled by chargers from above. When the drum magazine was used, the magazine lid was taken off and the follower and spring fell out. The drum magazine was inserted in the magazine stock until the locking spring (17) rested on the rear end of the magazine stock.

In case problems with the gas cylinder, gas piston or pressure rod appear, the connection between the coupling piece (3) and gas-pressure system can be detached with the help of the spring lever (10). Then the weapon can be used like a repeater rifle with straight bolt.

The Self-Loading Aircraft Carbine 15 has a hammer lock (19), which is mounted on the trigger panel, similarly to many break action hunting guns. The hammer is cocked again by moving the cylinder breech backward. When shooting, it strikes toward the end of a long, uncocked firing pin that lies loose in the bolt.

The breech of the "Self-Loading Aircraft Carbine 15", with cocking grip and coupling piece. The breech is shown locked (left) and half opened, with two of the three radial lugs visible on the front surface of the bolt (right).

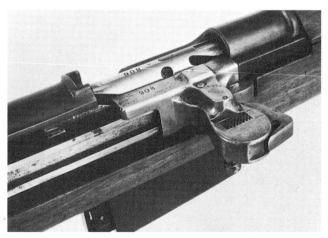

Bad Firing Performance was the Rule

The sevenfold locking of the bolt by three lugs on the front (which fit into grooves in the receiver) and four at the rear (that fit under the closed, tube-shaped rear section of the receiver) seems strikingly complicated to us today. And the arrangement of the gas drive is much too complex. Since Mondragon probably believed then, ninety years ago, that as perfect gas-tightness as possible had to be achieved, he equipped the gas piston with three copper reinforcing rings, similar to the piston rings of a combustion engine. In addition, the hollow piston rod had to be filled at regular intervals with weapon grease, "lubricated" regularly. We know now that it can be much simpler.

About the accuracy of the Mondragon rifle, it says in the service manual of 1917: "The unified construction of this self-loading weapon results in greater variations in the targeting position than exist in previously introduced weapons. Only deviations of more than 20 cm from the normal group are corrected . . ."

German Self-Loading Rifles Between the Wars

All the nations that fought in World War I had tested self-loading rifles (the USA alone tested almost a dozen different designs), but the results were never encouraging.

Although almost all self-loading systems known today were already designed and described in patents before 1914, the necessary experience that would turn these many good ideas into useful front-line weapons was lacking.

At the stage of development that prevailed then, the two principles of recoil and gas-operation were only usable within limits. At least they worked when it was a matter of setting up light weapons for the usual powerful standard cartridges. In the recoil loaders there were difficulties with case ejection, and the gas loaders then had very complicated jet systems and rods. They were also sensitive to dirt.

The most practical solution to the operation-problem, taking gas out through a hole bored in the barrel wall, was taboo in Germany in the Twenties

Cutaway drawing of the mechanism (above) and the gas cylinder (below) of the Mondragon self-loader.

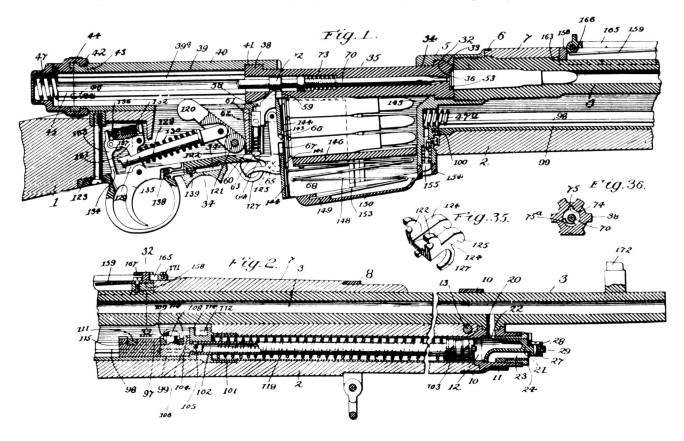

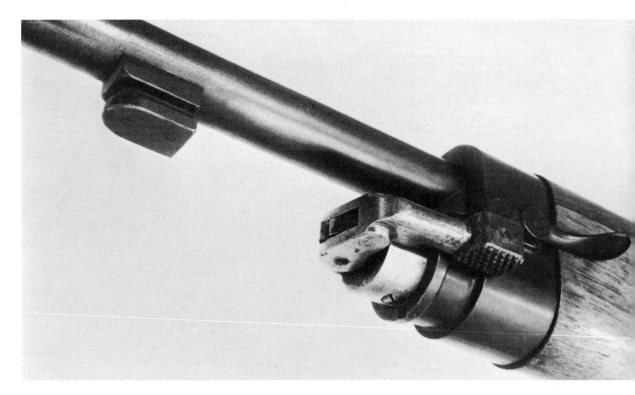

The front end of the stock with the cap of the gas cylinder. It was removed for servicing with the help of the ridged locking handle. The smooth lever above it to the right allows the removal of the upper band.

and Thirties because it was feared that a bullet would lose too much of its driving force through this vent. This fear was unfounded in view of the excess power of the long 7.9 mm cartridge. This prejudice against the gas-pressure loader at the Weapons Office crippled the German designers. There were also the Treaty of Versailles' weapon ban and the limitation of the army to 100,000 men, which eliminated any noteworthy need for self-charging rifles.

But at the end of the Twenties, when news of extended testing of self-loaders in Czechoslovakia, the USA and the Soviet Union became known, the development that had been interrupted in 1919 commenced — hesitantly at first — again.

In 1929-30 the Army Weapons Office approved two self-charging rifles for the long cartridge, which designer Karl Heinemann of "Rheinmetall"

and the Biberach machine-shop owner Heinrich Vollmer had presented. Heinemann's recoil operated weapon had a movable barrel and a lateral toggle-joint action, while Vollmer's rifle was gas-operated with an impact pressure vent at the muzzle.

In firing at the test center in Kummersdorf, both weapons achieved nothing better than limited success. The Reichswehr officers did not know just what to do with the new device that they had not ordered. For in Berlin nobody as yet had a concept of how heavy and expensive a self-loading rifle might be and by what system it should work.

Five years later — meanwhile the first short cartridges and the first fully automatic machine carbine had come upon the scene — the Weapons Office still had not worked out any detailed guidelines for acceptance. When Mauser went in a

The Mauser "G 35": An experimental self-loader with a movable barrel. In 1935 two slightly different versions of this weapon, Types "S" and "M", were tested but finally declined by the army.
(Photo: Vollmer Archives)

new direction in 1935 with a semi-automatic for the long cartridge, there was a small troop test with 600 rifles, to be sure, but nothing happened from there on. The Mauser "G 35" was a recoil loader with a movable barrel, developed by the Oberndorf designing team of Altenburger and Schweikle. The Vollmer "M 35" and Walther "A 115" prototypes, two gas loaders, also were unsuccessful. Testing of both weapons was halted in 1938. At that time the impending war was already expected, and at the Weapons Office they thought it better to concentrate at first on mass production of the tested but somewhat outmoded Model 98 repeater, despite the fact that the USA (Garand) and the Soviet Union (Simonov, Tokarev) had already introduced rapid-fire rifles to their infantries by this time.

Only after the war began, during 1940, did the Army Weapons Office request that the firms of Mauser in Oberndorf and Carl Walther in Zella-Mehlis present new suggestions for a semi-automatic gas-operated infantry rifle. The sS cartridges were specified as ammunition.

In addition, the Weapons Office had prepared, for the first time, a catalog of requirements that the designers had to meet. Here are the three most important points that defined the future self-loading carbine.

1. The barrel may not be bored to extract gas.
2. No part on the upper surface of the receiver may move along with the automatic loading movements.
3. If the automatic mechanism fails, the use of the rifle must not be halted. In the case of such a failure, the rifle must be manually loaded similar to that of the Model 98.

These requirements were at odds with reality. They narrowed the designers' parameters and prevented optimal solutions.

Only two years later did Berlin deviate from these requirements. But in the meantime two weapons that corresponded to the Weapons Office's requirements wholly or at least in part had arisen in Oberndorf and Zella-Mehlis: the Mauser and Walther 41 self-loading rifles.

The Mauser Self-Loading 41 Rifle-G 41 (M)

When the designers in the Mauser "Vl" department (test department for light weapons) set out to turn the Weapons Office's assignment to reality, they were able to build on a self loader prototype that had taken shape in the years after 1936. In any case, the weapon had to fit the new requirements, and the Mauser people were determined to take the Weapons Office's standards literally. The project was designated "S 42/D" (S 42 was then the code for Mauser).

Since the barrel could not be bored out for gas extraction, the self-charger was given an impact pressure vent on the muzzle. When the bullet had passed the jet openings, combustion gases were collected in the tube. The collected gas pressed on a steel ring that was pushed over the muzzle and sealed the tubular lengthening of the muzzle vent.

Under the pressure of the gases, the piston moved back. It slid a few centimeters along the barrel and in the operating rod covers, in the direction of the receiver, and thus pushed back an operating rod that lay under the barrel and, with its forked end, reached into the receiver assembly. The operating rod acted on the bolt carrier, pushed it back and thus indirectly brought about the release of the breech.

The cylinder breech of the G 41 (M) consisted of the bolt carrier and bolt. The bolt bore on its forward end two symmetrically located locking lugs. It was linked with the bolt carrier by a steep threading and could turn 90 degrees for locking and releasing. The bolt carrier, on the other hand, could only move forward and back in the direction of the barrel axis.

When the operating rod pushed back against the resistance of the recoil spring, the breech head, guided by the threading, was forced to turn 90 degrees. The locking lugs came out of their positions in the head of the receiver. In the process, the empty case in the chamber was first loosened and finally — moved by the remaining gas in the barrel — pushed out to the rear. The bolt assembly and carrier then ran farther back together, compressed the closing coil spring and ejected the empty case out. In the following frontward moving of the bolt assembly, a new cartridge was lifted out of the magazine in the usual way and pushed into the chamber, after which the bolt head was forced to turn to its locked position again. The weapon was ready to fire.

Instead of a cocking handle such as is customary in automatic weapons today, the 41 (M) rifle had a bolt action mechanism, which — fitting the prescription of the Weapons Office — could be activated as in the 98 carbine. During automatic operation the bolt action was disengaged.

With its wooden stock, short handguard and fittings, the 41 (M) rifle was very much like the 98 k carbine. At first glance, only the unusually shaped gas cylinder at the muzzle, the built-in magazine projecting from the stock, and the unusual length of the receiver catch the eye.

The front part of the case more or less resembles the breech case of the Model 98. The rear section is box-shaped with a lifting lid. The magazine holds ten cartridges. It could be filled from above by using clips, like the 98 rifle. The safety was activated by a turning lever that was set into the surface of the breech lid. A lever on the right side of the breech served to release the breech lock when the magazine was empty.

There are only vague references to the fate of the 41 (M) rifle. It is definite that troop test took place, presumably in groups of the Waffen-SS on the Italian front. The 41 (M) rifle is among the rarest weapons of World War II, as only 20,000 of them were built, and are scarcely to be found today, even in the large collections in English and American museums.

The Walther 41 Rifle - G 41 (W)

Type: *Gewehr 41 (Walther)* - G 41 (W)
Number: 4743
Year built: 1943
Manufacturer: "duv" (Berlin-Lübeck Machine Factory, Lübeck plant)
Function: Semi-automatic gas loader with muzzle vent
Total length: 1138 mm
Weight: 4.6 kg with empty magazine
Barrel length: 550 mm
Barrel caliber: 7.9 mm

Number of riflings: 4
Rifling direction: Right (other data same as Model 98)
Breech: Straight action with flap locking and hammer lock
Safety: Lever safety
Magazine: Built-in box for ten cartridges
Sight: Curved sliding sight (100 to 1200 meters)
Standard ammunition: sS cartridge (8 x 57)
Disassembly: see last section of text

The requirements that the Weapons Office had established for the Wehrmacht's first self-loading rifle have already been mentioned. In 1941 the firm of Carl Walther in Zella-Mehlis also presented its model. The weapon went into troop testing with the designation of "Rifle 41 (W)."

The (M) and (W) weapons are very similar in their weights and measures, as well as in their appearance. The Walther model too, with its long wooden stock and fittings, was made to resemble the 98 k carbine.

Since the barrel could not be bored into, the Walther designers set the same odd-shaped gas apparatus on the muzzle that has already been described for the Mauser model. They did, though,

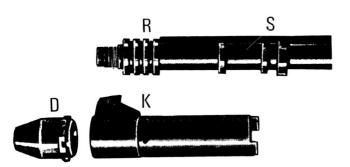

Gas drive of the 41 (W) rifle: Above: Barrel with operating rod (S), ringed piston (R) and threading for the jet (D). It secures the seat of the operating rod cover (K).

move the operating rod (which was under the barrel of the Mauser model) to the top, under the long plastic handguard, which extends from the upper band of the G 41 (W) almost to the receiver. The front end of the receiver, which also formed the base of the sight, lay over the barrel axis and was pierced parallel to it. The reamed-out slit held the end of the pushrod, which was stamped out of sheet metal.

It is interesting to see how bravely the Walther staff surmounted the Weapons Office's regulations. It was one of the conditions that no moving part could be located on the surface of the receiver. In addition, a repeater operation had to be present in case it was needed. But in the Walther rifle the heavy breech lid moves back and then forward after every shot. And instead of the old-fashioned but accepted bolt handle for repeating, which the Mauser designers had made their model to fit, the Walther rifle had only a short cocking handle on the right side of the bolt carrier.

Strictly speaking, the Walther test model should have been rejected by the Weapons Office because it did not fulfill the requirements. But reason triumphed over nit-picking in Berlin. The Walther G 41 worked better than its competitor. Above all, because the Walther breech was more efficient and also more economical than the Mauser's. In comparison calculations for the 41 (M) and (W) rifles, the Walther saved 100 minutes of work time, which amounted to about ten Reichsmark. A lot of money, when one realizes that only 56 RM were being paid for the 98 k carbine at that time. The "Berlin-Lübeck Machine Factory" received the order, presumably to produce 70,000 41 (W) rifles for a troop test on the front. The weapons had to be delivered at the end of 1942 or the beginning of 1943.

The Walther self-loading rifle had a straight bolt action with support flaps for locking. Its essential parts were the cylindrical bolt with two movable locking flaps, the steering piece that lay inside the bolt with its firing pin and a bolt carrier, which slid on two rails to the right and left of the housing.

The bolt carrier lid had a projection firing pin that reached through a long cutout into the inside of the hollow cylinder. There the point connects with the steering piece. So the movement of the lid (transmitted by this point) controlled the steering piece and thereby also the locking flaps and the cylinder. The weapon had a hammer lock that was housed in a box under the mechanism, The hammer struck on a firing pin extension set diagonally in the breech piece.

The Firing Process

On firing, gases collect in the impact pressure vent or "jet" at the muzzle. The gas pushes back the ring-shaped piston and the pushrod lying behind it. In the process, the rear end of the pushrod moves out of its course in the head of the breech housing and strikes against the front edge of the heavy breech lid. This follows the impulse and slides back on its rails; its point takes the steering piece in the chamber cylinder with it. In the process, the locking flaps are forced out of their positions in the head of the breech case and swung into the breech cylinder. Thus the lock is released.

As the breech lid moves farther back, its point pulls the breech cylinder with it. The lid and cylinder move back together, and the empty case is

The disassembled breech (G 43). From top to bottom: Bolt with locking flaps, operating spring and guide rod, steering piece with striker, lid and removable upper part of the breech housing.

pulled out of the cartridge bed and later ejected. In addition, the hammer and closing spring are cocked, as in the usual self-charging pistols.

In the ensuing frontward motion of the breech, the cylinder takes a cartridge from the magazine with it and seats it into the chamber. Finally the point of the lid pushes the flaps back into the locking position. The weapon is ready to fire.

At the rear end of its mechanism the 41 (W) rifle had a safety lever with an extension that activated the trigger mechanism. To set the safety catch, the wing was pushed to the right. In the rifles up to serial number 8000, setting it was possible but forbidden, because the firing mechanism could be damaged. As of number 8001, setting the safety catch was prevented by a locking lever when the hammer was released.

The magazine of the G 41 (W) held ten cartridges and was built in. Thus it could only be filled from above by using clips. A small locking lever on the left side of the breech lid was used for loading and for dismantling the bolt. If the lid, including the breech cylinder, was drawn back by the cocking handle, the whole mechanism was locked in an opened position.

Breech Disassembly

The following — abridged — instructions are taken from the operating manual, *The 41 Rifle*, issued by the Army Weapons Office on February 16, 1943:

"Pull the bolt backward and lock it with the bar. — Safely! — Press the leading pin projecting backward out of the bolt case forward and lift the breech up from the case. — Place the rear end of the breech on a firm foundation and push the leading pin into the case. — Push the bar on the lid to its resting position at left. — Let the bolt and its lid, under spring tension, (!) slowly slide upward out of the housing . . ."

The rest of the disassembly of springs and bolts is so simple that it does not need to be described here. Assembly was done in the opposite order.

The 41 (W) rifle was heavy, and especially at the muzzle, not easy to handle, because of the awkward gas cylinder on the muzzle. The built-in magazine, which could be filled only with clips, forced the rifleman to pause to load it, which lessened the advantage of the rapid-fire rifle. The breech, though, worked so well that the Walther firm was given the green light for further development of the "G 41 (W)" at the end of 1942. The result was the "43 rifle."

The 43 Rifle (G 43)

Type: *Selbstlade-Gewehr 43 - G 43*
Number: 4025
Year built: 1944
Manufacturer: "ac" (Carl Walther, Zella-Mehlis)
Function: Semi-automatic gas-operated rifle with barrel vent
Overall length: 1120 mm
Weight: 3.9 kg
Barrel length: 560 mm
Barrel caliber: 7.9 mm

Number of riflings: 4
Rifling direction: Right (other data same as Model 98)
Breech: Straight action with flap locking and hammer lock
Safety: Wing safety
Magazine: Ten-cartridge removable magazine
Sight: Curved sliding sight (100 to 1200 meters)
Standard ammunition: sS cartridge (8 x 57)
Disassembly: Like 41 (W) rifle

The Army Weapons Office's old prejudice against the self-loaders had prevented the designers at Mauser and Walther from presenting fully functional weapons in 1941. This statement is proved by the example of the Mauser model, in which all the conceptions of the Weapons Office were realized. And the Walther model was only capable of development because its creators had circumvented two decisive requirements of the Weapons Office.

When the German troops on the eastern front in 1941-42 saw themselves exposed to the unexpected effects of Soviet self-loaders and had no weapon that could come near equaling the enemy's rapid-fire rifles, the German designers were finally given the permission and freedom to make further developments.

Suddenly the short-cartridge machine carbine project emerged, and even the self-loading 41 (W) rifle, still undergoing large-scale troop testing at that time, was finally allowed to make progress. The Walther designers reworked the model thoroughly again and developed a new model that was lighter, more effective and less costly.

The self-loading 43 rifle was introduced by the Wehrmacht in 1943 and went into series production in the same year at both Walther and the Berlin-Lübeck "duv" factory. Since this model can often

The 43 rifle, complete and with its system removed.

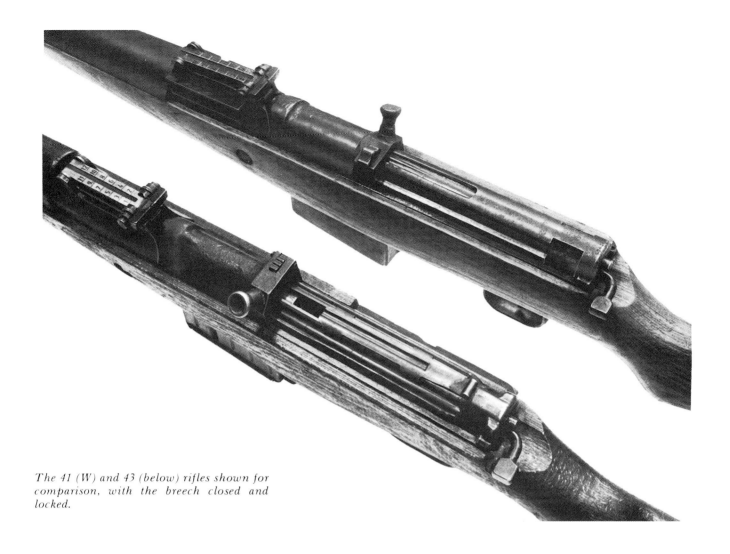

be found in collections to this day and examples built in 1945 have turned up, one may assume that total production was about 500,000 pieces. Exact statistics exist only for 1944: 324,300 pieces.

The self-loading 43 rifle was based on the slightly modified breech and firing system of the 41 (W) model. New features are the "gas drive" via the bored barrel, the half-stock and the removable magazine for ten cartridges.

The changes in detail:

Gas drive: About 30 cm behind the muzzle, a hole was bored into the top of the barrel. In firing, a small part of the combustion gases escape through this channel. The gases are led backward and flow into a gas chamber that is attached over the barrel axis and parallel to it. The chamber is fitted with a cylinder to receive a very short piston. Gas pressure expands in the cylinder driving the short piston violently back. The piston strikes the operating rod which extends backward into the receiver, this thrust imparted is transmitted to the bolt carrier on top of the bolt. The following releasing and loading functions take place exactly as in the 41 (W) rifle.

When the bullet has left the barrel and the pressure in the gas cylinder sinks to zero, it is pushed back into its original position by a coil spring wrapped around the transmitting pin. The new gas system with the bored barrel, which the Army Weapons Office opposed for so long, proved to be so insensitive to dirt that regular cleaning and maintenance was not asked of the soldiers. According to regulations, occasional maintenance was to be carried out only "by weapon-technical personnel."

Breech: The cocking lever on the bolt carrier (at right in the 41 (W) rifle) is now on the left side. In exchange, the pusher for the breech lock moved to the right. The removable upper part of the bolt case, still reamed out of solid material in the 41 rifle, consists of a stamped sheet-metal part in the G 43. In the G 41 the long perforation in the surface of the bolt case, into which the point of the lid fits, was

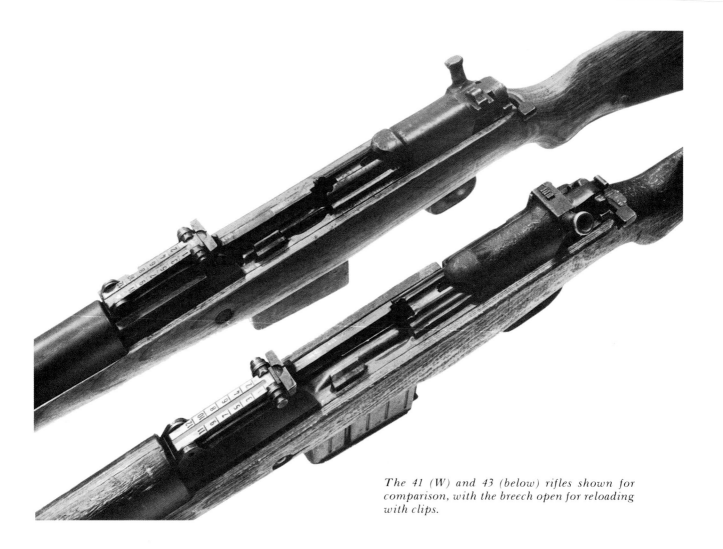

The 41 (W) and 43 (below) rifles shown for comparison, with the breech open for reloading with clips.

closed by a slide coupled with it. The slide accompanied the lid when it moved and thus made sure that no dirt could get inside the breech system. The slide of the G 43, a simple sheet-metal part that fit into the stiffening grooves of the bolt case, is no longer coupled with the lid. The slide can be closed by hand if necessary. For the next shot it has to be pushed back again by the lid.

The lid and the breech frame of the 43 rifle were raw components of which only the functioning surfaces had to be machined. The marks of rough filing can be seen on the surfaces. In war production functioning capability mattered; finish did not.

Repeating apparatus: A box magazine made of sheet metal and holding ten cartridges was pushed into the stock from below and held by a snap with a ridged head. The magazine could also be filled from above with clips while in the weapon (when the breech was drawn back and locked, as in the G 41).

Stock: The plywood stock in the rear part of the 98 k carbine was copied here. It ended about 25 cm

behind the muzzle. A covering band held the barrel, stock and handguard together and carried the swivel on the left side. The wooden handguard had two slits on each side near the front end. When the gas in the cylinder had done its work, it could escape into the air through these openings.

A bayonet was no longer planned for the G 43. The front third of the barrel ran free, and the foresight was mounted on a relatively high socket under a tunnel. A short external thread on the barrel could hold a cup discharger for firing rifle grenades, a silencer or a blank cartridge device.

Telescopic sight mount: On the right side of the breech housing there is a cast and precisely machined T-shaped rail about seven centimeters long. This rail holds the foot of the 43 telescopic sight mount (with fourfold magnification). The 41 (W) rifles were already prepared in series production for the mounting of a telescopic sight (at that time still the "40/41 telescopic sight" with 1.5-fold magnification). The G 41 (W) had two sym-

188

The removable magazine of the 43 rifle, made to hold ten cartridges.

mm caliber, followed in quick succession by other successful Walther pistols.

In World War I the staff of the factory grew from 75 (in 1914) to 500 workers, and the number of the machines from 50 to 750. After 1919 the firm took up the manufacture of calculating machines but also built civilian sporting weapons and a series of pistols (PP, PPK). At the end of the Thirties Fritz Walther was able to make another great success with the 38 army pistol. But he also devoted himself to the development of self-loading rifles, and later a machine carbine as well. In 1939, when World War II began, the Walther works employed a total of 2000 workers. By the end of the war the works were completely destroyed.

Fritz Walther fled westward ahead of the advancing Soviets and began anew in a shoemaker's shop in Heidenheim in 1947. Today his firm is located in Ulm on the Danube. Walther sport and defense weapons again have a worldwide reputation.

Fritz Walther (1889-1966)

metrically located rails for this purpose, to the left and right of the sight.

The quickly and precisely firing self-loading 43 rifle made a name for itself as a sharpshooter's rifle in World War II. The G 43 was originally chosen to gradually replace the 98 k carbine, for whose ammunition it was made. But the surprising success with the machine carbine and the short cartridge created a whole new situation.

Carl Walther Weapons Factory, Zella-Mehlis

The family of Carl Walther can trace its gun-smithing tradition back into the early 18th Century, but the world-famous weapons factory in Zella-Mehlis (near Suhl in Thuringia) arose only in the years after 1886, founded by Carl Walther (1858-1915). The firm's chief and his three sons, Georg, Fritz and Erich, brought the business from its small beginning to a high level of industrial development quickly.

Fritz Walther soon proved to be a talented designer. In 1908, at the age of nineteen, he designed the first usable German self-loading pistol in 6.35

Die Walther Werke in Zella-Mehlis 1939

The Walther factory in Zella-Mehlis in 1939. (Photo: Walther Archives)

Fallschirmjäger Rifle 42 (FG 42)

Type: *Fallschirmjäger Gewehr 42* (FG 42)*
Manufacturer: Krieghoff of Suhl
Function: Automatic gas-operated rifle with bored barrel
Total length: 975 mm
Weight: 4.98 kg (without magazine)
Barrel length: 500 mm
Barrel caliber: 7.92 mm
Number of riflings: 4

Rifling direction: Right (other data same as Model 98)
Breech: Turning cylinder with two lugs
Safety: Switch on handle operates on trigger
Magazine: Removable 20-cartridge magazine, inserted from left
Sight: Diopter (100 to 1200 meters)
Standard ammunition: sS cartridge (8 x 57)
* All statistics refer to the final Model III.

The 42 Fallschirmjäger rifle, the third model with bipod behind the muzzle and wooden handguard and butt.

The developmental history of the Fallshirmjäger (Paratrooper) rifle is as unusual as that of the weapon itself. The FG 42 arose at about the same time as the test-model machine carbines made by Walther and Haenel, with which it has — aside from the ammunition — much in common. One must wonder today whether it would not have been more sensible then, in the interests of the troops and the industry, to combine the two developments. Then, of course — and this can be said with assurance today — the Fallschirmjäger rifle never would have existed.

With its elegant design, its simple technology and problem-free handling, the machine carbine, the later 44 assault rifle, was superior to the Fallschirmjäger rifle. And the two weapons were more or less equal in performance. The greater power of the sS cartridge scarcely made a difference in the Fallschirmjäger rifle, as the barrel was only fifty centimeters long. The muzzle velocity of the bullet, which amounted to 785 meters per second for the 60-centimeter carbine barrel, fell to 685 meters per second in the FG 42. And only by technical tricks could the unpleasant side effects of muzzle flash, puff and recoil be kept at a bearable level.

The lighter short-cartridge bullet of the assault rifle was, at 650 meters per second, scarcely slower, and its effect was fully sufficient within the practical usable range of 600 meters. The small plus in performance that the sS cartridge gave the FG 42 was balanced in the assault rifle by greater readiness to fire, because the shooter's supply of ammunition and the magazine capacity were one-third greater.

So why was the Fallschirmjäger rifle ever built? The answer is found in the confusion of authority and the jealousy that existed between the Luftwaffe and the Army, which — as in most armed forces — also existed in the German forces during World War II.

Engineer Otto Schulze, a retired Lieutenant Colonel, was a specialist in on-board weapons in the Reich Air Ministry and took a major part in the development of the FG 42. In a letter that the *German Weapon Journal* published in 1970, he portrayed the remarkable early history of this weapon. It began in 1941, the year in which German paratroopers, despite heavy losses, conquered the island of Crete. Otto Schulze wrote: "One day the Fallschirmjäger turned up at Section GLC-6, On-board Weapons, at the office of Air Senior Staff Secretary Ossenbück and explained that, with the 98 carbine and the machine pistol, they were not sufficiently armed . . . They needed a weapon that was not longer than 100 centimeters, that could be used as a sharpshooter's rifle with a telescopic sight and was suitable for single shots and sustained fire. In addition, the weapon had to be able to fire rifle grenades and be usable as a club in close combat and thus be insensitive to damage. The weight of the weapon had to be that of the K 98.

It was explained that our section was responsible only for on-board weapons, and that the Army Weapons Office was in charge of infantry armaments.

Thereupon the gentlemen presented their wishes for a new paratrooper rifle to the Army Weapons Office.

The gentlemen in charge of the Army Weapons Office explained that such a request was utopian, and that they would have to make do with the coming self-charging rifle (G 41).

So they came back to our office . . . We were really disappointed that the Army Weapons Office had turned them down and believed we could fulfill the paratroopers' requests . . ." Balancing on the outer limits of their authority, the men of the Air Ministry set out to turn the paratroopers' idea to reality. That was a brave undertaking. For the development of a universal weapon, as described above, had to seem just as difficult then as the breeding of the "egg-laying wool-milk pig." At least if the sS cartridge was to be used as ammunition.

The Air Ministry wrote to all possible armaments firms and tried to interest them in the project. In the end, though, they found only two genuine and a half-hearted applicant for the job. The Krieghoff firm of Suhl and Rheinmetall-Borsig wanted to develop new weapons. Mauser of Oberndorf, on the other hand, offered a rebuilt aircraft "MG 81" that fulfilled almost all the conditions but, with a weight of 6.5 kilograms, was much too heavy and had to be eliminated.

Fallschirmjäger Rifle 42, first model with bipod in the middle of the barrel, sharply angled handle and metal butt. (Photos: Kaltmann)

Characteristics and Function

The Rheinmetall rifle works as a gas loader with bored barrel and a gas piston system underneath. It has a turning cylinder breech with double lug locking. The box magazine for twenty cartridges is introduced from the left.

When the bullet, having been fired, has passed the boring in the middle of the 50-centimeter barrel, a part of the combustion gases flows into the impact tube underneath. The gases spread out and press the front end of the long cylindrical breech carrier, which acts as a piston in the gas tube — the carrier then moves back.

At the rear end of this carrier is the firing pin holder. It directs the point of the firing pin forward against the end of the barrel. The turning breech cylinder is pushed over the rigid firing pin. Its jacket surface is cut by a screw-like guiding curve which the step of the firing pin holder enters. Thus as the breech carrier moves forward and back, it guides the turning movements by which the breech cylinder is locked and released.

Louis Stange, born in Sömmerda in 1888, died in Hassleben near Erfurt, DDR, in 1971, worked as a designer for "Rheinmetall" in Sömmerda from 1907 to 1945. His best-known creations are the MG 34 and FG 42. (Photo; Rheinmetall)

Individual parts of the breech: Turning cylinder with lugs, extractor and guiding curve (above), breech carrier with cutouts for the trigger rod, firing pin, firing pin spring and breech cap. the prototypes from Krieghoff and Rheinmetall arrived in Berlin. The Rheinmetall model, developed by the well-known machine-gun designer Louis Stange at the Sömmerda works in Thuringia, set the pace.

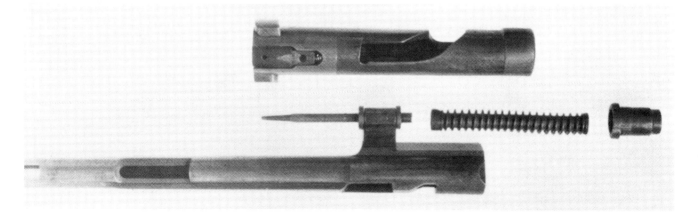

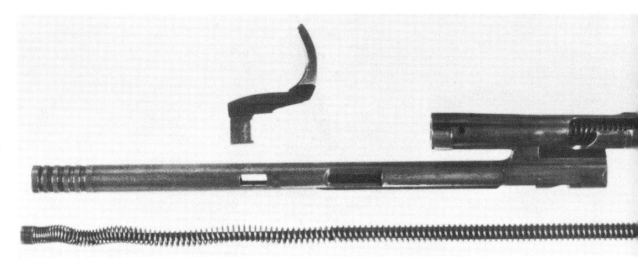

The complete breech, plus cocking handle (above) and closing spring with rod (below).

The special features of the FG 42 system are the different starting positions that the breech takes in single and sustained fire. For precision firing in semi-automatic single shots, the weapon is fired with locked breech. In sustained fire, though, the breech remains open in its rearmost position after every shot, so that the hot weapon cools more quickly. Open breeches — always the rule in air-cooled machine guns — are to prevent cartridges from igniting unintentionally in the hot barrel ("cooking off").

The clever combination of "open" and "closed" firing systems was achieved by the designer Louis Stange by simple means: The trigger bar in the handle contacts sockets in different sides of the breech carrier in single and sustained fire. So that the rod always enters the right socket, it is turned to the correct position in the handle by the fire selector switch.

This system requires two coil springs. The larger — guided by a rod — functions as a closing spring on the breech carrier. In sustained fire, it goes into action alone. For single shots, though, when the breech carrier is held 14 mm ahead of its foremost position between shots, a second, smaller coil spring must also move the firing pin on its short path. The power of the closing spring, which is almost fully expanded in this position, would no longer be sufficient for sure ignition.

The guiding curve on the underside of the breech cylinder ends in a short straight piece, that is, the two lugs on the head of the breech cylinder have

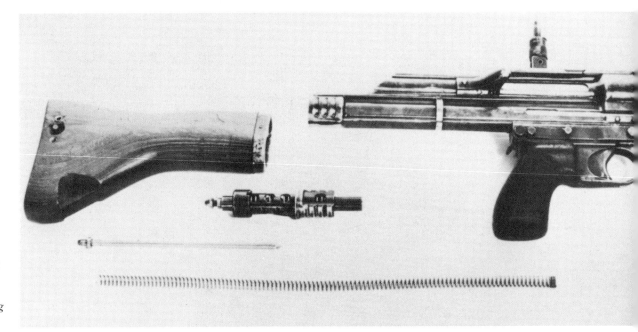

The detached butt, buffer, rear case, closing spring and rod.

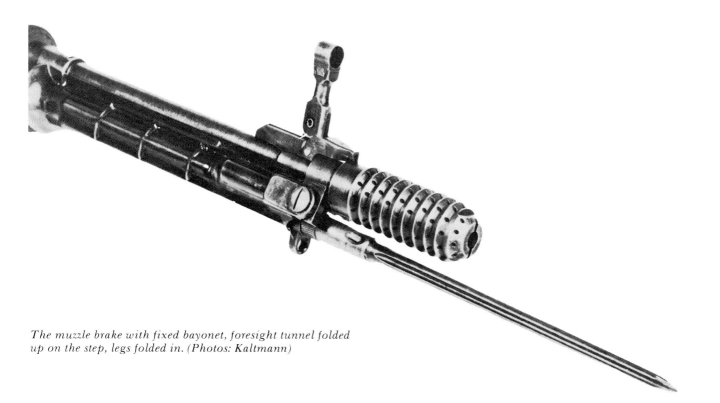

The muzzle brake with fixed bayonet, foresight tunnel folded up on the step, legs folded in. (Photos: Kaltmann)

already turned back into their locking positions when the breech carrier covers the last 1.5 centimeters of its path with the firing pin.

Since the Fallschirmjäger rifle must stand the long sS cartridges in sustained fire as well, it has all the characteristics of a light machine gun: a folding bipod, an added handle that forms a unit with the trigger guard and holds the trigger mechanism, and a sprung shoulder butt.

The straight lines of the weapon, without the otherwise customary bend in the butt, makes it better able to bear the recoil on the shooter's shoulder and eliminates the danger of the muzzle rising in sustained fire. But this design also necessitates a sight line that is unpleasantly high above the barrel.

This disadvantage, to be sure, is balanced by the diopter sight, new at the time, with its 53-cm sight line. The rear viewer, relatively close to the shooter's eye, is adjustable in height by using a milled ring, and there is a target hair in the foresight tunnel. Both parts of the sight are mounted on removable sockets.

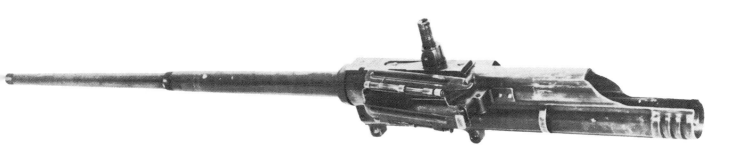

The left side of the housing with the magazine shaft, barrel without gas cylinder, diopter step folded up.

In place of the diopter sight, a telescopic sight can be mounted. The weapon's housing has a standard flat prismatic bar on its upper surface for this purpose.

As could be expected, the short FG 42 had a strong recoil, blinding flash and loud puff from the start, three unpleasant characteristics that — according to reports that agree — add up to an unbearable level under sustained fire. These were probably the main reasons why this brilliantly designed weapon had to be changed three times before it was ready for use. Louis Stange had already fitted the first model with a muzzle brake with a cup-shaped silencer over it, but this setup was not yet effective enough and was changed in Model II. To decrease the recoil, Model III was finally given a new shoulder butt with a longer spring distance.

At the same time it was possible to decrease the rate of fire, originally too fast, from 900 to about 600 rounds per minute. This, of course, caused the weight of the breech to be increased and its path to be lengthened. In the process the weapon became markedly heavier and longer.

The Fallschirmjäger rifle changed externally as well. The bipod, attached shortly before the middle of the barrel in Model I, gained a new attachment point behind the muzzle, and the shoulderstock, originally made of sheet metal, was — like the handguard — made of wood. The cartridge ejector opening was given a lifting lid and a deflector that directed the flight of the ejected case forward. The handle, sharply angled backward in Model I, returned to the usual pistol form in Model II.

The angled handle had originally been designed for firing downward. The *Fallschirmjäger* had hoped to be able to commence firing on defenders as they floated down on their parachutes. But the very first tests showed that this was an unfulfillable wish. A witness reported that after the very first bursts of fire from the FG 42, the recoil sent the paratroopers twisting and turning in all directions.

The pike bayonet of the Fallschirmjäger rifle remained unchanged, as it obviously worked well. It had a long, four-sided dagger blade and was always fixed on the weapon. In its resting position it lay under the barrel with its point backward. This bayonet, reminiscent of earlier French models, is a curiosity among German infantry weapons.

Tests in which Everything Went to Pieces

We have gotten ahead of the changes to the model which resulted from testing. Lieutenant Colonel Otto Schulze wrote of them: It "was our duty to place this weapon at the disposal of the Army Weapons Office again for testing . . . The tests (in Kummersdorf) were carried out so that nothing remained intact . . . After a few days they brought the weapon back to us in pieces.

On the basis of this experience, the components involved were immediately strengthened at their weak points by Rheinmetall and the new weapon was presented again. This repeated itself several times. Thus it was possible to develop a usable weapon fairly quickly through stringent testing."

But the Fallschirmjäger rifle, created in the tense area between Army and Luftwaffe, did not get off to a good start. Although the FG 42 held its own in an official comparison shooting test against the com-

A paratrooper with FG 42 on the day of Mussolini's liberation from the Gran Sasso in the Abruzzi on September 12, 1943. In the background is one of the freight gliders in which the commandos landed on the mountainous terrain.
(Photo: Bundesarchiv)

petition of the 98 carbine, 41 self-loading rifle and machine carbine and gave the best results in accuracy, it was still not officially introduced in 1943. Only after the personal intervention of Reich Marshal Göring with Hitler — as 1943 changed to 1944 — was permission finally given for a small series.

The firm of Krieghoff in Suhl (now in Ulm), which had not had its own prototype accepted, was finally given a contract to make 5000 FG 42 rifles, using stamped sheet-metal parts and carbon steel. And only in the last year of the war did each *Fallschirmjäger* unit receive a few GF 42 rifles. The plan to give the *Fallschirmjäger* units a new high-performance uniform weapon had long since failed.

The *Fallschirmjäger* carried out their most spectacular mission in the liberation of the Italian dictator Mussolini from the Gran Sasso on September 12, 1943. The *Fallschirmjäger* commandos that landed on mountain slopes in freight gliders and stormed the mountain hotel in which Mussolini was being held prisoner, were completely armed with FG 42 rifles. But not a single shot was fired in this hair-raising action.

It is not easy to assess the importance of the FG 42 in the history of weapons. With a somewhat longer barrel and belt feeding, the weapon would have been an outstanding super-light machine gun. Louis Stange knew that and had also built a prototype with belt feeding. The breech mechanism of the FG 42 was so good that the Belgians used it after the war, as did the Americans almost twenty years later in their Model 60 machine gun.

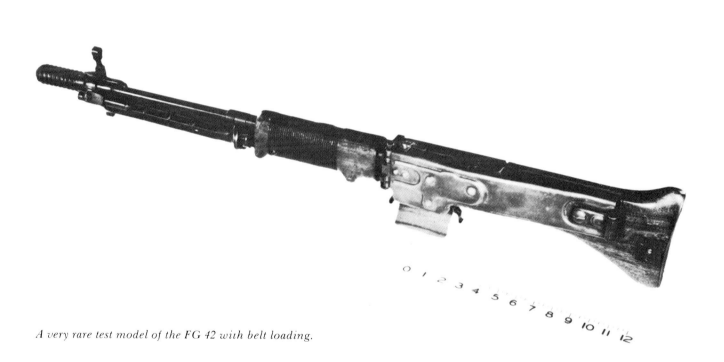

A very rare test model of the FG 42 with belt loading.

The German Short Cartridges

Only at the end of the Thirties, half a century late, did the military specialists in Germany recognize that something had gone awry in the development of ammunition for handguns: the performance of the 7.9-mm standard cartridge with the 57-mm case and 12.8-gram bullet could only be utilized fully in a machine gun. For the 98 k carbine, the main weapon of the infantry, the cartridge was much too strong.

What good is a rifle whose effective range extends to 2000 meters if in practice a rifleman can scarcely hit a human target beyond 500 meters at all?

The 1890s would have been the right time for these considerations. When the high-performance flake powder types were developed in Germany at that time, the voluminous case of the 88 cartridge, originally conceived for the weak Rottweil Cellulose Powder, could have been shortened without harm. Instead of that, the old cartridge was filled to the brim with the powerful new powder. In 1903, when the light pointed bullet was added, the cartridge was so overloaded that it was no longer possible to build a light, short weapon for this ammunition (See: Early History of the 98 a Carbine).

The only weapons in which the long cartridge could have their full effect were machine guns. And since they soon had a decisive effect on the tactical scene in World War I, the Reichswehr's Weapons Office used all its power to develop the machine gun further. The handguns of the infantry moved back to the second row in terms of their significance. Only in these terms is it comprehensible that officialdom turned to the short cartridge only hesitatingly, and ultimately too late.

The only valid argument against the short cartridge was a certain difficulty in supplying. For if they were introduced, an additional type of ammunition would have to be kept in stock and delivered.

But the advantages won out. Quite apart from the saving of material in ammunition manufacturing, the short cartridge created the conditions for the development of a completely new type of weapon: the short and inexpensively produced machine carbine, which could be used for either single shots

or sustained fire and showed practically no recoil even under sustained fire. These requirements could not be fulfilled with the long cartridge. (The example of the "FG 42" Fallschirmjäger rifle will not be cited here as an argument to the contrary, as this weapon was comparatively expensive and complicated, and because it could not utilize the power of the long cartridge at all economically.)

Development Before 1930

The short infantry cartridge is regarded throughout the world today as a German invention. And that is correct when we start at the point at which the first (Geco, 1935) short cartridge was ready for series production.

On the other hand, the Czech designer Karel Krnka and the Swiss F.W. Hebler were already working on the construction of a "miniature rifle" in 1892; it was a repeater for military purposes, and was to give practically equal ballistic performance but be one-third shorter and lighter than the usual army rifles of the time.

In his work *Firearms*, the Czech weapon historian Jaroslav Lugs quoted a letter in which Hebler wrote that the cartridge that went with it was "three times lighter, the gas pressure and recoil only half as great . . . as before . . ."

While Krnka and Hebler had only thought of reducing the customary repeating rifle of the times to reasonable size and weight, in World War I there was also a desire to increase the firepower of the individual infantryman. He should be able to fire faster at particular moments in battle than was possible with the repeater rifle.

The long "08 pistol" with its adjustable butt and drum magazine, the comparable model of the Mauser military pistol "C 96", and lastly the Bergmann machine pistol of 1918 certainly fired rapidly but were limited by weak pistol ammunition to effectiveness only at short range. For a light automatic handgun that could fire both bursts and aimed single shots over ranges of several hundred meters, a completely new type of ammunition was required.

Captain Piderit, Assistant to the Rifle Testing Commission, expressed this lesson of World War I in 1918 in the essay "The Practicality of Introducing a Short Cartridge." Piderit attracted some attention, but at first nothing happened. The internal political confusion in Germany, the weapons ban of the Treaty of Versailles, and probably also the Reichswehr leadership's lack of interest slowed the development. Only in 1927 were there said to have been initial experiments with a short cartridge at the "Berlin-Karlsruhe Industrial Works" (successor to the old DWM), of which, unfortunately, no data have survived. This work could have involved a predecessor of the 7-mm cartridge with which Walther and Mauser later experimented in developing the machine carbine.

The first authenticated report of a short cartridge that fulfilled all the current concepts of this type of ammunition comes from 1934-35. At that time the "Geco" Works in Karlsruhe-Durlach developed a short cartridge on their own. It was presented to the Army Weapons Office in 1935 along with a fully automatic test weapon and improved onto production stage. Competition came later from the "Polte" short cartridge of 1938, which had been developed at the request of the Army Weapons Office. More about these two most important German types will be found below.

"Geco" and Polte

Geco: Director Winter of the "Gustav Genschow & Co. A.G." developed the first genuine short cartridge ("Kurz-Patrone") in 1934-35. It had a caliber of 7.75 mm, a bottle-shaped case 39.5 mm long, and a pointed bullet weighing nine grams. The gas pressure amounted to about 3000 atmospheres, the bullet's velocity (V_{25}) was 695 meters per second. The whole cartridge originally was 55 mm long (58 mm as of 1938). The zenith at 300 meters was 285 mm. During the course of later tests "Geco" reduced the cartridge caliber from 7.75 to 7.62 mm in 1942.

The shape of this cartridge almost completely corresponds to the Soviet short cartridge (Kalashnikov), which was for thirty years the standard cartridge of the Warsaw Pact (and still is), of Red China and many other nations. The Geco short cartridge was tested by the Army Weapons Office in conjunction with the "Vollmer Machine Carbine

The "Geco" M 35 short cartridge (left) and the Soviet short cartridge (right). The resemblance is not accidental. (Photo: Vollmer Works)

M 35" until 1938 and approved. But it was never introduced by the Wehrmacht.

Polte: One of the greatest German ammunition factories, the firm of Polte in Magdeburg, received an assignment from the Army Weapons Office in 1938 to develop a short cartridge too. Polte solved the problem in the same year by shortening the 7.9 mm standard cartridge. The bottle shape, the measures of the cartridge base and the mouth of the case were retained unchanged. But the case length was shortened to 35 mm at first and later, in its final form, to 33 mm. The pointed bullet (with an iron core during the war) weighed seven grams (6.95 grams), the powder charge originally weighed 1.4 grams, and two grams as of 1943. The entire cartridge was 45 mm long, the bullet had an initial velocity of 650 meters per second (later 685 m/sec) and still penetrated a steel helmet at a range of 700 meters. The Polte short cartridge, with a painted iron case, was introduced by the German Wehrmacht in February of 1943 as "Pistol Cartridge 43 m.E." (with iron core), for use in the "M/P. 43" (later the "Assault Rifle 44").

There were still other short-cartridge developments: The Walther firm, for example, experi-

"Pistol Cartridge 43" (Polte). An original package from 1944, plus a clip.

mented until 1938 with a 7-mm cartridge, and Mauser made tests from 1942 to 1944 with a DWM development in the same caliber. Neither type progressed beyond the testing stage.

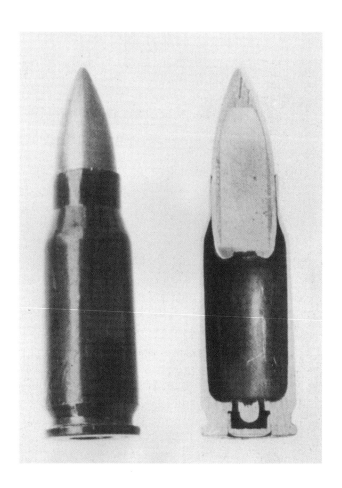

A short cartridge with painted iron case and iron-core bullet, complete and cutaway.

The "Vollmer" M 35 Machine Carbine

The Vollmer Machine Carbine, Type "A 35/II" of 1938.

Without a doubt, the first German machine carbine did not originate from Oberndorf or Suhl, as one might have expected. It was the creation of an inventive outsider, who had many good ideas but too few connections to make a name for himself in the realm of weapons. He was Heinrich Vollmer, a

Heinrich Vollmer (1885-1961), manufacturer and weapon designer.

machine-shop owner and designer from the Swabian town of Biberach on the Riss.

In World War I Vollmer had invented a beltless cartridge feed for the 08/15 machine gun, which was not introduced only because the war ended first. Afterward, despite the Allied ban, Vollmer developed a machine pistol (the production of which he had to turn over to ERMA in 1931 for economic reasons), and one of the first really light machine guns, the introduction of which was planned by the Reichswehr in 1929.

In the same year, the prototype of a self-loading rifle for the 7.9-mm cartridge was finished at Biberach. This weapon, to be sure, was produced regardless of the market, since the Army Weapons Office was not thinking of introducing semi- or fully automatic rifles at that time. The Vollmer self-loading rifle gained nothing more than attention at its introduction in Berlin but was later to gain importance as the basis of Vollmer's first machine carbine. It happened this way:

On February 13, 1935 Heinrich Vollmer received a letter from the retired Major Runnebaum, a directing colleague of the Weapons and Ammunition Works of Gustav Genschow (Geco) in Berlin, who knew Heinrich Vollmer personally. Runnebaum wrote of a secret matter that had suddenly become serious: "It concerns the prompt production of a *locked* machine pistol for special ammunition, which has been created by a colleague in our company . . ."

The short cartridge, later designated M 35 by the firm, has already been described (caliber 7.75 mm, case length 39.9 mm, 9-gram pointed bullet, V25 695 m/sec). Heinrich Vollmer seized the opportunity and, in just four months, built his first machine carbine for the new ammunition. The weapon was 96 cm long, weighed 4.2 kilograms, had a slightly curved removable magazine for 20 cartridges and looked a lot like the 98 k carbine.

The "Machine Carbine 35" (works designation) had a long wooden stock and wooden handguard, both held together by bands. As yet nobody thought of using stamped sheet-metal parts.

Vollmer had taken the task of producing a "locked machine pistol" literally and designed an "open" weapon whose breech only moved forward, pushed a cartridge into the bed, locked itself and fired when the trigger was pulled.

This "open" design, long since proved in the unlocked "blow-back" systems of machine pistols, has the advantage of letting cooling streams of air flow through the hot barrel during pauses in firing. In addition, cartridge self-ignition, such as could occur in hot closed systems, was impossible. A certain disadvantage nevertheless appeared in aimed single shots, because the weapon was shaken when pulling the trigger by the breech moving forward quickly.

The two types of firing (single and sustained) and the safety catch could be combined in a selector switch on the right side, above the trigger guard.

The Vollmer machine carbine functions as a "remaining gas-pressure loader" by an original system. Since bored on barrels and gas-piston systems were still unwanted in Germany in the Thirties, Vollmer invented the following:

Just in front of the muzzle, and exactly in the barrel axis, lies a ball-shaped jet with a bore about the size of the caliber. When the bullet passes this jet, gas pressure builds up briefly and pushes the jet some 20 to 25 mm forward into a case that slides over the barrel.

The jet's forward motion is transmitted by a rod hidden in the stock under the barrel to a sliding lever that turns the movement and throws the breech back. In the process, the upper arm of the lever moves out of a groove on the right side of the head of the breech case and pushes back the side guiderail of the breech carrier. When the breech carrier goes into motion against the resistance of

The muzzle area with foresight and jet system. The transmission rod is in the box under the barrel.

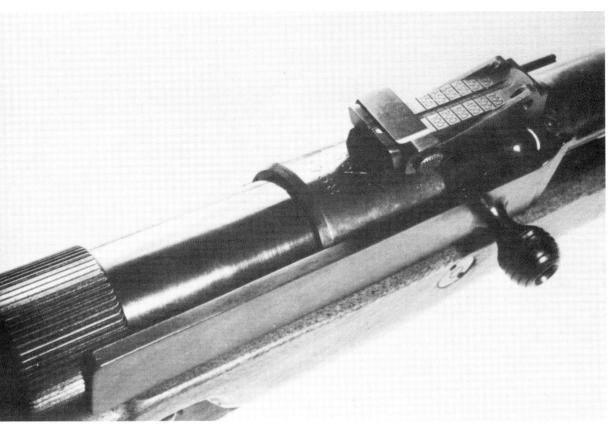

The opened breech, with the heavy guide rail with its cocking handle in the foreground.

As seen from the right side: Next to the cocking handle, the front edge of the guide rail is visible. The sliding lever strikes against this edge.

the closing spring, it forces the breech head, which has a thread inside it, to turn. The two lugs on the breech head come out of their beds, the breech is released and moves back, aided by the gas pressure still present in the barrel. The empty case is ejected to the right. In its rearmost position the breech is caught by the trigger (for single shots) or immediately moves forward again for the next shot (in sustained fire).

At first the Vollmer machine carbine fired 700 to 1000 rounds per minute, much too fast for practical use. But at the same time, that was the only justification that resulted from the tests at the test center of the Army Weapons Office in Berlin-Kummersdorf.

In his Model 35/III Heinrich Vollmer solved the problem of too-rapid fire with a pneumatic brake element, and in the summer of 1938 the Vollmer weapon with this "air brake" satisfied all the requirements that the Army Weapons Office had set. Twenty-five machine carbines (costing 4000 RM apiece handmade) were delivered for a small troop test. But then everything ended at once. On August 30, 1938 the Army Weapons Office suddenly withdrew from the matter; someone at the highest level had presumably objected.

One Vollmer machine carbine, with which work on improving the Geco short cartridge had been done at Genschow in Berlin, including during the war, fell into Soviet hands in 1945. The occupiers had 20,000 rounds of ammunition made for it, meanwhile reduced to 7.62-mm caliber, and shortly thereafter brought out their own, surprisingly similar short cartridge.

The last Vollmer Type "A" 35.III:. In the center of the picture is the pneumatic brake element by which the rate of fire could be regulated. (Photo: Vollmer Works)

On the Way to the Assault Gun

In retrospect it looks as if the Army Weapons Office played a dirty trick on the Genschow and Vollmer firms when, in the autumn of 1938, it withdrew from further testing of the 35 machine carbine and the Genschow short cartridge. The ammunition and weapon were ready for series production after three years, but Berlin justified the halting of the project by citing the possibility of iminent war. The situation, they said, did not at the moment allow any further experiments with new weapons. All energy had to be concentrated on the production of proved types.

We know today that this justification — to put it mildly — was an excuse. For the Weapons Office had meanwhile given two other firms secret developmental assignments for a short cartridge and a machine carbine.

Why the Weapons Office rejected the Geco short cartridge at that time will probably always be a riddle. Why it rejected the Vollmer machine carbine can be guessed: The weapon fulfilled all the performance requirements, to be sure, but it was probably not too well suited to mass production because of several very expensive components. Thus the Weapons Office threw away a three-year advantage over other countries and, in the spring of 1938, began again at the beginning in the development of the machine carbine.

At the beginning of the year the ammunition firm of Polte in Magdeburg had received a contract to design a new short cartridge. Since the development was based on the basic form of the long sS cartridge and could use available machines, the miniaturization succeeded in a short time. In April the ammunition tests had already proceeded to the point at which the Weapons Office could give a contract for the weapon to go with it. They went to the well-known machine pistol designer Hugo Schmeisser, the proprietor of the "Weapon and Bicycle Factory of C.G. Haenel" in Suhl.

The contract with Schmeisser of April 18, 1938 described the weapon to be built as follows: Usable at ranges up to 800 meters, optional single or sustained fire, suitable for mass production.

Two years went by before Hugo Schmeisser could present his test piece to the Weapons Office.

The unusual length of the design phase may have been linked with the discussion of how to build gas-pressure loaders, which had not yet been concluded. And it appears that Schmeisser, in 1940, was the first German designer to successfully cure the Weapons Office of its decade-old prejudice against bored on barrels.

Schmeisser's machine carbine had a new type of tipping breech, as novel as it was effective, in which there were no single turning part, no locking lugs of the usual kind, only simple, solid components (the mechanism is described in detail under "MP 43").

A Revolution in Gunmaking: Stamped Sheet Metal

The Haenel prototype was an all-metal weapon with wood used only on the simple shoulderpiece. Schmeisser had used some shapes and components of the "MP 38", and as in it, the case of the weapon was machined out of solid metal. But that seemed too expensive to the Weapons Office. "Sheet metal" was the magic word then. After the first successful attempts to replace solid fittings of the 98 carbine with pieces of stamped sheet metal, this new technology had already become so widespread by 1940 that even complicated parts, such as weapon casings, could be made of sheet metal. A cleverly worked-out system of deeply-cut stiffening grooves gave the sheet metal the needed stability. The raw material was cheap, weight was saved, as were costly machine and work hours.

At that time, most weapons factories already had their own developmental units that worked on sheet metal stamping techniques. Obviously the small firm of C.G. Haenel was not one of them.

Thus it happened that the Schmeisser design had to be reworked by another firm before it could go into production. The main weapon branch of the Reich Ministry for Armaments and War Production gave the contract to the "Merz Works" in Frankfurt, an office-machine factory with sheet-metal experience. At the end of 1941 Merz delivered the first carbines with sheet-metal cases and, right on

The Machine Carbine 42 (H).

time according to the contract, a total of fifty test pieces on July 1, 1942. Thirty-five of them went directly to a first troop test on the eastern front. The weapon was given the designation "Machine Carbine 42 (Haenel)" — MKb 42 (H).

The "(H)" was a necessary differentiation because a competitor had meanwhile appeared on the scene: the firm of Carl Walther in Zella-Mehlis also applied for the lucrative armament contract with a model of its own.

Machine Carbines by Haenel and Walther

The development and testing of such a revolutionary new weapon as the machine carbine could not have been kept secret long in the weapon-building center of Suhl. Fritz Walther, chief of the

Carl Walther firm in nearby Zella-Mehlis, heard of it and made his own suggestions to the Weapons Office. At the end of the Thirties Walther had already undertaken testing of a semi-automatic system which was designated "A 115" at the works.

It was a gas-pressure loader with two holes bored in the barrel, and its original gas drive had the advantage of being fully insensitive.

The barrel was enclosed by a sheet-metal tube that served simultaneously as handguard and gas cylinder. At about half its length the barrel was bored on both sides. Behind it was a solid tightening ring around the barrel, which could be pushed

The Machine Carbine 42 (W).

forward and back. When gases escaped through the barrel holes into the gas cylinder on firing and expanded there, they pushed the ring in the direction of the barrel end. It struck against the breech carrier and transmitted its impulse to move. The breech carrier resembled a tube whose lower front half had been cut away. It slid over the end of the barrel, carrying in its rear section the cylindrical breech piece with the two locking lugs.

When the breech carrier moved backward against the pressure of the closing spring, the breech piece was guided over a twenty-degree curve, turning it just far enough so the lugs lifted out of their places and released the lock.

The remaining gas pressure in the barrel and the inertia of the heavy breech parts caused further backward motion, the empty cartridge case was pulled out of the bed and ejected, the closing spring was cocked. Next the breech unit moved ahead again under the pressure of the closing spring, a cartridge was taken from the magazine and pushed into the bed, the breech locked and the ring around the barrel moved forward to its original position again. The weapon was ready to fire again.

The Walther "A 115" system had a hammer lock housed in the attached grip piece. When firing, the hammer head moved in an arc. In the process, it struck the end of a short firing pin which projected from the rear of the breech piece.

For use in a machine carbine, the available — semi-automatic — system was modified only insofar as the hammer bolt now allowed sustained fire too.

Around the slightly modified A 115 system, Erich Walther now built a weapon that corresponded to the specifications of the Weapons Office in its dimensions, its surface and its material.

At the end of 1940 he presented his design and, since the model appeared to be capable of development, he received an order in January of 1941 to produce 200 test pieces for the planned great test in July of 1942. The weapons were to be equipped with long, curved thirty-shot magazines, which Walther's competitor Hugo Schmeisser had already developed for his machine carbine. This magazine later came in for a lot of criticism because it made using the weapon difficult when lying down behind low cover.

The assault-rifle magazine could not be refilled in the weapon. Short cartridges could only be loaded into the removed magazine, either individually or with an inserted magazine filler, stripped off a clip.

The close cooperation of the two firms with the Army Weapons Office resulted in two weapons that could hardly be told apart from outside. In the comparison tests at Kummersdorf in the summer of 1942, though, the Walther firm was at a disadvantage from the start, as it had delivered only two prototypes of their Carbine 42 (W) instead of the 200 that had been ordered, while its competitor Haenel appeared with fifty guns.

Both machine carbines, though, proved themselves so well that the office at first hesitated to decide to introduce one or the other. A large troop test on the eastern front was to clear things up. Both the Walther firm and the Haenel Weapon Factory put their models into small-series production.

According to American sources which are based on captured German production data, some 200

Waffen-SS men in bivouac. A 98 k is leaning on the wall of the shed. The soldier at right is armed with a Walther assault rifle.
(Photo: Federal Archives)

machine carbines of each type were to be finished by December of 1942.

As Lieutenant Colonel Dr. Rudolf Forenbacher reported in the journal "Wehrkunde" (I/53) after the war, the machine carbines experienced their first acid test with the "Scherer Battle Group", which had been enclosed in a pocket at Cholm during the Soviet 1942-43 winter offensive. The battle group, Dr. Forenbacher wrote, "was extensively (?) equipped with assault rifles. According to reports from the defenders it was this circumstance that made it possible for them to hold out . . . until they were relieved . . ."

Only in February of 1943 did machine-carbine production gradually get going. By July of 1943 it had grown to a monthly production of about 1400 pieces. At this point in time, when some 8000 weapons of both types were in the hands of the troops, the decision was made in favor of the Haenel machine carbine, which had been improved by using Walther components; it was designated Machine Pistol 43 (MP 43). The Walther firm then withdrew completely from production.

The 43 Machine Pistol (MP 43)

It looks as if the Haenel and Walther machine carbines came out of troop testing at the front with equal scores. For the successor weapon with the designation "Machine Pistol (MP) 43" combined essential parts of both systems. It consisted of the sheet-metal housing of the Haenel machine carbine, developed by the Merz works, was a modified Schmeisser gas and breech system and the hammer lock of the Walther prototype. The fact that more components of the Haenel prototype were adopted was due to the simpler process of manufacturing the Schmeisser weapon. The MP 43, in comparison to the MKb 42 (H), shows the following essential differences:

The gas cylinder of the MKb 42 (H) extended over the connecting piece to the muzzle and was closed off by a screw cap. This arrangement certainly increased the stability of the weapon and made cleaning the gas cylinder easier, but it made the weapon heavier. In the MP 43, the cylinder ended at the connecting piece and was closed off by a screw

The front of the MP 43: the gas cylinder is closed by a screw cap with a rod.

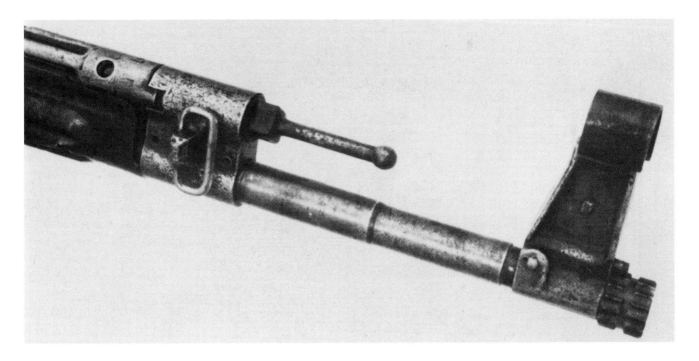

cap that bore a rod used in stacking several weapons. The front of the barrel thus stood free and had a particularly high, sloping foresight carrier.

The Firing Process

The MKb 42 (H) was an "open" weapon. That means that before firing, the breech block was held back by the trigger rod behind the magazine when the closing spring was tightened. Only when the trigger was pulled did the breech shoot forward under the pressure of the spring and push a cartridge out of the magazine into the chamber; then its rear end tipped downward into the locked position and the contact point of the following bolt guiding piece struck the end of the firing pin, which stuck out some two millimeters from the breech block. The cartridge was thus ignited.

When the bullet had passed the hole bored in the barrel, combustion gases pushed into the gas cylinder lying over the barrel and threw the piston backward. (After moving two to three centimeters of its way, the piston already had absorbed the necessary energy for the loading process. Then it passed a hole bored in the wall of the gas cylinder, which led to the open air. The driving gases could escape from the gas cylinder into the atmosphere through this "valve").

The gas piston turned into the piston rod at the rear. It reached back into the housing and ended there in the bolt guiding piece. This part had a unique cutout on its underside and a "hook" that corresponded to a similar part on the top of the breech block. The closing spring worked on the rear of the bolt guiding piece, which was angled off to the bottom.

When the gas piston and rod moved the bolt guiding piece backward, its hook reached under the corresponding point on the breech block, lifted its rear end some 2.5 millimeters and thus released the breech block from its locked position. The breech block and steering piece moved together into suitably formed grooves on the sheet-metal housing,

The MP 43: The bolt guiding piece and breech block. Under it is the four-sided firing pin.

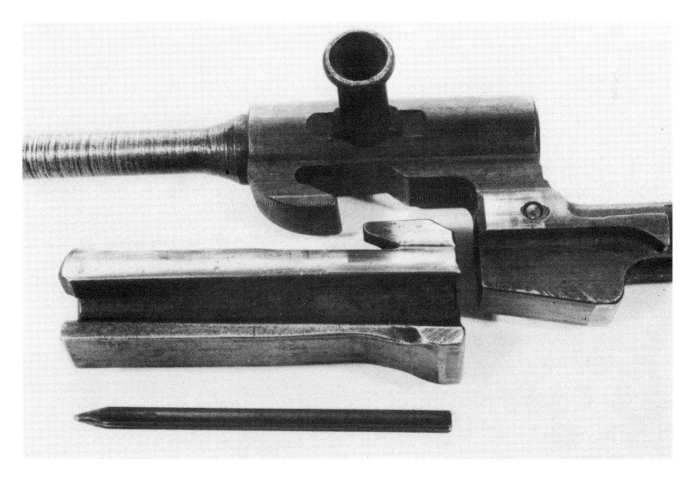

the empty cartridge case was pulled out of the bed and ejected, and the closing spring was cocked. (The first examples of the Haenel machine carbine had a telescopic spring like the MP 38/40, but this was soon replaced by the simple coil spring.) When the heavy breech parts were driven forward again by the closing spring, the trigger rod caught the breech block and held it (for single shots). The process described here applies to the Machine Carbine 42 (H).

The Machine Pistol 43 has the same breech, of course, but is fired not in an open but in a closed position. The breech parts complete their forward motion unchecked, push a new cartridge into the chamber and lock the weapon. But a shot is not yet fired, because the firing pin arrangement of the MP 43 is different.

The bolt is shorter, no longer projects from the breech block at the rear, and thus remains uninfluenced by contact with the guiding piece.

The angled-off rear part of the guiding piece, on the end of which the closing spring acts, in lengthened in the MP 43, reamed out on the underside and equipped with an inset spring bolt. When the shooter pulls the trigger, the hammer moves upward out of the holding piece of the weapon, its head strikes the spring bolt in the guiding piece, and this passes the shock on to the firing pin in the breech block.

MP 43: Safety and Choice of Fire

A positive change was made in the safety catch of the Machine Pistol 43. The MKb 42 (H) had a cocking handle that turned around the gas piston rod and could be placed in a hook-shaped cutout in the left wall of the housing as a safety catch. The designer Hugo Schmeisser had taken his machine pistols as models and necessarily transferred its shortcomings to the machine carbine: The shooter could bump the projecting cocking handle and thus release the safety catch unintentionally.

Operation, Disassembly, Cleaning

By adopting the Walther firing pin bolt in the handle piece, the MP 43 gained a safety catch that was set by a turning switch on the left of the handle piece and acted on the hammer. To set it, the switch was moved upward and the letter "S" became visible.

The type of fire could (as in the Schmeisser MP 28, II) be selected by using the push-button that passed horizontally through the housing. For single shots the switching rod was pushed to the left so that an "E" became visible. For sustained fire it was pushed to the right and a "D" became visible. Another push-button, located the upper left behind the magazine shaft, served to release the magazine.

The right side of the MP 43. The dust-protector lid over the cut out for case ejection is open and the arrangement of the breech parts can be seen. The milled button over the handle piece is the selector for single and sustained fire.

In both the MKb 42 (H) and the MP 43, the empty cartridge cases were ejected through a window in the right case wall. The opening could be closed by a dust-protector lid. In firing, the lid was automatically pushed open; it lifted under the pressure of a spring.

The weapons were held with the right hand on a handle piece. All operating handles with the exception of the safety catch and selector button were operated with the left hand.

To load, set the safety catch. Insert the filled magazine into the magazine shaft from below until it snaps in audibly. Pull the cocking handle back on the left side to its rearmost position and let it snap into place. Select the desired type of fire by using the selector switch, release the safety catch. The weapon is ready to fire.

So as not to let the weapon get too hot, only short bursts of fire in series of five shots at most should be fired. The MP 43 fires about nine rounds per second in sustained fire, and about 500 per minute. In single fire, the MP 43 is effective up to about 600 meters. For sustained fire, the operating manual cites a (very generously measured) effective range of 300 meters at most.

Unlike the 43 machine carbines, the MP 43 and its successor types had done away with a mount for a bayonet. But the weapons still had a thread in front of the foresight carrier on the outer wall of the barrel for mounting accessory devices. Normally a protector nut was screwed onto the thread. Accessory devices were: Blank cartridge device, rifle grenade device, curved barrels with periscope sights for firing from cover, and silencer. A part of the weapon was prepared for mounting the fourfold 43 telescopic sight.

For minor disassembly of the MP 43, as far as was necessary for cleaning, only the spring pin down on the attachment of the wooden shoulderpiece had to be pulled to the right until it made contact; then the shoulderpiece could be drawn out of the housing along with the closing spring, the breech parts could be taken out and the handle piece folded downward. To clean the gas cylinder with a chain and gas-cylinder brush, the cap with the stacking spike at the front end of the cylinder could be unscrewed.

The individual pieces of the assault rifle. To disassemble it, only one bolt on the shoulderpiece had to be loosened.

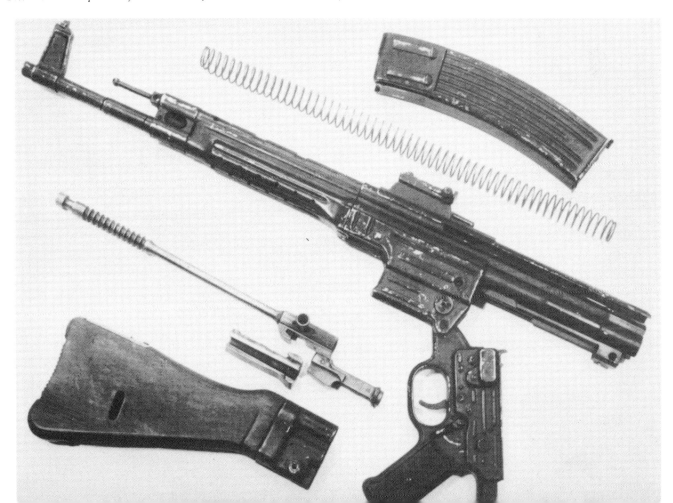

MP 43, MP 43/I, MP 44, Assault Rifle 44

Type: *Sturmgewehr 44* — StG 44*
Number: 4633
Year built: 1944
Manufacturer: C.G. Haenel Weapons Factory, Suhl
Function: Fully automatic gas loader with bored on barrel
Overall length: 950 mm
Weight: 4.6 kg (with empty magazine)
Barrel length: 410 mm
Barrel caliber: 7.9 mm
Number of riflings: 4
Rifling direction: Right

Breech: Locked tipping breech block
Safety: Turning switch on handle (left)
Magazine: Arched midstock removable magazine for 30 cartridges
Sight: Curved sliding sight (100 to 800 meters)
Standard ammunition: "Pistol Cartridge 43" (8 x 33)
Initial velocity (Vo): 685 meters per second (increased velocity, as the charge of the short cartridge was increased to two grams of powder in 1943.)
Performance in sustained fire: ca. 500 rounds per minute
* The Assault Rifle 44 is identical to the Machine Pistols (MP) 43, 43/I and 44 in form.

The confusing designations that the highest Army command and the Weapons Office got together and created in 1943-44 in naming the machine carbine can only be explained partially via psychology.

It began when the improved MKb 42 (H) was suddenly no longer called a "machine carbine" but "Machine Pistol 43." As a result, the ammunition used with it was called the "Pistol Cartridge 43" from that time on.

One must understand that there was a great deal of opposition to the new weapon in the Wehrmacht High Command, but particularly to the new types of ammunition that would have to be produced and delivered to the front additionally in case it was introduced. Influential members of the General Staff at the Führer's Headquarters also feared that the new short cartridge could force out the old standard cartridge and thus cost the infantry their "long arm." One may assume that it was this

particular argument that inspired the highest commanders to refuse the machine carbine and even expressly forbid its production.

Under the new nameplate of "machine pistol", the Army Weapons Office nevertheless continued its development and prepared for its production secretly. But even the "MP 43" could not stay alive under the Führer's eyes. After a presentation of the weapon in the spring of 1943, Armaments Minister Speer, on Hitler's orders, requested a cessation of all work on it for a second time. In spite of that, production went on in small series. A new type even originated, the "MP 43/I", which differed from the basic model only in having a different threading on the muzzle. The "Rifle Grenade Device 43" could be screwed onto the MP 43/I, while the MP 43 was set up for the attachable rifle grenade device of the Carbine 98 k.

Of this weapon, which was actually not supposed

to exist, barely 1500 pieces had been made by September of 1943, and despite the ban, the numbers delivered continued to grow steadily. German production data show a monthly production of 5000 of the weapons for February 1944, which even increased to 9000 in April. All in all, some 30,000 machine carbines were already with the troops by that time. As of April 1944 the weapons' housings were stamped with "MP 44." Why that happened can no longer be determined. In the summer of 1944, when the fortunes of war had already turned away from the German Reich, Adolf Hitler reversed his two former bans on production and instead ordered that the MP 44 and its ammunition be given priority in production, effective immediately. In his desperate situation, Hitler even tried to increase the weapon's value with a suggestive name: "Sturmgewehr" (Assault Weapon) was to be the machine carbine's name from then on. (See the notes on page 214.)

The 44 Assault Rifle, its Costs and Faults

A whole series of firms shared in the production of the assault rifle. Housings and stamped sheet-metal parts were supplied by the "Merz Works" of Frankfurt and the "Württemberg Metal Goods Factories" (WMF). The final assembly was done by Haenel in Suhl and ERMA in Erfurt. Production of the assault rifle continued until the factories were occupied by the Allies at the end of the war.

With a production time of fourteen hours and a total cost of about seventy Marks, the Assault Rifle 44 was considerably above the price range of the 98 k carbine (56 RM). This happened because the weapon had originally been made by its designers in very expensive, conventional methods, using machined parts. The later attempt to concert the machine carbine to sheet metal was only partially successful. Among experts, the result was referred to as the "machined weapon wrapped in tin."

Because of the high cost of the assault rifle, the Army Weapons Office invited various industrial firms to participate in a competition with the goal of reducing the production time of the machine carbine. This invitation included the condition that all suggested constructive changes to the assault rifle had to be able to be made in ongoing production without modifications and made to already delivered weapons by exchange.

The Mauser works, which were originally supposed to supply the complete stock of housings for the assault rifles won the competition. The suggestions of the specialists from Oberndorf succeeded in reducing the production time by one hour and forty minutes.

When it was seen that the trend was toward an even simpler weapon than the Assault Rifle 44, Hugo Schmeisser entered the field again. He tried, starting with his "original model" MKb 42 (H), to simplify it radically and create an even cheaper weapon, the "MP 45." Other weapons firms made similar attempts. Chief Designer Barnitzke of the "Gustloff Works" in Suhl worked on a very primitive semi-automatic version of a short-cartridge carbine in which the recoil of the unlocked breech was to be delayed by gases streaming out and being directed in the opposite direction. The "Johannes Grossfuss Metal and Locier Goods

"Machine pistol 45", a test model by Hugo Schmeisser.

Factory" in Döbeln, Saxony, at that time one of the leading German firms in the working of sheet metal, also worked on a primitive short-cartridge weapon in which ducted-off combustion gases were to counteract the recoil of the breech piece.

Little is known of weapons of this type; they never went into service. The war's end interrupted the development of simple automatic weapons, which in their own way were highly amazing achievements in German weapons building.

Hugo Schmeisser

His father, Louis Schmeisser (1848-1917), had worked as a gunsmith and designer for the "Rheinish Metal Goods and Machine Factory" in Sömmerda and the Bergmann Weapon Works in Gaggenau (later Suhl and Berlin). The son Hugo followed in his father's footsteps.

His first successful design was the MP 18, I, which became world-famous under the Bergmann firm's name. Hugo Schmeisser later developed this model intich Schmeisser tried to capitalize on his first great success. Perhaps even more important than his machine pistols are his machine carbines, which he developed after 1938. He is considered the "father" of the assault rifle.

After World War II, Hugo Schmeisser was dispossessed in the GDR. His firm of C.G. Haenel became the "VEB Ernst Thälmann Works."

A semi-automatic "Volkssturm" carbine made by the Gustloff Works.

Notes on Pages 212, 213:
About the fight over the introduction of the machine carbine, the former Armaments Minister Albert Speer quotes in his "Memoirs" the Führer's orders of June 28-29, 1942, Point 55: "The Führer declares very definitely that the production of a machine carbine has never been agreed upon as long as it does not have rifle ammunition. Moreover, he is very thoroughly convinced that the rifle . . . fulfills its purpose better."

The tactics through which the Army Weapons Office circumvented all orders to stop production of machine carbines is depicted by a competent witness, General of the Artillery Emil Leeb, Chief of the Army Weapons Office, as follows: "In the autumn of 1940 the Army Weapons Office decided to have an automatic rifle with sufficiently accurate single fire up to 400-600 meters (hence cartridges with a weaker powder charge, called short cartridges) and the same weight as the 89 short rifle developed and to let only the finished weapon be presented to the competent authorities. The automatic rifle with short cartridge could replace the machine pistol (MP 38), so that, as before, two types of cartridge would be on hand in the smallest infantry unit . . .

The military authorities could not be convinced of the necessity of accepting the assault rifle. In a presentation to the Supreme Commander of the Wehrmacht in the presence of the Chief of Army Equipment, by whom, though, the Chief of the Army Weapons Office was ordered, on higher command, to stay away, so that he could not discredit the erroneous two-cartridge theory, the Supreme Commander of the Wehrmacht refused the assault rifle in about the spring of 1942 in regard to the two types of cartridges.

Nothing concerning this decision was officially communicated to the Army Weapons office, so that the manufacturing preparations and slow development of mass production of weapon and ammunition went on; only on the part of the Reich Ministry of Armament and Ammunition did opposition gradually appear. In May and June of 1943 the Chief of Army Equipment suddenly ordered verbally that all ammunition production for the assault rifle should be stopped on July 1. Through officers at the front, though, it was achieved in about September of 1943 by the Supreme Commander of the Wehrmacht that the assault rifle would be introduced."

Mauser "Device 06 H"

Type: Mauser *Gerät 06 H*
Year made: 1942-43
Manufacturer: Mauser Works A.G., Oberndorf
Function: Fully automatic gas loader *
Overall length: 900 mm
Weight: 4 kg with empty magazine
Barrel length: 400 mm
Barrel caliber: 7.9 mm
Number of riflings: 4
Rifling direction: Right

Breech: Originally rigid roller lock breech. After rebuilding, early in 1943, semi-rigid roller lock
Safety: Selector switch on handle (acts on hammer)
Magazine: Removable magazine, as in MKb 42 (H)
Sight: Curved sliding sight (100 to 800 meters)
Types of fire: Semi- and fully automatic
Standard ammunition: "Pistol Cartridge 43" (8 x 33)
Initial velocity: ca. 650 meters per second
Performance in sustained fire (cadence): ca. 650 rounds per minute
* After rebuilding: Fully automatic recoil loader

In the developmental history of the assault rifle, one misses the name of Mauser. What was wrong in Oberndorf when the competitors in Suhl created a piece of German weapon history by themselves?

The German Weapons and Ammunition Factories (DWM), to which the Mauser works belonged, had originally been passed over by the Army Technical Bureau (HTB) in the development of the assault rifle. But the designers in Mauser's Development Section 37 (small weapons up to 10 mm) had naturally recognized the signs of the times too. When the introduction of the Polte short cartridge was being discussed (DWM, incidentally, had also developed its own 7-mm short cartridge), a team under Chief Designer Altenburger worked intensively on this new type of ammunition. Designers Illenberger, Jungermann, Stähle and Vorgrimler first developed a gas operated system with rigid roller lock, but soon found a considerably better solution: the semi-rigid breech, which is just as modern today as it was when it was created, more than forty years ago.

We find the semi-rigid roller breech in a whole family of weapons all over the world today, including the "G 3" rifle of the German Bundeswehr.

Wilhelm Stähle (1901-1974) invented the semi-rigid roller lock.

The history of this system's origin is depicted in the following excerpt from a sworn statement made by the former Mauser designer Wilhelm Stähle in 1957:

The Semi-Rigid "Roller Breech"

Wilhelm Stähle wrote: "In November of 1942 I was given the assignment of developing a machine pistol. At first there was no agreement on the question of ammunition, as to whether the 9 mm Mauser, 9 mm PARABELLUM, or short cartridge (7.9 x 33) should be chosen. After the decision had been made in favor of the short cartridge, I thought about the breech. A breech block without locking would have been too heavy for the short cartridge. Therefore I looked for a breech that was to have any kind of locking but worked without a drive. After various considerations, I found the semi-rigid roller breech and put it right on paper . . .

After repeated discussions with Mr. Altenburger, in which Mr. Vorgrimler also took part, I was then given the authorization to build a principle model. From this model, which was finished in December of 1942, one could see clearly how capable of variation this breech was. There were three steering pieces with different locking angles involved.

In order to arrive at a firing model as quickly as possible, I built the roller breech into an already available assault rifle. The functioning firing, in February and March of 1943, was almost without trouble; only the sustained fire was still irregular in, because the barrel had no grooves . . ."

The "already available assault rifle", a test piece designated "06 H" by the works, originally had a rigid locked roller breech that was unlocked by a conventional gas-pressure drive (with cylinder and piston over the bored on barrel). The weapon had a sheet-metal housing and was about 90 centimeters long (barrel: 40 cm).

After rebuilding for a semi-rigid lock, the weapon was given the unofficial designation "Machine Carbine (MKb) 43."

The test weapon worked well from the beginning; still in all, its further fate was quite uncertain in the spring of 1943. For at that time the Haenel and Walther machine carbines had long since passed their tests at Kummersdorf, the manufacturers' factories were already being set up for series production, and the first machine carbines, the 42 (H) and 42 (W), had been able to gain points on the eastern front. It was clear to see that Haenel and Walther would run the race against each other, at least at the beginning.

In the long run, though, the Mauser assault rifle had a real chance, because it — with the same performance — was considerably simpler and cheaper to produce than the two competitors' models.

The roller breech (head with guiding piece) of the MKb 43/StG 45 (M).

A sketch of the principle model of 1942. R = rollers, S = steering piece with locking angles, V = breech head, P = rocker to provide lock resistance.

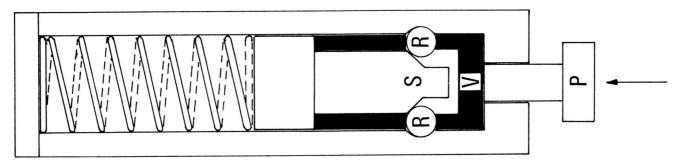

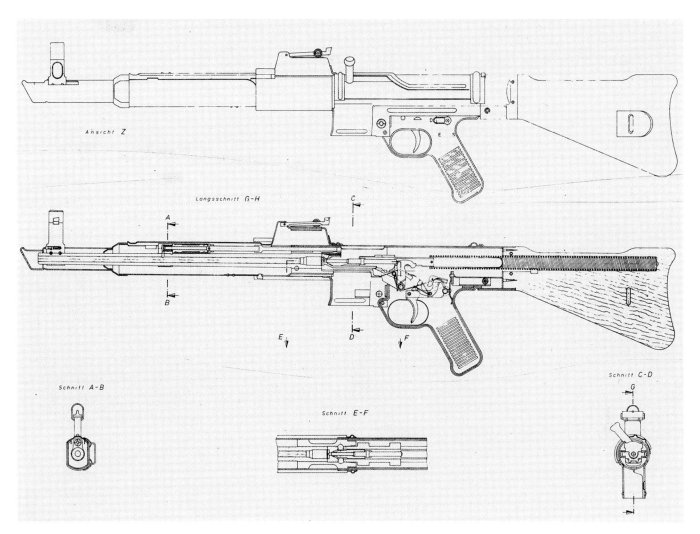

An original drawing of the Mauser "06" device. This predecessor of the 45 (M) assault rifle still has gas drive above the barrel and a compensator over the muzzle. The roller breech is still rigidly locked.

The semi-rigid breech of the Mauser machine carbine had the following layout: A breech head with two locking rollers is flexibly linked with the breech carrier by a steering piece. A striker piece runs behind it, which neutralizes the rebound of striking the breech head on the barrel end.

The four-sided breech head carries the extracting claw and takes up a flat, arrow-shaped steering piece from the rear. The two slanting surfaces make contact with the rollers, which are mounted movably in cutouts on the sides of the breech head.

The steering piece, through the central axis of which the firing pin passes, is coupled with the breech carrier at its rear end. The closing spring acts on the rear end of the striking piece (with a short closing spring rod). The striking piece has a cutout area that allows the hammer to reach the end of the firing pin.

The Firing Process

When the entire breech hurries forward under the pressure of the closing spring and the breech head has pushed a cartridge out of the magazine into the chamber, the breech carrier drives the arrow-shaped steering piece linked with it to make contact with the breech head. In the process, the two locking rollers are pushed sideways out of the breech head and into two cutouts in the locking piece at the end of the barrel. Thereby a connection between the breech head and the locking piece is established, which relaxes only when, in firing, the gas pressure in the barrel reaches its highest value. Then the pressure on the cartridge base and breech head overcomes the locking powers acting against it, and that happens as follows:

The pressure acting on the cartridge base is trans-

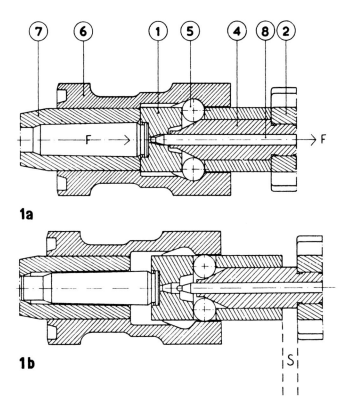

1a

1b

The functioning of the semi-rigid roller breech, shown schematically in two phases. Phase 1a: The breech is locked, with a cartridge in the bed. Phase 1b: Shortly after firing. The bullet has already left the barrel. Under the effect of the base pressure on the cartridge, the rollers have withdrawn into the breech head and pushed the steering piece backward along the distance "S." The numbers indicate: 1. Breech head; 2. breech carrier, 4. steering piece, 5 locking rollers, 6 locking piece, 7. barrel end, 8. firing pin.

mitted to the rollers in the cutout areas of the locking piece and to the arrow-shaped inclined surfaces of the steering piece, which is nevertheless under opposing pressure from the closing spring.

Delayed by the powers of friction, the locking rollers retreat into the interior of the breech head and thus press the steering piece, as well as the breech carrier and the striking piece, backward at a transmission ratio of 1 to 3.

Thus the locking is released, the remaining gas pressure in the barrel pushes the cartridge case out of the bed. The breech carrier, its speed increased, takes the breech head back with it and the cartridge case is ejected in the process.

The Soviets Provide a Good Idea

The semi-rigid locking with its simple components certainly met all the requirements for quick and cheap mass production, but it was not completely

problem-free. Suddenly they had to wrestle with the same recoil-loader problems in Oberndorf that the firm's founder, Paul Mauser, had come to grief on forty years before: sticking cases, torn cartridge bases, jammings. The causes were known: The gas pressure inflated the case and pushed it so tightly against the wall of the chamber that the friction involved in extraction became too great. Paul Mauser had tried to solve the problem with greased cases; the Altenburger team found a better way.

In studying Soviet aircraft machine guns that the *Legion Condor* had captured in the Spanish Civil War, the Mauser designers had noticed the chambers. Grooves had been cut in the walls of the bed. "Gas-release grooves", as we say today. They let the gas pressure also act on the outside wall of the case and thus drastically lower the friction in the chamber. When irregularities in sustained fire showed up during the first functioning firing of the rebuilt "06 H Device", releasing grooves were added to the chamber experimentally and success was instantaneous. The weapon fired faultlessly.

Mauser Machine Carbines: Almost 50% Cheaper than the 44 Assault Rifle

In the spring of 1943 extended tests of the rebuilt 06 H Device began in Oberndorf. The weapon with the semi-rigid roller breech came through its test of strength with sustained fire of 6000 rounds unharmed and impressed the invited observers from the Army Weapons Office so strongly that the officials ordered four prototypes for their own tests in Oberndorf and Kummersdorf the same year.

The new model, barely changed externally, was given the works designation "Machine Carbine (MKb) 43." Early in 1944 the four ordered weapons were sent off for official testing at the "Army Proving Grounds" in Kummersdorf and passed all the tests there too.

Meanwhile the calculations for the Mauser machine carbine were at hand. The "Dürenberg Agency", a production technology firm in Bad Riesa, Saxony, an independent company, had calculated a work time of only seven hours. That represented a value of about 40 Reichsmark at that time and was well under the production expenses of the Haenel assault rifle (14 work hours, or 70 RM).

In 1944, the year in which the German war industries turned out their highest performance by using all their powers to the fullest, 400 saved production minutes were an argument that could hardly be refuted.

For that reason the Weapons Office ordered a zero series of thirty machine carbines from Oberndorf for a small troop test; the weapon parts were to be produced, as much as possible, on the final tools.

For the model, which had been simplified externally one more time, the designation "Sturmgewehr 45 (Mauser) — StG 45 (M)" was planned. The new weapon was to replace the Haenel Assault Rifle 44 gradually. But it never happened.

The Victors Finish the Job

The preparation of the "final" stamping tools and the other necessary production equipment delayed the delivery of the zero series. When the war ended, the individual parts of the thirty ordered rifles were finished, but not a single Mauser assault rifle was assembled.

In spite of that, the victors recognized the significance of the design at once and had the parts assembled by captured Mauser employees at the English base in Eschede.

How many weapons were assembled in this way after the war ended is not known. Without exception, they went to collections and museums in France, England and the USA.

Since only a few years there has been a single example of the legendary 45 assault rifle on German soil. The former Mauser designer Ludwig Vorgrimler was able, with the help of friends in the USA, to obtain a complete set of original parts from the 1945 zero series. Missing small parts were made and mounted expertly from the original plans.

Parts from the Assault Rifle 45 zero series in the condition in which they were captured by the victors. From top to bottom: locking piece and lock, barrel with foresight carrier, housing of sheet metal with plastic handguard and closing band. Below: Hammer-lock housing, safety wing, pins and springs. The magazine, several small parts, the dust cover and the wooden shoulder piece are missing.

Assault Rifle 45 (Mauser) - StG 45 (M)

Type: *Sturmgewehr 45 (Mauser)* — StG 45 (M)
Year made: 1945
Manufacturer: Mauser Works A.G., Oberndorf
Function: Fully automatic recoil loader
Overall length: 900 mm
Weight: 4 kg with empty magazine
Barrel length: 400 mm
Barrel caliber: 7.9 mm
Number of riflings: Four
Rifling direction: right

Breech: Semi-rigid roller lock
Safety: Selection switch on handle, acting on the hammer
Magazine: Removable magazine as in MKb 42 but for only ten cartridges
Sight: Curved sliding sight (100 to 800 meters)
Types of firing: Semi- and fully automatic
Standard ammunition: "Pistol Cartridge 43" (8 x 33)
Initial velocity: ca. 650 meters per second
Firing performance in sustained firing (cadence): ca. 450 rounds per minute
Disassembly: By two pins, similar to Assault Rifle 44.

At first glance it becomes clear that this weapon was produced very deliberately at the least possible expense. The two sides of the housing, including the magazine shaft and handgrip, are stamped out of sheet iron. Even the ridged plates of the handgrip are made of one piece along with the frame. The long cylindrical part of the housing, in which the breech and the closing spring move, opens at the front into a likewise round, ridged handguard of plastic, that extends to the middle of the barrel. The front half of the barrel is free and carries a high foresight socket at the muzzle.

The backsight (to 800 meters) and the wooden shoulderpiece (attached to the housing by one bolt) are reminiscent of the 44 assault gun.

The hammer lock is attached inside the rigid handle piece by a second bolt. On the left side of the handgrip is a switching lever for single fire, sustained fire and safety catch. Also on the left side of the housing, in a cutout in the semicircular arched dust cover, is the cocking lever. Unlike all other German World War II machine carbines, the zero series of the Assault Rifle 45 (M) was equipped with only a small magazine for ten cartridges. But

the normal 30-cartridge magazine could also be used.

From Assault Rifle 45 (M) to Assault Rifle G 3

If we trace the postwar fate of the last significant German handgun design, we turn, after a wrong-way trip through half of Europe, back to our point of departure: Oberndorf on the Neckar.

"G3" assault rifles are made there for the Bundeswehr today, with a semi-rigid roller breech on the principle of the Assault Rifle 45 (M).

This "G 3" production is in the hands of Heckler & Koch of Oberndorf and Rheinmetall of Düsseldorf, because the Mauser firm, in the process of being liquidated by the French occupation powers after the war, surrendered their rights to the semi-rigid locked breech and got them back only after a long struggle for patent rights.

When the rearmament of the German Federal Republic was at hand in the mid-Fifties and the "Blank Office" in Bonn (the subsequent Federal

Defense Ministry) surveyed the international market for a suitable standard weapon for the Bundeswehr, the Spanish "CETME" rifle also got on the short list.

A group of former Mauser designers, who had gone to Spain after the war, had developed the weapon for the Spanish armed forces at the "Centro des Estudios Técnicos de Materiales Especiales" (CETME).

The CETME rifle is a machine carbine that looks like the Haenel 44 assault rifle in its lines and workmanship, but its functioning is based on the Mauser Assault Rifle 45. The CETME model was set up for a special Spanish short cartridge. Since the Bundeswehr, as a NATO force, was committed to the 7.62 x 51 "NATO Cartridge", the Spanish machine carbine had to be modified first to use the new, considerably stronger ammunition if it was to qualify for introduction in the Federal Republic.

Ludwig Vorgrimler, the director of the German-Spanish team in Madrid, succeeded in converting the automatic weapon from the short to the "long cartridge" in a remarkably short time. In the process, the universality of the semi-rigid roller breech proved useful to him, for by modifying the arrow angle on the steering piece it can be modified to take any new type of ammunition.

This advantage had already given the designers in Madrid the idea of developing a whole "family" of light weapons using the semi-rigid system. In recent years the firm of Heckler & Koch has proved that this is possible.

In their Oberndorf factory the CETME model has been slightly modified since its introduction in 1957 to suit the wishes of the Federal Defense Ministry and developed further into the "Assault Rifle G 3." Machine pistols and machine guns with semi-rigid roller breeches have since been created by "H & K" too.

Weapons of this type are being used today by the armed forces of Norway, Sweden, Denmark, Portugal and Pakistan and many others today.

Ludwig Vorgrimler

Born near Freiburg in 1912, he began his weapon-technological activity as a graduate engineer with Krupp. In the early Thirties Vorgrimler worked on the establishment of firing tables for Krupp's long-range guns. In 1936 he transferred to Mauser in

Ludwig Vorgrimler.

Oberndorf, and remained in the developmental department for light weapons until 1945. He played a formative role in the tests of the semi-rigid locked breech and the "Assault Rifle 45" project.

Because of his special knowledge in this realm, the French Defense Ministry brought him to Mulhouse, Alsace at the end of the war. There Vorgrimler designed a machine pistol with a semi-rigid breech, and in 1950 he went to the "Centro des Estudios Técnicos Materiales Especiales" (CETME) in Madrid. As the director of a German-Spanish team, he developed the CETME rifle on the basis of the Mauser assault rifle for a new short cartridge that Dr. Voss, another German designer, had created. For their successful work, Ludwig Vorgrimler and Dr. Voss received the beribboned medal of the Order for Art and Science from the Spanish government.

In the summer of 1956 Ludwig Vorgrimler returned to Germany in the service of the Mauser parent firm "Karlsruhe Industrial Works." Till 1975 he was the Director of the (IWKA) Weapon Development Department in Schramberg-Sulgen, near Oberndorf. Vorgrimler died in 1983.

The German Machine Pistols

When the first pocket pistols with unassisted blow-back breeches came on the market at the beginning of this century and became tremendously successful, it is probable that no designer thought of using this problem-free system for an automatic shoulder weapon. The reasons are simple enough:

For the self-loading rifles that were being developed then, the unlocked system was not even considered, for it was not equal to the pressure of the long military cartridges. And for weapons of that type that we call "machine pistols" today there was then no need.

Around 1910 the military plans and tactical models in Europe were still essentially based on the experiences of moving warfare in 1870-71. To be sure, soldiers had first had to dig themselves in during the Russo-Japanese War of 1905-06 to find cover from machine-gun fire, and in the Imperial German peacetime army techniques of static warfare were then being practiced. All the same, when the war began in the autumn of 1914, trench warfare for months at a time, such as was soon to develop at Verdun, was still outside the bounds of military thinking.

When the unimaginable suddenly became reality, weapons for close combat had to be developed in a hurry. The machine pistol was one of them.

In assault and defense of the narrow trench system, in the chaos of barbed wire and trench material, the long, slowly firing repeater rifle proved to be a hindrance. And even the heavy and relatively immobile machine guns of the time could not be relied on for sufficient fire protection in dramatic situations. A light weapon that could be carried and used by one man and could send out a hail of bullets was needed. It was to be a close-combat weapon for practical shot ranges of no more than 200 meters, as simple as possible, robust, and suitable for an already available type of ammunition: the 9-mm cartridge of the 08 pistol.

These requirements had already been set up by the Rifle Testing Commission at Spandau at the end of 1915. It was planned at that time to convert the long 08 artillery pistol, with its 20-cm barrel and shoulder stock to sustained fire, but the attempt failed. The pistols fired much too fast and could not be kept on target because of their light inherent weight. It was soon clear that the Commission's requirements could only be fulfilled by a completely new type of weapon. The first German designers who began to occupy themselves with the problems of the machine pistol were Andreas Schwarzlose in Berlin and Hugo Schmeisser in Suhl. Schmeisser's prototype, which came into being with the co-operation of the Bergmann Weapons Factory, received the approval of the Rifle Testing Commission in 1918.

With the Schmeisser MP the German Reich put itself at the forefront of progress in weapon technology, and it remained the leader in the realm of machine pistols until the beginning of World War II. But the machine pistol was actually "invented" — if one can say that at all here — in Italy.

As early as 1916 the Italians had introduced a small, original twin machine gun, with two legs and double handgrips, which fired pistol ammunition. The mechanisms were unlocked, the cartridges entered from the sides via stick magazines. Shortly before the first German machine pistol was delivered, there was already a Beretta model in Italy that showed all the typical characteristics of the machine pistol. In Steyr too, they were working on a machine pistol in 1918. But this weapon was not finished by the time the war ended.

Machine Pistol 18, I - MP 18, I

Type: *Maschinenpistole 18*, I - (MP 18, I)
Number: 17667
Year made: No data
Manufacturer: Theodor Bergmann Weapons Factory, Suhl
Function: Fully automatic with blow-back system
Overall length: 820 mm
Weight: 4 kg (with empty magazine)
Barrel length: 200 mm
Caliber: 9 mm
Number of riflings: Six
Rifling direction: Right
Sight: Folding scope with two notches
Sight settings: 100 and 200 meters
Safety: Safety notch for chamber grip in housing

Magazine
Capacity: 20 cartridges (32 cartridges)
Standard ammunition: 08 pistol cartridge (9 mm Para)
Initial velocity: 360 meters per second
Rounds per minute: 350 to 450
Safety catch: Pull chamber grip back and put in notch of guiding slit marked with "S."
Disassembly: Push button and remove magazine, release breech, press lock bar on rear case end, tip entire case forward, turn base cap to left and remove with closing spring. Pull firing pin with breech cylinder out at rear.
Notes: Original troop use with drum magazine of long 08 pistol. Available and new MP's fitted later in the Twenties with new "insertion socket" for Schmeisser staff magazine.

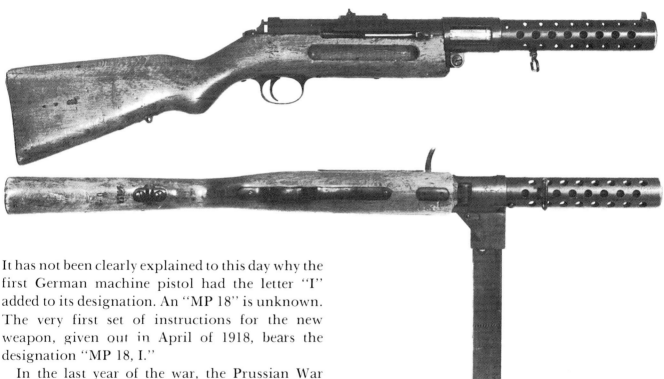

It has not been clearly explained to this day why the first German machine pistol had the letter "I" added to its designation. An "MP 18" is unknown. The very first set of instructions for the new weapon, given out in April of 1918, bears the designation "MP 18, I."

In the last year of the war, the Prussian War Ministry had ordered 50,000 machine pistols from the Theodor Bergmann Weapons Factory in Suhl. Plans were made to establish six machine pistol detachments consisting of one shooter and one ammunition carrier in each company. Every detail was to have a supply of about 2500 cartridges for action, some in filled magazines, others in folding boxes.

This plan could not be carried out, for on Armistice Day there were not even 10,000 machine pistols with the troops.

In the end, the stipulations of the Treaty of Versailles banned the further development and production of machine pistols. In spite of that, the "illicit" manufacturing continued at the Bergmann factory until 1920.

Hugo Schmeisser, the designer, had turned his rights over to the Bergmann firm. This explains why the weapon became known as the "Bergmann" machine pistol. After their own production ended, the Bergmann firm granted a license to the Swiss Industrial Company (SIG) in Neuhausen. There the weapon was built in various versions during the Twenties for the world market (especially for Japan).

The MP 18, I is the first really simple infantry weapon. It has (counting the detached magazine but not the screws) only 34 individual parts and is excellently made.

The essential parts:

The walnut half-stock, with the same shape as the 98 rifle, carries the rear half of the long casing tube in its bed. The jacket encloses the 20-cm barrel at the front and the breech at the rear. The front half of the casing, as far as it encloses the barrel, has numerous holes. It serves as a cooling jacket and handguard. About in the middle of the casing an "insertion socket" is attached, a magazine holder, into which the magazine is pushed from the left. The insertion socket and casing are pierced on the right side of the weapon. The rectangular opening, the "window", serves for cartridge ejection.

In the rear section of the casing, the 700-gram breech cylinder moves forward and back in firing. It bears a sprung extractor and a hook-shaped chamber grip that reaches out through a long slit on the right side of the weapon. On the rear end of the casing, the guiding slit is interrupted by a bend. The chamber grip can be hooked into this bend and thus secured.

The coil closing spring leads between a closing-spring bolt (that sticks into the breech base at the end of the casing) and the tubular extension of the firing pin. The spring thus acts on the firing pin, but the latter remains in the breech cylinder and transmits the pressure.

On the left inside of the casing, shortly before the magazine shaft, the rigid extractor reaches into the chamber rail. The breech cylinder has a fitting radial groove on its left side.

The trigger housing is screwed to the underside of the casing. For disassembly the whole unit can be swung upward on a hinge at the front end of the half-stock. To do this, the spring-lock piece on the end of the casing must be pressed down.

The Firing Process

The principle of the MP 18, I is typical of all German machine pistols up to 1945 and, in fact, for almost all the world's machine pistols. To avoid repetition in this book, the firing process will be described just once, here:

The MP 18, I is an "open weapon", meaning that the breech is in its rearmost position before firing, with the closing spring tightened, held by the trigger rod.

When the trigger rod frees the breech, the heavy steel cylinder moves forward under pressure from

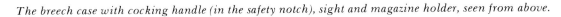

The breech case with cocking handle (in the safety notch), sight and magazine holder, seen from above.

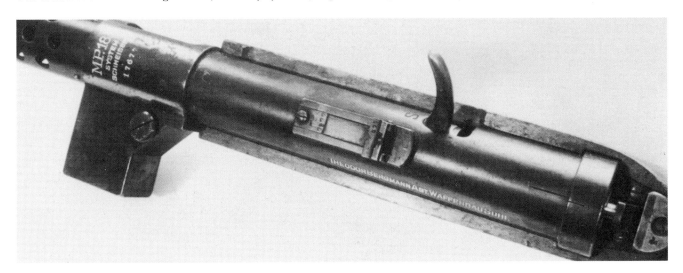

the closing spring. The firing pin is set in the breech with its point always projecting from the front surface.

The breech takes the topmost cartridge out of the magazine along, pushes it into the chamber and immediately strikes against the barrel end. At this moment the firing pin point hits the percussion cap of the cartridge. The shot is fired and the gas pressure in the barrel acts both on the bullet and on the breech. Both begin to move in opposite directions. Since the breech, though, is about a hundred times heavier than the bullet, it moves considerably more slowly. When the bullet leaves the barrel, the cartridge case has not been drawn completely out of the bed, thus the barrel end is still closed.

Only later is the cartridge case freed and immediately thrown out through the "window" at the right by the ejector. Meanwhile the breech moves farther back and thereby tightens the closing spring until its motion reaches its end and reverses.

Performance of the MP 18, I

The first German machine pistol was made only for sustained fire. In the 1918 "guidebook" it is said of the weapon: "Its design and the ammunition used with it allow the use of:
a) Sustained fire — converging and shifting fire,
b) Spray fire — done by quickly releasing the trigger while firing — in all shooting positions.

When using 'shifting fire' the 32 rounds of a drum magazine are shot in 3.5 seconds. In the process, a field some 15 meters wide can be covered with a barrage fire impenetrable to unarmored living targets."

Magazine Types

The original version of the MP 18, I was equipped with the drum magazine of the long 08 pistol,

The MP 18, I with staff magazine, disassembled.

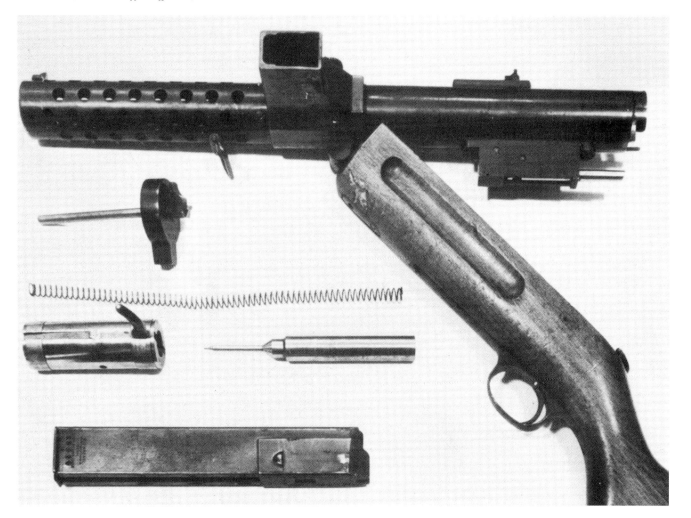

which was inserted at an angle from the left, into a magazine holder, the "insertion socket", which was angled some sixty degrees to the rear.

Weapons from postwar production, though, were equipped with a Schmeisser staff magazine, inserted vertically on the left, that had a smaller capacity of twenty cartridges but was cheaper to produce and easier to fill than the drum magazine.

This magazine, in which the cartridges were placed in zigzag order to save space, did not fit into the mouth of the old insertion socket. The new magazine holder was therefore added to most of the old wartime MP 18, I. In these weapons the casing bears the trade name of Bergmann and the magazine holder that of Schmeisser's firm, C.G. Haenel, of Suhl.

It is significant that Hugo Schmeisser had foreseen staff magazines for the MP 18, I from the start and had equipped the weapon with the already available drum magazine only at the request of the Rifle Testing Commission.

The drum magazine of the MP 18, I. It corresponds to the magazine of the long "Pistol 08" and was later replaced by the staff magazine.

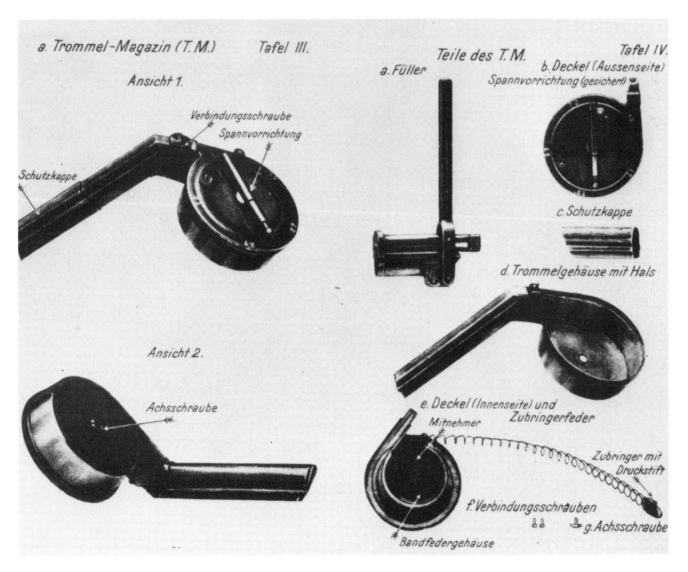

Machine Pistol 28, II - (MP 28, II)

After World War I, when Hugo Schmeisser had bought into the C.G. Haenel Weapons Factory in Suhl, he developed his "Bergmann" MP 18, I design further on his own.

In 1925 the "Inspection of Weapons and Equipment" (IWG) of the Reichswehr tested an improved Schmeisser model in Kummersdorf. Machine pistol tests were then not uncommon, despite the Versailles ban, as we shall see.

Schmeisser's new machine pistol, which was finally designated "MP 28, II", can scarcely be told from its predecessor externally. The stock with the hinge on its front end, the casing with the cooling louvers forward and the spring bar at the end, the holder for the staff magazine and the cocking hook were retained from the MP 18, I. There were only slight changes in the mechanism.

The most important innovation is the built-in interrupter that now allows single shots. The desired type of fire can be set by pushing a button on the trigger guard to the side (as was later done in the Schmeisser machine carbines).

Individual parts of the MP 28, II.

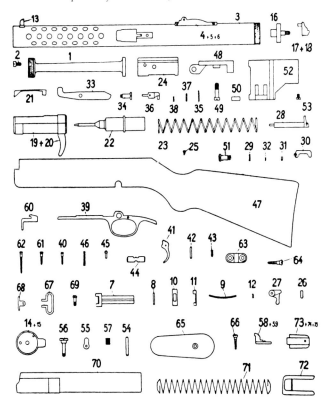

Instead of the old folding sight notches for 100 and 200 meters, the weapon now had a curved sliding sight with markings up to 1000 meters. This measures the range more than generously, for the chance of hitting a target with this machine pistol with its 20-cm barrel essentially ends, even with aimed single shots, at 400 meters. The zenith of the slow 9-mm bullet's trajectory then is barely three meters above the sight line.

Inside the casing, the barrel is attached somewhat differently than in the MP 18, I, and the coil diameter of the closing spring has been enlarged considerably, which increases its stability in use. The spring is now pushed forward "over" the cylindrical end of the firing pin and backward over an extension of the breech plate. The "spring bolt" of the MP 18, I no longer exists. Since the Reichswehr's Inspection of Machine Pistols required a magazine capacity of 35 cartridges, Schmeisser had to lengthen his existing 20-cartridge magazine. With a capacity of 32 rounds he finally reached the limit of capacity for a staff magazine with zigzag positioning. Because of the great friction of the 9-mm cartridges, on each other and on the magazine walls, disturbances in feed are not impossible.

Production and Distribution

Although the Reichswehr unofficially tested machine pistols in the Twenties and even financially supported some firms in developing them, an official introduction of the forbidden weapon naturally could not be considered. They presumably wanted to prepare for the day when the limits of the Treaty of Versailles became pointless. Thus Schmeisser transferred the production of his MP 28, II to the Pieper weapons factory in Herstal, Belgium. The Belgian Army later introduced the weapon as "Mitraillette Modele 34", and deliveries also went to South America, Spain, China and Japan. In Germany the MP 28, II originally played a subordinate role in police use. In World War II old supplies of 18 and 28 machine pistols also turned up individually in the hands of the troops.

ERMA Machine Pistol (EMP)

Type: *ERMA Maschinenpistole* (EMP)
Manufacturer: Erfurt Machine Factory, Berthold Geipel GmbH
Function: Automatic with blow-back system
Overall length: 880 mm
Weight: 4.1 kg with empty magazine
Barrel length: 230 mm
Barrel caliber: 9 mm
Number of riflings: Six
Rifling direction: Right
Sight: Fixed sight with flap for 100 and 200 meters
Safety: Safety notch for cocking grip and auxiliary turning safety

Magazine: Staff magazine for 32 cartridges, inserted from left
Types of fire: Single and sustained fire
Performance in sustained fire: 350 to 450 rounds per minute
Standard ammunition: "Pistol Cartridge 08" (9 mm Parabellum)
Disassembly: Set switching lever for sustained fire. Index finger pulls trigger through, middle finger pushes breech lever back (on rear end of trigger guard). Left hand holds casing at magazine holder and turns barrel, including casing, some 60 degrees to left. Now the unit including breech inside it can be drawn forward out of stock. Slide breech out of casing by cocking grip.

The name in the title is the official one, if not the only one. The first machine pistol made by the "Erfurt Machine Factory, Berthold Geipel GmbH" is also known at times as the "Vollmer-ERMA" or simply "Vollmer MP." And there is reason for that.

The Biberach machine-shop owner Heinrich Vollmer (see also the Vollmer machine carbine) had developed the weapon between 1925 and 1930 in cooperation with the "Inspection of Weapons and Equipment" (IWG). The Reichswehr supported the project but finally had to withdraw from its development because there was obviously no chance of introducing the weapon.

Vollmer, working on his own, had been able to build some 350 to 400 machine pistols in 7.63, 7.65 and 9-mm calibers and sell them outside Germany.

A Vollmer machine pistol of 1930 (disassembled). The ERMA produced the design almost unchanged. (Photo: Vollmer Works)

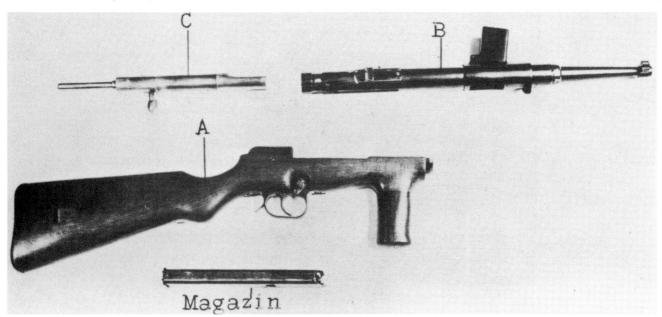

These small sales did not cover the expenses. When the weapon was fully developed in 1930, the manufacturer had no choice but to turn his design over to a financially stronger company for production.

After signing a licensing contract (10/31/1931), ERMA produced the Vollmer machine pistol under its own name and placed it — with slight external changes — on the international market successfully. France, several South American countries and Spain bought the "EMP." After 1936 the SS also ordered it.

Vollmer's first prototype of 1925 still had a cooling jacket like the MP 18, I, a drum magazine for 25 cartridges and, as a typical identifying mark, a wooden handgrip projecting from the front end of the half-stock. This stock pattern was retained later when, after 1926, the cooling jacket was eliminated and, in 1928, the drum magazine was replaced by a 32-cartridge stock magazine inserted from the left. In 1930 the Vollmer machine pistol finally gained a new breech cylinder, with which the closing spring was linked by a telescopic tube.

The ERMA left the weapon almost unchanged, but later added a block safety catch on the upper right side of the breech case and restored the old cooling jacket that Heinrich Vollmer had done away with in 1926. Vollmer had preferred the "mass cooling" of the barrel to "air cooling." To afford better understanding, here is a brief explanation of the difference between the two types of cooling:

Mass-cooled barrels are strongly conical and more strongly made overall. Because of their great mass, they can absorb much heat energy without suffering damage or burning the shooter's hands.

Air-cooled barrels, on the other hand, have thin walls. They become very hot very soon and thus need a barrel jacket with ventilating louvers to support the barrel and make handling it easier. This barrel cools off more quickly than the thick, mass-cooled type.

It is noteworthy that the ERMA later returned to mass cooling in its successful 38 and 40 models. And the Vollmer idea of stabilizing the closing spring by a telescopic tube (Reich patent no. 580 620 of 7/13/1933) remained a typical mark of German World War II machine pistols.

Description of the Weapon

The EMP is made for single and sustained fire; the switch is on the right side in a cutout in the wooden stock above the trigger guard. When the closing spring is tightened, in its rearmost position, the breech can be locked by hooking the cocking grip into a safety notch (as MP 18, I). The block can also be secured by a turning lever on the breech case. The magazine is inserted into its holder diagonally from the left front and held there by a spring lever.

The breech cylinder is unusually long because it holds half of the closing spring inside it. The other half is contained by a sheet-metal tube that, when the spring is released, sticks out the rear of the cylinder and, when the spring is compressed, disappears into the breech piece. The front end of the spring acts on a plate of the long firing pin, the rear half of which is surrounded by the spring.

The "EMP" fires 350 to 450 rounds per minute in sustained fire. It was produced in various, slightly modified versions from 1931 to 1938. The biggest change was in barrel lengths.

Cutaway drawing of the ERMA machine pistol with block safety.

229

Rheinmetall (Steyr-Solothurn) MP - MP 34 (ö)

Type: *Rheinmetall (Steyr-Solothurn)-MP - MP 34 (ö)*
Number: 8323
Manufacturer: Steyr Weapons Factory
Function: Automatic with blow-back system
Overall length: 780 mm
Weight: 4.1 kg with empty magazine
Barrel length: 200 mm
Barrel caliber: 9 mm
Number of riflings: 6
Rifling direction: Right
Sight: Curved sliding sight from 50 to 500 meters
Safety: Block safety on breech lid
Magazine: Staff magazine for 32 cartridges
Types of fire: Single and sustained fire

Performance in sustained fire: 400 to 450 rounds per minute
Standard ammunition: "Pistol Cartridge 08" (9 mm Parabellum)
Safety: Press block safety lever on lid and push forward
Release: Push lever backward. The weapon can be secured whether cocked or not.
Disassembly: Remove magazine, be sure chamber is empty! Release breech. Right thumb presses button on rear end of case lid downward, index finger simultaneously presses lid bolt forward. Lift lid at front, lift out breech with guiding piece and spring rod. Turn breech guiding piece 90 degrees to right, take it off breech cylinder. Remove cocking grip, firing pin and firing pin spring.

The Rheinmetall (Steyr-Solothurn) MP is the most elaborate of German machine pistols. It was produced from 1929 to about 1940 in the weapons factory at Steyr. When the whole weapons industry shifted to simpler production, complicated quality products such as this one were simply not practical any more.

The origin of the design can be found at the "Rhenish Metal Goods and Machine Factory" in the early Twenties. As early as 1925, along with the Schmeisser and Vollmer machine pistols, a Rheinmetall model had also been tested in Kummersdorf.

Manufacturing was also done then at the Swiss Weapons Factory in Solothurn, as Rheinmetall had obtained the majority of their stock in order to overcome the limitations of the Treaty of Versailles. In 1929 the Steyr Weapons Factory obtained a license, and in 1934 the Austrian Army and police introduced the Rheinmetall-Solothurn machine pistol as "Model 34."

The military weapons were made for the 9-mm "Mauser export" pistol cartridge, the police weapons, on the other hand, used the 9-mm Steyr cartridge. In addition, weapons were made for Japan (7.63 Mauser) as well as Yugoslavia and Portugal (9 mm Parabellum). After the union with Austria (1938) Steyr switched all production to the German "Pistol Cartridge 08" (9-mm Parabellum). The post-1938 weapons bore the Steyr works code (660). In the "Great German Reich" the MP 34 had an "ö" added to its designation, for "österreichisch" (Austrian). During World War II these weapons were used by the police.

The Closing Spring is Hidden in the Stock

The construction of the breech and spring system is original, if somewhat laborious. One has the feeling that the designers simply had to come up, at any price, with something different from the work of their great competitor Hugo Schmeisser, whose machine pistol set the pattern in the Twenties.

The closing spring of the Rheinmetall model is in a tube that leads diagonally from the rear end of the breech case through the wood of the butt to the butt plate. The coil spring, with its pressure and

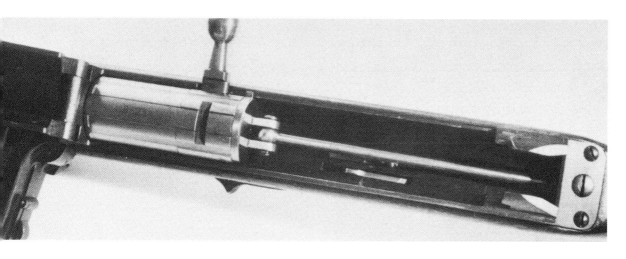

The MP 34 with its lid raised and breech cylinder in foremost position. The spring rod is in contact with the closing spring hidden in the stock. Under the rod the notches for single and sustained fire can be seen.

advancing spring bolts, can be drawn out of the rear of the stock if necessary. The connection between the breech cylinder and the spring is made by a guiding rod, the end of which sticks into the closing spring tube. This arrangement has the advantage that the breech case can be made somewhat shorter than in the other machine pistols.

In the breech piece, which narrows in a step at the front, the firing pin is housed, with the firing pin holder and a small coil spring. The rear end of the breech cylinder is enclosed by the rather complex "breech guiding piece", to which the guiding rod is also attached.

The MP 34 (ö) is a dream for people who know how to appreciate quality. The casing, angular on the outside, with a round inner cross-section, is machined out of solid material and has a precisely closing lid whose hinge is shortly behind the magazine holder on the left side. The box magazine for 32 cartridges is inserted at an angle from the front. On the lid is the curved sight, adjustable to 500 meters, as well as a block safety catch by which the breech piece can be held in its cocked or released position.

The cocking grip with its knob is located at the right. By a switch on the left side of the stock, single or sustained fire can be selected. This function corresponds to the MP 18, I and 28, II.

Two special features of the MP 34 (ö) are the bayonet mount on the right side of the cooling jacket (for the Austrian M 95 bayonet) and the built-in magazine filler in the magazine shaft. For filling, the magazine is pushed into the window of the magazine shaft from *below*. In this position cartridges can be stripped off clips into the magazine.

Since the German "Pistol Cartridge 08" was not delivered with clips, this practical magazine filler later lost its importance.

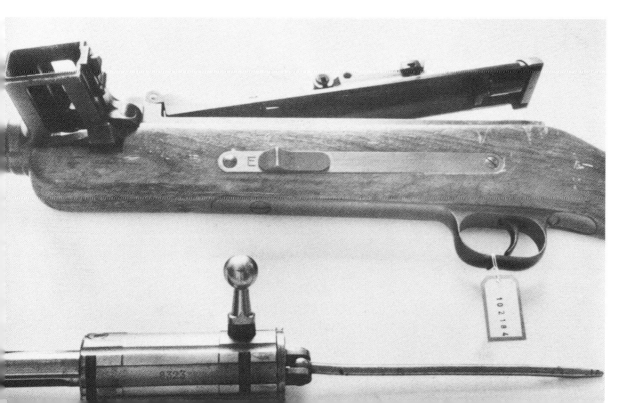

The MP 34, partly disassembled. In the foreground is the breech cylinder with the movable rod. The fire type selector on the stock is set for single shots.

"Bergmann" Machine Pistol 35 - MP 35 Bgm

Type: *Bergmann Maschinenpistole 35* (MP 35 Bgm)
Number: 461
Year made: 1944
Manufacturer: Junker & Ruh, Karlsruhe (ajf)
Function: Automatic with blow-back action
Overall length: 810 mm
Weight: 4.3 kg with empty magazine
Barrel length: 180 mm
Barrel caliber: 9 mm
Number of riflings: 6
Rifling direction: Right
Sight: Curved sliding sight, 50 to 1000 meters
Safety: Pusher blocks trigger and breech cylinder

Magazine: Staff magazine for 20 or 32 cartridges
Types of fire: Single and sustained fire
Performance in sustained fire: ca. 350 rounds per minute
Standard ammunition: "Pistol cartridge 08" (9 mm Parabellum)
Safety and release: Move lever on left side of breech case forward or back. This is possible whether cocked or not.
Disassembly: Press bolt holder on left side of case (behind safety) with left thumb, lifting breech handle with right hand. Draw breech out of case as a unit. Press breech base in arrow direction and turn 90 degrees to right. Now the breech mechanism falls into its individual pieces.

The Theodor Bergmann Weapons Factory in Suhl (later Berlin) had produced the first German machine pistol in 1918. The weapon became known worldwide as the "Bergmann MP", though it could also have been called the "Schmeisser MP" after its designer.

When Hugo Schmeisser brought out an improved version of his machine pistol (MP 28, II) through his own firm after the war, the Bergmann firm was compelled to go on the market with a completely new development.

The first model, of 1932, was not called a "machine pistol", but rather the Bergmann "Machine Carbine" (BMK). This was a completely new concept at the time, but one which soon was to take on a new significance in connection with the short cartridge. Hugo Schmeisser, moreover, was still experimenting with a "machine carbine" in 1936 too, though it was really just an ordinarily 9-mm MP with an unlocked breech, though it possessed the form and dimensions of the 98 k carbine.

The Bergmann "Machine Carbine" of 1932 also had much in common with the 98 carbine externally: the breech handle and the cocking procedure before the first shot. These characteristics remained through the entire developmental series to the MP 35. They raise the Bergmann weapon above the masses of machine pistols.

Judged from our present-day standpoint, the Bergmann MP deserves to be called "solid and dependable" but also "complicated and somewhat laborious."

At first glance, with its perforated cooling jacket and wooden half-stock, the MP 35 looks like most machine pistols of the Thirties.

The only remarkable feature is the magazine guide from the right, with the straight bolt lever at the rear end of the breech case. When it is raised and drawn back (as with a repeating rifle), a genuine bolt comes into view unexpectedly; its parts can be seen in the picture on the opposite page.

The mechanism consists essentially of four parts: the *breech base* with bolt lever and catch stock, the *breech cylinder* with a narrow hole bored in front for the firing pin and a widened rear for the catch stock, the *firing pin*, that is forged flat approximately in the middle, and the *closing spring*.

In the cocking process (breech cylinder in forward

position), what happens is briefly as follows: By raising the bolt lever, the breech base is uncoupled from the end of the weapon's housing, and at the same time the catch cam of the catch stock is coupled with the breech piece. By drawing back the bolt lever, the breech cylinder is moved in back of the trigger rod. When the bolt lever is pushed forward, the closing spring is cocked, and when the lever is moved to the exiting position, the breech base and catch stock are released from the breech again and coupled with the breech case. The mechanism is now cocked.

The whole thing seems rather complicated in comparison to the simple cocking procedures of the other machine pistols. But the fact that the Bergmann machine pistol imitated the very familiar repeating process of the infantry rifle seemed then, in military circles, to be a weighty argument in favor of this weapon.

Yet the Bergmann MP had other things to offer as well. For example, a very clever apparatus that held back the firing pin until the breech, at the end if its forward motion, has pushed the cartridge completely into the bed.

In most of the machine pistols, the point of the firing pin always projects from the front surface of the breech, which means that if something goes wrong, a cartridge can be ignited before the breech is fully in place. Generally, nothing serious happens. But such potentialities indicate a weak point in the classic arrangement of the machine pistol's firing pin.

In the Bergmann case, the firing pin is held back by a small tipping lever that rests on the underside of the breech cylinder and slides into the chamber rail. Its upper joint moves into the flat forged part of the firing pin. At the right moment, at the end of the breech's forward motion, the lower joint tips into a perforation of the breech case. In the process, the upper joint of the tipping lever, called the "striking hammer", drives the bolt forward for ignition.

The Bergmann MP 35 disassembled. Lower right: the breech base with bolt lever, above it the firing pin with its flattened section for the tipping lever.

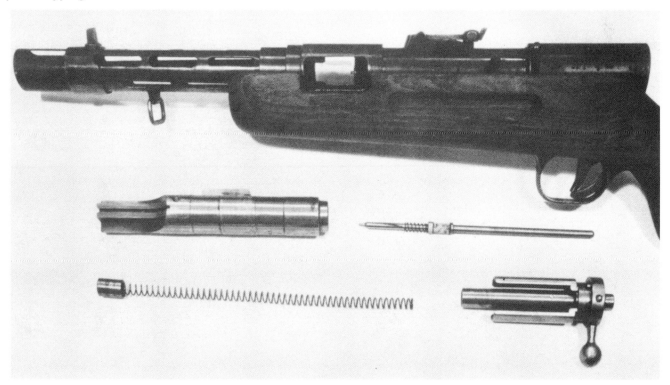

Light Finger Pressure: Single Shots; Heavy Pressure: Sustained Fire

The Bergmann machine pistol will fire either single shots or sustained fire. Thanks to an original trigger construction, the transition from one type of fire to the other is smooth and possible without switching. With light finger pressure (short movement of the trigger), the weapon fires single shots, the interrupter catches the breech cylinder after every recoil. With stronger pressure (long movement of the trigger), the trigger comes into contact with the crescent-shaped switching lever that lies in back of it and moves it backward. Thus the interrupter is switched off and the weapon fires sustained fire until the shooter releases the trigger (or the 20- or 32-cartridge staff magazine is empty).

The safety catch of the Bergmann machine pistol is outstanding. It is switched on and off by a lever on the left side of the breech case and has double action; on the trigger and the breech piece. It can be applied whether the gun is cocked or not (a few specimens of the MP 35 have an additional turning safety on the right of the case, similar to that of the "EMP").

Production and Distribution

The forerunners of the Bergmann MP 35 were called "BMK 32" (made by "Schultz & Larsen" in Otterup, Denmark), "MP 34 Bgm" and "MP 34, I Bgm" (made in Denmark and Germany). The forerunners differ from the last model, the "MP 35 Bgm", mainly in their barrel lengths.

For the international market, Bergmann machine pistols were made in 7.63-mm Mauser, 7.65-mm Para, 9-mm Mauser Export and 9-mm Bergmann-Bayard calibers. In 1939 Sweden introduced a Bergmann MP in 9-mm Para caliber.

In Germany the Bergmann MP 35 was of major importance only in that the SS decided to use this unusual weapon. Production was carried out exclusively by "Junker & Ruh" in Karlsruhe. The Bergmann MP was also made there in somewhat simplified form during the war (Junker & Ruh — code ajf). In all, some 40,000 of the MP 35 are believed to have been made.

Machine Pistol 38/40 (MP 38, MP 40)

Type: *Maschinenpistole 40* - (MP 40)
Number: 1030
Year made: 1943
Manufacturer: "ayf" - ERMA, Erfurt (the breech base is stamped "cnd" and was made by "Krupp National Cash Registers" in Berlin)
Function: Fully automatic with blow-back action
Overall length: 600 mm
Weight: 4.3 kg with empty magazine
Barrel length: 230 mm
Barrel caliber: 9 mm
Number of riflings: 6
Rifling direction: Right
Sight: Fixed sight (100 m) and flap (200 m)
Safety: Locking cap on cocking lever and safety notch in case
Magazine: Staff magazine for 32 cartridges, inserted from below
Types of fire: Only sustained fire
Performance in sustained fire: 350 to 400 rounds per minute

Standard ammunition: "Pistol Cartridge 08" (9 mm Parabellum)
Notes: Firing process same as MP 18, I
Safety: Pull cocking grip all the way back on left side and place in safety notch (marked "S"). Press spring cap of cocking grip. The chamber can also be fixed in foremost position by pressing the spring cap when the closing spring is released.
Disassembly: Remove magazine! Make sure there is no cartridge in chamber! Release breech, pull out "breech pin" (ridged plate on underside of stock) and turn 90 degrees. Press trigger and turn breech case 90 degrees clockwise, then pull forward out of the stock. Take breech cylinder and telescopic closing spring out of the case.
Handling the shoulder brace: Press the square ridged button of the joint and turn the fork back until the button pops out again. Turn oval shoulder brace to the right position, it locks in. Release in opposite order.

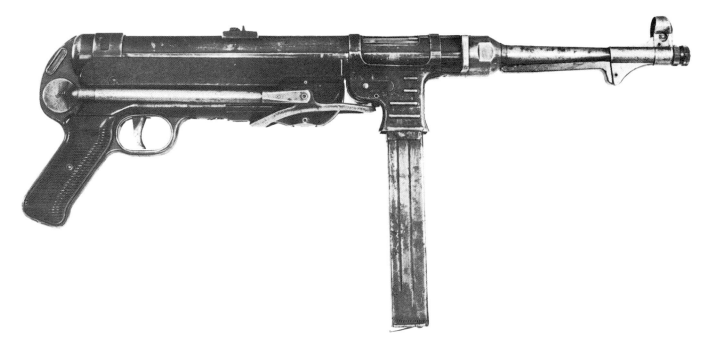

To this day no military historian has explained clearly why the German Wehrmacht began to take a serious interest in a machine pistol only one year before the war began.

It was probably the experience of the German *Legion Condor* in the Spanish Civil War, reinforced by the requests of the paratroopers and Panzer troops, that finally gave the advocates of the machine pistol in Berlin the support they needed.

Thus at the beginning of 1938 the Erfurt Machine Factory received a request from the Army Weapons Office to present a machine pistol model. The

ERMA, internationally successful with their "EMP" for years, must have had their new model ready in advance. This is the only explanation for the short time span between request and acceptance (August 1938).

The "Machine Pistol 38" (MP 38) had what was then a completely new form, meant primarily to meet the needs of the tank crews. The influence of Schmeisser and Vollmer on the design and mechanism can be detected.

The free-standing barrel with mass cooling goes back to the Vollmer machine pistol, which the

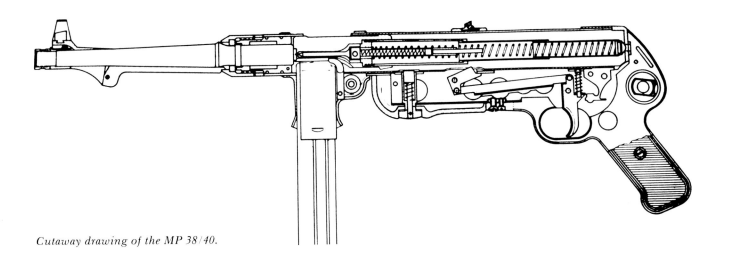

Cutaway drawing of the MP 38/40.

ERMA had built under license. The magazine holder shaped as a handgrip is a functionally sensible further development of the typical wooden Vollmer handgrip. This arrangement forced the insertion of the magazine from below, which was certainly an advantage for carrying the weapon, though it made the weapon difficult to use when lying behind low cover.

The metal cap fastened to the frame and closing the rear end of the casing was also retained from the forerunner model. The result was that the casing had to be pulled forward out for disassembly.

The cylindrical breech piece with the hook-shaped cocking grip is very reminiscent of the chamber of the Schmeisser MP 18, I and 28, II. And the three-piece telescopic case that covered the closing spring and bore the fixed firing pin was based on a 1933 Vollmer patent.

The stock is original by ERMA, if one can apply this concept to the MP 38 at all, for it consists exclusively of metal and plastic. There is no more rear stock (butt). The ERMA designers had replaced this long, heavy piece only used in exceptional cases on machine pistols with a folding steel shoulder brace. Thus the MP was only 60 centimeters long.

The fixed sight for 100 and the flap for 200 meters limited the effective range of the MP (as in the "EMP" before it) very realistically. A plastic rail was set into the flat underside of the conical barrel and meant to absorb the vibration of the barrel during inclined shooting (such as out of a tank hatch). The muzzle had an external thread with a protective nut. A blank cartridge device, and later also a silencer and a *bent barrel attachment* for "shooting around the corner", could be attached.

The MP 38 and its successor model, the MP 40, were made only for sustained fire. Because of the relatively low cadence of 350 to 400 rounds per minute (six to seven per second), it was possible for trained marksmen to fire single shots as well.

The only problem with the MP 38 was its unreliable safety catch. The cocking grip, as in the old MP 18, I, had to be set in a hook-shaped notch in the breech case. An auxiliary lock, such as almost all other machine pistols had at that time, was lacking in the MP 38. The insufficient safety provisions and the originally very expensive production of the MP 38 — the parts were almost exclusively machined — led to minor modifications to the model. Here are the differing features:

Machine Pistol 38/40 (MP 38/40)

It corresponds to the MP 38 in all components but simply has an improved safety-cocking grip. A spring cap has been inserted over the grip bolt in the breech cylinder, which must also be pushed when the cocking grip is in the safety notch. The spring cap locks the cocking grip against unintentional releasing. In the same way, the chamber can be locked when not cocked.

Machine Pistol 40 (MP 40)

In the spring of 1940, in a period of general industrial changeover to war production, the model of the MP 38 was made to suit the requirements of cheap mass production. All the machined parts except the barrel and breech piece were successfully replaced by simpler parts, usually of stamped sheet metal, without changing the form and function of the weapon.

The breech case of the MP 38 had parallel longitudinal grooves in its outer surface. The surface of the MP 40's case is smooth except for a stiffening step at the top. The closing cap of the breech case is smooth in the MP 38, while the MP 40 has two rectangular recesses (for locking the breech case) stamped in. The magazine holder of the MP 38 has a round window on the side. The corresponding part of the MP 40 is not pierced but has five parallel gripping ribs on each side. (The first run of the MP 40 lacked these ribs.)

MP 40 with Twin Magazine (Presumably MP 40, II)

In the literature of weapons there are various photos and descriptions of this model, sometimes called "MP 40, II." Definite information as to by whom and in what quantities this weapon was built is lacking to this day. The MP "40, II" has a magazine holder in which two rod magazines (each with 32 cartridges) could be inserted side by side. When the first magazine was empty, the second was

The Machine Pistol 40 disassembled. At lower right above the magazine is the telescopic closing spring with the firing pin.

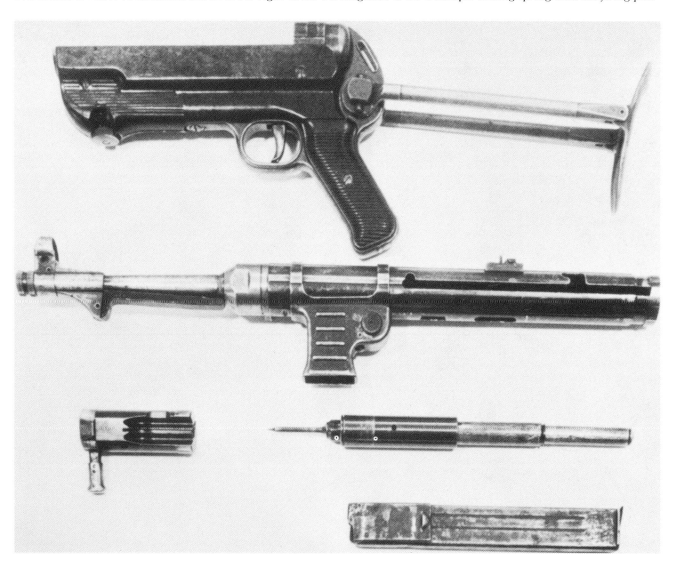

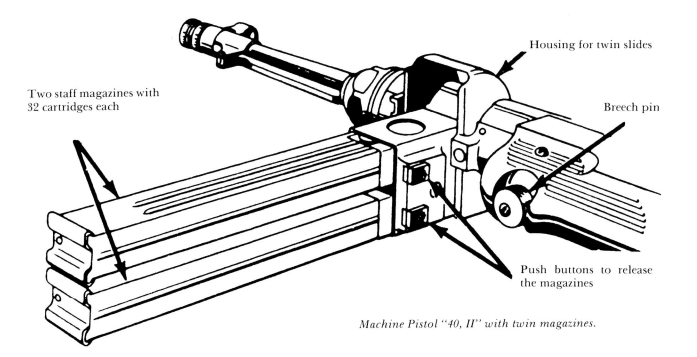

Two staff magazines with 32 cartridges each

Housing for twin slides

Breech pin

Push buttons to release the magazines

Machine Pistol "40, II" with twin magazines.

moved under the barrel with the help of a sliding guide. Thus one could go on shooting almost without interruption.

The existing MP 40's with twin magazines all bear the letter code for the Steyr Weapons Factory (bnz). Presumably only a small test series was made. These machine pistols were probably not very practical, for the weight of the weapon with two filled magazines must have risen to about six kilograms.

Significance of MP 40 and its Manufacturers

Although there was really no lack of German machine pistol types in World War II, the MP 40 was and still is meant when German machine pistols were talked of. Its handiness and functional form assured it a popularity that was attained by no other German infantry weapon in World War II.

The MP 40 was highly regarded by the enemies too. The "Aberdeen Proving Ground", the best-known American government institution for testing handguns, tested the German MP in 1941 and evaluated it very highly. There also exists a remarkable quantity of photos in which American or British soldiers are seen in battle with captured MP 40's.

It is said that by the end of 1944 about a million MP 38 and MP 40 weapons had been produced. The

most important manufacturing firm was naturally ERMA (Pre-1941 code "27", post-1941 "ayf"). In 1940 the MP 40 was also produced in series by Steyr (codes "660" and "bnz"), and as of 1941 by C.G. Haenel in Suhl (fxo). Parts were delivered primarily by the "Merz Works" in Frankfurt, "Krupp National Cash Registers" in Berlin and other smaller companies.

Schmeisser Machine Pistol 41 - MP 41

Type: *Schmeisser Maschinenpistole 41* - (MP 41)
Number: 17545
Manufacturer: C.G. Haenel, Suhl (no code)
Function: Automatic with blow-back action
Overall length: 850 mm
Weight: 4 kg with empty magazine
Barrel length: 230 mm
Barrel caliber: 9 mm
Number of riflings: 6
Rifling direction: Right
Sight: Fixed sight (100 m), flap (200 m)

Safety: as MP 40
Magazine: Staff magazine for 32 cartridges, inserted from below
Types of fire: Single and sustained, selected by push button
Performance in sustained fire: 350 to 400 rounds per minute
Standard ammunition: "Pistol Cartridge 08" (9 mm Parabellum)
Notes: Functions like MP 18, I
Safety and release: as MP 40
Disassembly: Remove magazine, check chamber, release breech, release spring lock on rear end of breech case (as MP 18/28) and remove breech cap. Take breech cylinder including closing spring out of case.

This weapon ranks among the rarest German machine pistols of World War II and, with its old-fashioned wooden stock, looks quite antique next to the MP 40. Hugo Schmeisser had tried to combine elements of his basic model MP 28, II with the technology of the MP 40, which was in series production at the C.G. Haenel Weapons Factory in Suhl as of 1941.

The stock form and trigger apparatus (with settings for single or sustained fire by push button) are almost exactly like those of the MP 28, II. The cylinder and the three-part telescopic closing spring are taken from the MP 40. That is essentially true of the breech case and magazine holder too.

The only new feature is the rigid attachment of the case to the stock. To remove the breech cylinder and closing spring of the MP 41, the breech cap has to be pulled off the case. It is attached with a spring clip as in the MP 28, II.

The attachment of the barrel is also new. It is slimmer than the barrel of the MP 40, and at the attachment point to the housing there is no heavy octagonal nut. The barrel has a round cross-section and no plastic cover on the underside. The safety is that of the MP 40.

The weapon shown here bears the seal of acceptance of the Army Weapons Office, but it is not clear whether the MP 41 was actually produced for the Wehrmacht. There is no record of its use by the troops. The high-quality workmanship suggests that only a small series was built. The trigger guard, for example, is a heavy machined piece of peacetime quality.

In the middle of the war a dispute flared up between Hugo Schmeisser and ERMA about the rights to the telescopic closing spring. Schmeisser was able to prove earlier use of the three-section type (in prototypes of 1935-36), but the principle of

The Schmeisser MP 41 disassembled.

the telescopic casing had already been patented by Heinrich Vollmer. Thus the license rights belonged to ERMA. Schmeisser lost the case at the Berlin Kammergericht.

Beretta Machine Pistol Model 38/42 - MP 38/42

Type: *Maschinenpistole Beretta Model 38/42*
Number: 2330
Year made: No data
Manufacturer: Pietro Beretta Weapons Factory, Val Trompia
Function: Automatic with blow-back action
Weight: 4.3 kg with empty magazine
Barrel length: 205 mm
Barrel caliber: 9 mm
Sight: Fixed sight (100 m) and flap (200 m)
Safety: Lever on left side of breech case
Magazine: Staff magazine)10, 20 or 40 cartridges) inserted from below

Types of fire: Single or sustained, controlled by front or rear trigger
Performance in sustained fire: ca. 400 rounds per minute
Standard ammunition: "Pistol Cartridge 08" (9 mm Parabellum)
Notes: Function as MP 18, I. After cocking forward, the cocking grip **must** be moved back to its starting point.
Disassembly: Remove magazine. Check chamber, release breech, press the spring knob of the breech cap at the rear end of the case, turn the cap 90 degrees and remove. Slide closing spring with tube and rod, plus cylinder, out the back of the case.

When the "Berlin-Rome Axis" broke in the summer of 1943, the "Duce" Mussolini fell from power and the government of Marshal Badoglio signed an armistice with the Allies, half of Italy was still occupied by German troops. Just as they had previously done in Czechoslovakia and Belgium, the German authorities had taken over the weapons industry in Italy for their own use.

Among the most important suppliers was the firm of Pietro Berretta in Val Trompia, near Gardone in northern Italy, which was already world famous thanks to its hunting rifles, pistols and machine pistols.

The factory ran under German control until the arrival of the Allied troops. Beretta delivered 20,000 Model 38/42 machine pistols a month as of 1944, among others. This type had been created by simplifying the Beretta MP 38, a dependable but rather heavy weapon, weighing about five kilograms.

The Beretta MP 38 had a 31-cm barrel with a cooling jacket, a curved sliding sight up to 500 meters and a wooden three-quarter stock.

In the MP 38/42 the barrel was shortened to 20.5 cm and switched to mass cooling. To increase the cooling area and make heat exchange easier, the barrel was given six longitudinal grooves.

The forestock was shortened, reaching only to the magazine holder. The sight range (fixed notch: 100 meters, flap: 200 m) was reduced to the effective range of the weapon. The muzzle brake of the MP 38/42 won great renown by effectively reducing the weapon's recoil and the natural tendency of all machine pistols to shoot high.

Two deep notches in the top of the barrel shortly behind the muzzle work like jets, directing the gas backward when it exits after firing. Their action simultaneously pushes the muzzle forward and downward. As a result, the weapon is very steady, even in sustained fire.

Another Beretta quality, which is somewhat reminiscent of the "Bergmann MP 35", is the use of two triggers, one behind the other in the trigger guard. The front one acts on an interrupter and is thus intended for single shots; the rear one is directly connected to the trigger notch and triggers sustained fire. Thus the transition from one type of fire to the other is done without switching, just by moving the trigger finger.

The safety catch of the MP 38/42 can be turned on

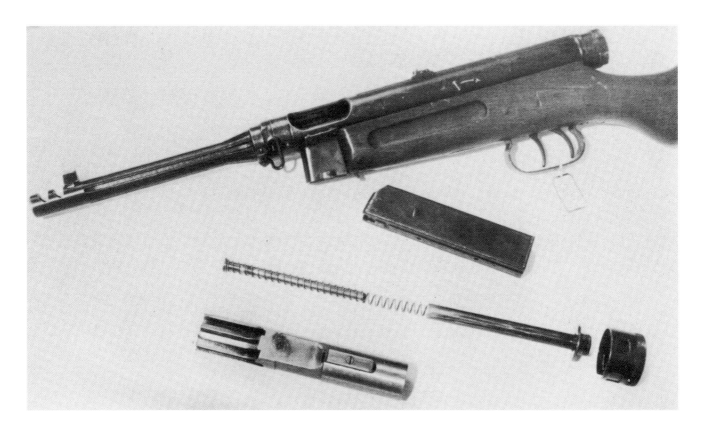

The Beretta MP 38/42 disassembled. At upper right by the breech case is the safety-lever.

and off by a push lever on the left side of the breech case. The staff magazine (they were made in different lengths for ten, twenty and forty cartridges) were introduced from below, and the empty cartridges flew out of the weapon at the upper left. Unlike the German machine pistols (with the exception of the Bergmann), the cocking grip of the MP 42 is not directly linked to the breech piece. It is on the right side of the breech base, on a sheet-metal plate that covers the guiding slit. After cocking, the pusher *must* be moved forward again to its original position, otherwise it will knock the moving cylinder forward in firing. If this happens, the cocking mechanism can also be damaged or the chamber so badly braked that its power is no longer enough to push a cartridge out of the magazine and ignite it reliably. The only argument in favor of the indirectly acting cocking grip is the fact that no external part of the weapon moves in firing.

In the breech of the MP 38/42, the Italian designers dispensed with everything that was not absolutely necessary. The surprisingly long chamber piece has a rigid firing pin. The closing spring fits into a tube in back and is guided by an inserted bolt in front. This is very simple but effective.

A metal cap with a bayonet attachment and spring lock closes the rear end of the breech case. For disassembly the cap must be removed.

The workmanship of the MP 38/42 is not particularly good (quite unlike the Beretta MP 38). There are many stamped or spot-welded sheet-metal parts, as is to be expected in wartime production.

With the German "Pistol Cartridge 08" the Beretta MP had a cadence of some 400 rounds per minute. With the considerably more powerful Italian 9-mm Model 38 cartridge (its case shaped like the German cartridge), the rate of fire increased to 500 rounds per minute.

A rare picture: A German paratrooper with a captured Beretta MP 38 gives a war correspondent (with movie camera) covering fire.
(Photo: Federal Archives)

Machine Pistol 3008 (Neumünster Device)

Type: *Maschinenpistole 3008* (Gerät Neumünster)
Year built: 1945
Manufacturer: Unknown
Function: Automatic with blow-back action
Total length: 780 mm
Weight: ca. 3 kg with empty magazine
Barrel length: 180 mm
Barrel caliber: 9 mm
Number of riflings: 6
Rifling direction: Right
Sight: Fixed sight, adjustable foresight

Safety: Notches in cocking lever guide
Magazine: Staff magazine for 32 cartridges, inserted from below (MP 38)
Types of fire: Single and sustained fire, switch on trigger housing
Standard ammunition: "Pistol Cartridge 08" (9 mm Parabellum)
Notes: Remove magazine, check chamber, release breech. Press sprung bolt in stock-holder panel and simultaneously pull stock down with panel. Release closing spring, pull cocking lever from cylinder, slide breech piece out rear of case.

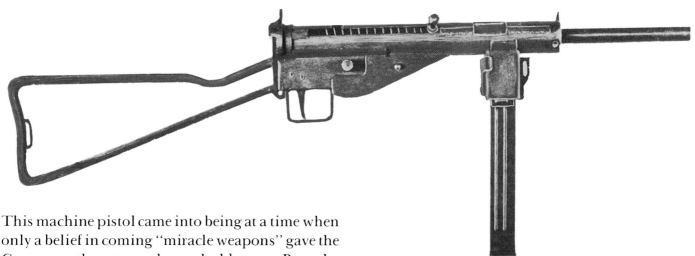

This machine pistol came into being at a time when only a belief in coming "miracle weapons" gave the Germans the strength to hold out. But the "Neumünster Device" was neither decisive nor mysterious. It was not even original, but merely a copy of the British STEN Mark II.

This machine pistol, developed in 1941 at the Royal Small Arms Factory, Enfield and built (three million in all) by various manufacturers during the war. took a direction that was not followed by German firearms until the summer of 1944: decentralized mass production using the slightest possible means.

When a new generation of primitive carbines, self-loaders and machine pistols had to be developed to arm the *Volkssturm*, the Main Weapons Branch of the Armaments Ministry turned to the hostile STEN model. The Mauser designer Vorgrimler reworked the British machine pistol and reduced the assembly time to about one hour. The hand-guard tube of the British model was dropped from the German copy. The magazine holder, located on the left side of the Sten and set in resting position when turned downward, it attached rigidly to the underside of the "Neumünster Device." The parts

of the trigger mechanism (which allows single and sustained fire) are somewhat simplified and riveted in the casing. For the shoulder brace, three different shapes were planned. The one, with a stable tube frame, was almost exactly like the British model. The second, with a bow that formed the outline of a wooden stock, is found almost all the time. A board stock was also planned.

It is scarcely necessary to waste words on the mechanism of the MP 3008. A massive cylindrical piece with a trunnion-shaped extension, onto which the end of the coil closing spring is pushed, forms the breech. Instead of a firing pin, the MP 3008 just has a small point in the middle of the front surface of the cylinder. This projection, worked from solid material, imitates the point of the firing pin. The housing consists of very simple shaped and spot-welded sheet-metal parts. As a safety catch there is only the well-known cutout on the rear end of the guiding slit for the (removable) cocking grip. As we know, this is an unsatisfactory arrangement. The normal magazines of the MP 38/40 fit into the MP 3008.

Making Weapons in the Backyard

The makeshift weapons for the *Volkssturm* and the planned "Werewolf" partisan commands were not to be built in one or two large weapons factories, but in a great number of small workshops all over the country. In the last months of 1944 the military authorities of the Nazi party and the SS offices tried to build up a network of suppliers on a regional level. At the beginning of 1945 the production of the MP 3008 slowly began in the Rhineland, Thuringia and Württemberg. About a hundred of the MP 3008 were made at the Mauser Works in Oberndorf, their parts delivered by small workshops all over the state. The finished barrels, for example, came from a locksmith's shop near Stuttgart.

The quick collapse nullified the plan of a great organization of gunsmiths covering the entire country. By the end of the war, the various producers had delivered only 3000 to 5000 machine pistols.

Thus the "Neumünster Device" did not even play a minor role in the battle for Germany.

The Mauser Copy of the "STEN Mark II"

Even more of a secret than the origin of the German *Volkssturm* machine pistol was the contract for an exact copy of the STEN machine pistol that the Mauser Works in Oberndorf received in the autumn of 1944.

Within six months, 25,000 weapons were to be delivered that could not even be distinguished from the British originals by specialists. The leadership in Berlin, usually rather stingy when it came to production costs, were prepared to pay 1800 RM for this special production. This unbelievably high price (compared to 56 RM for a 98 k carbine) leads one to suspect that the weapons would be used for some "big operation." But what it might have been is unknown to this day.

Ostensibly, the Mauser copies were to be para-dropped in containers of 25 guns over free France to "pro-German partisans." But naturally there were no such partisans who would have taken up these weapons for the defeated German Reich. And even if they had existed, why were they to be armed with copies of British weapons? This riddle can no longer be solved by the complicated logic of psychological warfare.

Another unanswered question is what finally happened to the Mauser STEN copies. It can be proved that 25,000 machine pistols were delivered, but not one single specimen has ever been shown in the international literature on the subject. Perhaps because nobody can tell the copies from the originals! They match not only in terms of fine dimensions but also by bearing authentic English lettering.

The weapon shown here could be one of those Mauser copies; at least the circumstances of its discovery speak for it. The machine pistol was salvaged from an Austrian Alpine lake by divers in the summer of 1972. Six machine pistols, along with magazines and a large quantity of ammunition, had been lying on the lake bottom in a soldered metal box.

The container was very rusty and overgrown with weeds on the outside, but the contents were factory-new. The location and circumstances of the discovery allow the suspicion that the weapon shown here is one of those STEN counterfeits, and that it was dumped in the Alpine lake by German troops on their retreat into the "Alpine fortress."

This is only a suspicion, an attempt to solve one of the many riddles from the chaotic last days of the German Reich.

STEN Mark II, stamped "Long Branch 1943", possibly one of the 25,000 Mauser copies.

Sources and Bibliography

The information on the development of German military rifles up to 1918 is based essentially on the study of files on armaments and weaponry in the former Bavarian War Archives (Main State Archives, Munich, Section IV). The author has reconstructed the period from 1918 to 1945, whenever possible, through his own research with firms and witnesses of those times. Along with the applicable military service orders, the following works were used:

Deutsch, F.W., *Waffenlehre*, Berlin 1935.

Eckardt-Morawietz, *Die Handwaffen*, Hamburg 1957.

German Submachine Guns and Assault Rifles, Aberdeen Proving Ground Series.

Gothsche, *Die Königlichen Gewehrfabriken*, Berlin 1904.

Major Hailer, *100 Jahre K.B. Gewehrfabrik Amberg*, Munich 1901.

Handbuch, betreffend die Munition für Handfeuerwaffen, Rifle Testing Commission 1904.

Hassler, F., *Geschichte der Mauser-Werke*, Berlin 1938.

Janssen, Gregor, *Das Ministerium Speer*, Berlin 1968.

Korn, R.H., *Mauser Gewehre, Mauser-Patente*, Oberndorf 1908.

Leeb, Emil, *Aus der Rüstung des Dritten Reiches*, Berlin 1958.

Mieg, Armand, *Die Verwendbarkeit des Infantriegewehrs M 71*, Berlin 1876.

Schmidt, Rudolf, *Allgemeine Waffenkunde für Infanterie*, Bern 1888.

Schoen, Erich, *Geschichte des Deutschen Feuerwerkswesens*, Berlin 1936.

Schwarz, *Vom braunen Pulver zum R.C.P.*, Rottweil 1938.

75 Jahre Waffenfabrik Carl Walther, Ulm 1961.

Smith, W.H.B., *Small Arms of the World*.

Speer, Albert, *Erinnerungen* Frankfurt 1969.

Thomas, Georg, *Geschichte der deutschen Rüstungswirtschaft*, Boppard 1966.

Vollmer, Udo, *Der Unternehmer Heinrich Vollmer als Waffenkonstrukteur*, n.d.

Wagenführ, Rolf, *Die deutsche Industrie im Kriege 1939-1945*, Berlin 1963.

SCHIFFER MILITARY HISTORY

Specializing in the
German Military of World War II

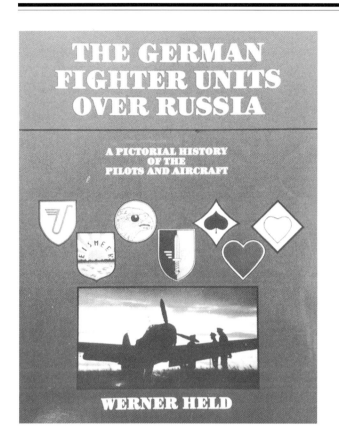

THE HG
PANZER DIVISION

by
ALFRED OTTE

THE
HEAVY
FLAK
GUNS

GERMAN
• 88mm • 105mm • 128mm • 150mm GUNS
AND BALLISTIC DIRECTIONAL EQUIPMENT

1933-1945

Werner Müller

THE
WAFFEN-SS

A PICTORIAL DOCUMENTATION BY HERBERT WALTHER

PANZER

A PICTORIAL DOCUMENTATION

HORST SCHEIBERT

SCHIFFER MILITARY

THE GERMAN NAVY AT WAR
1935-1945   VOLUME 1
THE BATTLESHIPS

A
HISTORY OF THE
"BIG SHIPS"

• POCKET BATTLESHIPS • CRUISERS •
AIRCRAFT CARRIER "GRAF ZEPPELIN"

SIEGFRIED BREYER   GERHARD KOOP

THE GERMAN NAVY AT WAR
1935-1945   VOLUME 2
THE U-BOAT

SIEGFRIED BREYER   GERHARD KOOP

THE U-BOAT•LIGHT NAVAL WEAPONS•NAVAL INFANTRY DIVISIONS•NAVAL AVIATION•
HARBORS AND BASES•WARSHIP CONSTRUCTION YARDS•NAVAL CITATIONS•
UNIFORMS INSIGNIA OF RANK AND SERVICE U-505